LIFE ALL OVER AGAIN

A NOT-QUITE NOVICE AUTHOR'S JOURNEY TO SELF-PUBLICATION

B. A. PAUL

CONTENTS

INTRODUCTION

Welcome, dear readers! Thanks for picking up this second volume of blog post compilations from bapaul.com.

Life Along the Way holds the first one hundred blog posts I created for my website.

Life All Over Again contains the second hundred.

Two hundred! Some came easy—all I had to do was watch myself be a fool in the kitchen or follow a cat around for a day, or the Hubs, and voila! The blogs wrote themselves.

Others required more reflection, and at times, a little more guts to put myself out there, give you a peek behind the Big Top CIRCUS and share parts of my jumbled-up creative process.

In the first volume, the tagline was: A novice author's journey toward self-publication. I hadn't sold anything when I first started the blogs — not via the self-publishing route or otherwise.

For this volume, the tag line reads: A not-so-novice author's journey toward self-publication. Not-so novice because I have sold a few things here and there, self-published and otherwise. (Enough to have to pay a dab of taxes on the bounty!)

Life All Over Again covers the timeframe from Fall of 2020 to Spring of 2023.

Yeah, you read that right.

2020.

And 2021.

And 2022.

Years and years of outside stressors for everyone—literally everyone—on the planet.

I touch on some of those heavier issues—it was, after all, 2020—but I tried not to dwell. We've all had enough of that stuff, and I've now been on a news-free diet for months and I don't miss knowing things. At all.

I've got enough to "know" within my own four walls, like:

Where's that sound coming from?

There's smoke in here. Is that normal?

Why's there a mess in my freezer?

Again, with the sound.

Who missed their medication?

What's burning?

What's leaking?

Who's leaking?

If you took your medication, would you still be leaking?

These are the most pressing questions of my days and nights... No major news outlets required.

Many of my blogs address my very own CIRCUS (all caps for reasons you'll discover as you read) and trying to navigate life while, well, having a life.

Little Miss Muse joins me for each "looking back" section, adding in her two-cent's worth, or as she'd rather me put it, her billion-dollars' worth to how the journey's going so far. (If you'd like to get a sense of Little Miss, visit bapaul.com. She's got her own landing page there!)

When I revisited these one hundred posts, I noticed a few things.

1. I don't always remember what I write; at times, it was like reading a long-lost diary of a stranger.
2. I need help. Pro-level help.
3. My Muse is psychotic.
4. My ducks never want to line up.
5. I'm living in a loop of the same patterns I had in *Life Along the Way*: Procrastination. Blessings. Grief. Happiness. Loss. Joy. Frustration. Productivity.

Then repeat it all. Month after month. The highest of highs and lowest of lows.

I guess that's life all over again.

It's all giving me whiplash and a bit of carsickness, but there you have it.

My hope with this project is that you'll see yourself in some of my maniacal days. Perhaps have a laugh with me—or at me. Cry with me. Roll your eyes and nod your head because, even though you'd never admit it in writing, you're as messed up as I am.

Whether you're a fellow writer or creative, or whether you couldn't imagine your way out of a brown paper bag, you're welcome to journey along whatever path you've chosen for yourself, and I'll journey alongside on mine, and we can try to hang onto this crazy, spinning orb together.

And as long as my CIRCUS and your circus never join forces, we'll be just fine. ☺

Little Miss is bored of intros, now. She's ready to get to the meat and potatoes and grape bubblegum of the posts. "Perhaps by Volume 3, you'll be able to tag-line that baby: A pro-author and her invaluable Muse's guide to ruling the universe."

"Cool your jets, Little Miss. We need a few more titles under our wings before we can fly that high."

She lays her new quiverful of bottle rockets at my feet and begins wiring them up in sequence.

"How high we talkin'?"

101

MOMENTUM 101

I t's the 101st blog.
101.

I remember college. Eons ago. When things were simple.

English 101. US History 101. Physics 101.

That 101 has a certain nostalgic ring to it even if it meant you were a low-on-the-totem-pole schmuck with no clue the torment that awaits in English 201, let alone British Literature 809.

I'm currently in an online writing class called Covers 101 through WMG Publishing (though I've elected to sit in the back and watch and not turn in my assignments for this one. I'm a slacker, but, well. Life...).

At any rate, school's back in swing for those of a certain age, or at least it should be. Many of the kiddos in our area can't get traction on their education due to, well.

We all know what it's due to.

I'm counting myself blessed that I don't have to make those schooling/sports/extracurricular decisions during this upheaval. All of my charges are senior citizens—which presents whole new dilemmas that require the application of a different law of physics and the wrangling of many dastardly ducks into ridiculous-looking rows...

I think every one of us—school-aged to seniors—are craving traction. Some sense of "forward."

A "Let's get going already" attitude.

Because what we've got here is a classic example of Newton's First Law of Motion: An object at rest stays at rest (unless kicked, licked by a sandpaper tongue wanting tuna RIGHT NOW, or the cable goes out); and an object in motion remains in motion (unless doctor visits, viruses, government mandates, and civil unrest ground said object in a state of shock and despair).

I paraphrased just a little bit. I hope you'll forgive me. If Newton had only known what was in Earth's future, maybe he would've phrased his laws differently. (All of the science geeks just died a little... that's okay. You'll respawn in a second or two).

Those who bother to watch commercials may remember the pharmaceutical company's rendition of the middle-to-elderly aged folks going for a hike with Newton's law encouraging them along (something about joint health). Their now-agile bodies rise from their benches and venture into the mountains. Because, well, momentum (and drugs, but that's another blog post).

I can hear that voice-over guy in my office today. "A work-in-progress in motion will remain in motion." Then he holds out his hand with a Diet Coke. "Here, honey, another swig of caffeine and keep going, the mountains await!"

My work in progress at the moment isn't the same work in progress as when I started the work in progress at the present moment. (And there go the English nerds to their very own "contemplation corners" to frown about and analyze that sentence. It's okay. You'll be alright. I may not be, but you will...)

I lost momentum on that fiction piece and had to generate a new kind of momentum somewhere else. To "write but not write" on something to keep my sanity and to keep my hands in the publishing and book-ish things.

And to practice on a new software and, and, and...

Something.

So a nonfiction bit that's 85% with good forward momentum. Until I had to stop and work on this blog, so I'll have to find the swing of it again.

Or until the creative juices break free on my "stuck" fiction work in progress.

The last time that happened on a piece, when Little Miss sprinkled my rusty gears with her magic glitter grease, the forward momentum was so powerful that I finished the last third of the novel in two settings.

I'm hoping for that same burst-and-move-forward kick in the teeth from Little Miss Muse here any day now.

But alas. I think Little Miss may have found her momentum elsewhere—like her very own campaign trail.

Little Miss Muse for President.

Vote Little Miss!

Oh, well.

Hang on. Another slurp of Diet Coke.

That's better. My Amazon order of "Creative Gear Grease" should be here soon, so Little Miss has time to prep her acceptance speech.

Unless they screw it up like last time and send me another box of utterly useless Creative Gear for Geese...

Looking Back: Wow. I still have that lost momentum-itis condition 803 days later due to, well, life. (Yes, exactly 803 days... I asked Google and everything). If you're the kind to jump forward and skip around in nonfiction books (okay, I just died a little...), check out Acceptance in Chapter 178. That level of intensity is still raging as I write this 803 days later. I frequently refer to it in current blog posts as the CIRCUS (all caps because when I think about it, I want to scream).
On the positive side, I'm learning to write daily in this new normal which is, in fact, total chaos.

Little Miss Muse enjoys the CIRCUS, stating that it gives her gobs of story fodder, but blaming me for lack of momentum to keep my butt in the chair long enough to transcribe her ideas.

102

LOPSIDED

Over the last few weeks, I've been working on a compilation project. I've gone back through those first hundred blogs and did a reassessment.

Where have I been?

Where am I going?

What patterns emerge (good habits, bad habits, hidden habits that one doesn't see unless one has a massive sampling of data to analyze).

The results were, quite frankly, stunning.

Not my progress as an author mind you, stunning as in eye-opening.

Doing a massive swoop like that brought back memories of Grandma and other losses. I knew that would happen. I cried a little. Memories of happy little "jump and squeal" moments. I smiled a little. Bits and pieces of memories not recorded in the blog, but happening in real life nonetheless made me cringe, cry, and smile.

You know, life. In all its up-ness and down-ness.

And then I noticed odd little things, that, well, made me shake my head. Mostly with Little Miss. Lots of cat issues. And then...

I noticed lots of "guys" who make appearances all over the blog.

Some are fleeting mentions (like pre-pandemic Face Mask Guy) while others are constants in my world.

I have "my guys" meaning the hubs and the son. They lift things, reach high-up things, make noise, make messes, always need fed, interrupt, and generally encourage me to keep writing. I'll put up with the noise and hollow stomachs and keep my guys.

I have a Web Guy who keeps the blog alive, guards the gate of website/tech purgatory, and generally nags me about where he landed on the Top 100 list. I'll put up with the nagging and keep my Web Guy.

I have an Eye Guy who tortures me with stinging drops and searing slit lamps and generally helps me not go blind. I'll put up with the torture and keep my Eye Guy.

I have a Mexican Restaurant Guy who feeds our family when I can't bring myself to stand in the kitchen and decipher that all-too-complicated list of directions on the back of the macaroni box. No complaints at all about the Mexican Restaurant Guy, only that he closes the restaurant up for the night and some holidays and doesn't serve breakfast. I can put up with the limited hours of availability and keep this guy. And all of his friends, too.

And I have Back Guy who I've been seeing quite a bit of lately. A chiropractor that keeps me upright with adjustments of the spine and attitude.

He pops, cracks, stretches, and otherwise snaps me back into alignment.

I saw him yesterday and surprised him because I was so off-kilter.

"Wow. You're lopsided today."

No kidding, Sherlock. That might be why I randomly kiss hallway walls as my knee gives and I grasp empty air and vertical planes for some kind of stability. Otherwise known as face-in-wall syndrome.

And then the popping, cracking, stretching, and snapping commenced with a fevered fury as he worked to alleviate what ailed me.

He called me lopsided again and sent me on my way. With a follow-up for next week, lest I lean too far the other direction.

Lopsided.

Thanks, Back Guy. (Eye Guy would tell me at this point I'm a few clicks off normal. I think they must share my records with each other.)

And as I laid there and he popped every vertebra in my spine, I remembered the blog review. Then I got mad because he's right.

Back Guy nailed it.

I'm lopsided.

I'm lopsided in my learning. Lopsided in goal-setting. I have lopsided attention spans.

Even my Little Miss Muse dances with an ever-so-slight-sway-to-the-left, occasionally causing her to bounce off random walls with her face as she trips over her high heels.

Lopsided. All-or-nothing at the expense of a well-rounded existence.

I've no idea how to fix it. I think I'm hard-wired to hyper focus on one thing at a time, despite appearing to juggle brightly colored balls belonging to four other people's circus clowns.

Focus on publishing, no new words written.

Write new words, no editing happens.

Caretake others in times of need, no groceries in our house and Mexican Guy's phone rings off the hook.

Insert any life activity here, and I can find a way to tilt it off-center.

Lopsided.

Is there a Guy for this? (Some of you are nodding your heads up and down real slow as you read this, and you're thinking of *your* Guy who sits in a nice chair, legs crossed, with a nice notebook while you recline on the leather couch, tissue in hand, and spill out the details of your own lopsided week. If you want, you can email me the name of your Guy, and I'll seriously consider adding him to my list.)

Anyway.

I'll put up with Back Guy's popping, cracking, and stating the obvious to stay upright and mobile.

Because we all need someone, once in a while, to point out just how lopsided we are.

Looking Back: I still have all my guys—except Web Guy (due to no fault of his own) had to decline keeping up my blog site shortly after that 100th blog, and now I'm battling it out solo with another provider. But all is well, the blog is still up and running and I have a storefront for my wares.
Unfortunately, I do also still have other people's clowns.
I am, at the time of this writing, actively looking for a Couch Guy (or Gal) to tell my CIRCUS troubles to. In that arena, I'm so lopsided, I'm nearly horizontal.
Little Miss Muse agrees I need therapy. "I wouldn't say so right up front. I was waiting for you to realize it on your own..."
Gee. Thanks.

103

MISHANDLED

As I type this, my left eye waters and my right eye twitches. Nearly five days of intense light sensitivity. Retina-searing, even.

Every screen I use for work/writing has been de-brightened, de-blue-lighted, or decommissioned altogether.

I wear sunglasses in the kitchen. (When you're as bad of a cook as I am, one doesn't need to see what one is doing, anyway.)

I wear sunglasses while doing laundry (stain? What stain?).

I wear sunglasses while I work. (I hope *that* works out...)

Wearing sunglasses in the grocery store? It must appear to others that I'm coming off some wild bender. Add to that the mask, and I'm sure I flag suspicion on the security cameras.

I've taken to throwing blankets on the floor to dull the sun's morning rays, lest my walk from the office to the garage blind me further. The cats aren't sure what to think about this. They enjoy those rays, their furry bodies soaking up the UV. They also enjoy the blankets on the floor. I'll have lots of laundry after this is over.

Still working on the cause of the matter. I got the all-clear from Eye Guy just last month. So, I'm leaning toward something else.

The first theory was migraine headache. I did have a little pain. A little nausea, then a lot of pain and a lot of nausea, then back to only blinding glare from any reflective surface. Like Eye Guy snuck into my bedroom Saturday night and dilated my pupils without my permission. (Wouldn't *that* make for a creepy horror story???)

The second theory was a bad startup of fall allergies with the harvest. Our area has been so dry that there's more dust kicking up than usual. And the weather has been so gorgeous that I've had the windows open round-the-clock enjoying not paying for climate control. More dust inside. More dry air, etc., etc. So I've started my little pink allergy pill, which comes with a few days of adjusting to "medicine head" and extreme thirst.

And, on the off chance that my little thyroid gland is tap dancing in my neck, I had a blood draw at the Local Lab. But the Far-Off Lab called me the next day. "Your specimen was mishandled. We'll need to do that again."

I liked the way the Far-Off Gal put that. "Mishandled." Not lost. Not dropped. Not left out on the counter too long.

Mishandled. Leaving the possibilities wide open should I decided to pursue legal action...

Little Miss Muse liked the "mishandled" angle and began thinking up one-thousand-and-one ways to "mishandle" a tube of blood. Out came the bottle rockets. And the lighter. Which I begged her to put away because I can't handle the lights right now.

Dull the sparkle a bit, Little Miss, just until this is over.

Mishandled specimen.

Well. Gee.

What choice did I have but to get another stick?

So Local Lab draws more tubes to send to Far-Off Lab (each place blaming the other place for the mishap, I'm sure). And to be on the safe side, Local Lab Gal drew more tubes than needed to appease Far-Off Lab.

Local Lab Gal reassuringly tells me that they'll let me know what happens to all those extra "unused" tubes. Like I'm gonna lose sleep over it. It's not like I want it back. You know, once certain things are out of the package, the resale value goes way down...

Or maybe they believe I have a stockpile on my pantry shelf. (Another horror story writing prompt, I do believe. Or maybe sci-fi. Unless I've got dragon DNA in my blood, then we could go fantasy, too.)

Now my right eye is watering and my left lid is twitching, so time to wrap it up, give both orbs a rest from the screen...

...and hope Little Miss Muse doesn't run off too far chasing her own twisted storylines of evil optometrists and mishandled specimens while I'm too blind to chase her.

Looking Back: Neither Local Lab Gal nor Far-Off Lab told me what they did with all those extra tubes of blood... but I'd forgotten about the possible storylines here, so I've added them to my hand-printed list of possible plots.
(If I don't physically write things down, they don't get done).
Little Miss Muse believes we should do a mash-up of every possible story idea from mishandled blood work, bending every genre ever created into a single tale.
Little Miss Muse would be wrong here...

104

AND THE WINNER IS...

From last week's Footrace of the Maladies, a fight to the finish for the Championship of Underlying Causes of retina-searing special effects, eyelid twitches, and otherwise annoyingly exhausting symptoms...

A death-defying photo finish, sorted out by the outstanding modern medical community:

Ding, ding, ding.

The winner is:

Thyroid flare by a hair, followed a close second by seasonal allergies.

That dumb gland loves to dance in my neck.

Tap, polka, tango, river dance. You name it. It's doin' its trophy-worthy, bi-yearly jig and demanding a medication adjustment before it sends me into coma-ville for two months.

The trouble with thyroid exhaustion is that I always have something else to blame the exhaustion on—some other drama, trauma, or turmoil that appears to be in the lead on the racetrack. But alas, the gland won out.

So...

New medication dose on board (takes several weeks to reach full effect, so, a hurry-up-and-be-patient deal).

Allergy medication on board (making me extremely thirsty and a bit medicine-heady).

But hopefully, by this time next week, I'll be firing on more than one cylinder.

I'm so thankful that Far-Off Lab and Local Lab didn't "mishandle" my bloodwork redraw.

I am beginning to wonder what they may have done with the extra three tubes of "just in case" blood. Little Miss Muse wonders, too.

At any rate, short and sweet this week while the Footrace of the Maladies winners cool down on the sidelines. I've two self-imposed publishing goals to hit by Friday:

1. A new collection, Volume 3 of All the Feels, done and into cyberspace (meaning my muddled brain has to tackle InDesign and remember what it did on the previous volumes).
2. Mailing list setup. Oh joy. More learning. Learning is fun. I love learning. Just not so much a fan of the *techy*-learny stuff.

Stay tuned for the release announcement and a cool offer for being on my not-quite-ready-yet mailing list.

Looking Back: I successfully set that list up... and promptly forgot about it. Once my millions of readers find me, I'll certainly have to relearn more techy-ish stuff.
Little Miss hates tech and is still trying to bribe me to write that all-genre blood loss story.

105

FOR ALL YOUR HOLIDAY ESCAPE NEEDS...

The holidays are coming.

And boy, will they look different this year. Massive election stress hangs over our heads and will likely continue to hang over our turkeys come Thanksgiving.

Add to that the never-ending game of dodge-a-virus and things get really interesting.

But.

There's a way to escape.

Yessirreee.

Escape the politics. Escape the virus of doom. Escape Aunt Agnes and her cheek-pinching, butt-smacking greeting-at-the-door. Escape Uncle Abner's fruit cake takes. The screaming from the kids' table.

The teens with their faces in their phones.

The fire in the kitchen.

The cat that just piddle-pawed his way through the sweet potatoes, dragging marshmallow topping across Great-Grandma's vintage lace tablecloth.

Throw in the dishtowel. Let the pumpkin pie smolder.

Run to your bedroom.

Or the bathroom. Or the cellar. (We don't judge here).

Slam the door.

Escape it all... For just a moment:

Taken from WMG Publishing's Kickstarter Description:

"...this year the **WMG Holiday Spectacular** is back, with 37 brand new and original stories by over two dozen top fiction writers. This year subscribers will get the first story on November 26th, 2020 and then a new story **EVERY DAY** through January 1st, 2021.

That's right! **A Brand New Original Holiday Story Every Day!**"

In advent-calendar style, a new story in your inbox each day. And this year, the stories don't stop with the New Year. Also available are shorts for February and October 2021, again with stories delivered to your inbox.

I've got a couple of tales tucked in this special event, but I can't tell you which ones or when they'll pop up—I don't even know what day my stories are slotted for. That's the fun.

Each day a new surprise.

Each day a new short story told by pro writers who grab you by the imagination and transport you, well, somewhere else.

So take a gander at the Kickstarter—You've got until November 17th. Read the dates on the specials carefully, some options are for 2019's tales. Others are for this year's advent. You can get just the calendars in email/electronic form or you can get the books, too, once they're ready next year.

Keep an eye out here or on the Facebook feed for more announcements about this amazing project and for B.A. Paul and Little Miss Muse to get their collective act together for their own project announcements coming soon...

Have a great week!

Looking Back: Since this announcement is a couple of years old, I can talk about it now. (Note to new authors: Always, always read the terms of your contract so you stay in the good graces of those who care enough to give you cold, hard cash for your work.)

The stories I sold to the 2020 WMG Holiday Spectacular were "All the Bells and Whistles", which you can find in Hijacked Holidays. "I Remember

Paperclips" is in *Spunk and Spice Volume 2. Both collections are available at bapaul.com or Amazon.*

WMG still puts out a yearly calendar of holiday short stories. Very cool project and something totally different from the norm...

Little Miss Muse fondly remembers the fun she had at the shark swimming pool in the Golden Nugget in Vegas while I was at the anthology workshop where these sales went down.

Yes. She had fun. But our second trip to Vegas... well, you'll just have to keep reading to find out what trouble she caused this go-round.

106

IT COULD HAPPEN

Today is October 29th. I'm writing ahead a bit. When this goes live on the blog on 11/9, October will be over. At least I think so. I'm doing one of those don't-know-the-day routines. And it's still 2020, so we may have gotten some weird Daylight Savings Time extension for this month. Or someone finally got their magic wand in the mail and reset this awfulness ahead or behind or to wherever the world screwed up for a do-over.

It could happen.

But I don't think my magic wand order from early March was ever received. I didn't get the email verification and figured Wands-R-Us went out of business...

By the time you read this, the election will be over. At least I think so, though it wouldn't surprise me if we don't have a winner figured out. Or someone else came in and declared themselves POTUS and the other two old white guys and their respective posses decided this mess we're in would be better off dealt with by someone else. Anyone else.

It could happen.

And my quarantine will be over. I hope.

Yup. That's right. I'm the unhappy recipient of a small dose of

Covid. Very small, I think. For that, I'm thankful. But it came on the convergence of all that lab work, thyroid hoo-ha, and the onset of allergies. Or was it just allergies?

Who knows where I picked it up. Likely multiple lab and doc visits had something to do with it. Or the flu shot I got a few days before taxed my immune system and Covid came in for the sneak attack.

That could've happened.

And, as grumpy as I'd been about the previously listed maladies, I'm grateful they stymied my already diminished out-and-about-around-human interaction opportunities. I'd been hanging close to home simply because of bright lights, headaches, and generally not feeling well. No fever though—until the flu shot took hold, sending a six-inch bright red streak down my arm from the injection site.

Yeah. That happened.

At any rate, the very morning of the day I was to have lunch with my mother, I discovered my taste buds had packed their bags for an extended vacation.

It took trying a multitude of breakfast items, tossing each into the trash with a gag and an "Oh my word! All the food in my kitchen went bad at once." Biscuits, bananas, sausage. All of it rancid. All at once.

What on earth did Walmart Grocery do? Send us bad food? When they picked my order, did they leave it in the hot sun? They're gonna get a phone call...

Then slowly, slowly (remember, thyroid fog, right?) it dawned on me. Then I panicked and tried a potato chip. Nothing.

Peanut butter. Nothing. Just my tongue stuck to the roof of my mouth by a tasteless paste.

Sherbet. Ditto.

Peanut butter on top of lime sherbet. (Can you sense my desperation?)

Nothing.

Zip. Zilch. Nada.

Then I heard Stella Marie kicking around in the litter box.

But I didn't *smell* Stella Marie.

Now, Stella is the most drop-dead gorgeous cat with the sweetest little personality. But man. Her litter box trips usually send us all scrambling for the pooper scooper, a Walmart sack, and a trip to the outside bin for fresh air if nothing else.

But I couldn't smell Stella.

Then I *knew*.

And I called my mom and cancelled lunch. And called my doctor who sent me on a wild goose chase to track down an open appointment slot in our area to get the infamous NG swab.

Again, I think my case may have been the mildest of mild. Vague aches. Weakness. No smell. No taste. One night of an excruciating headache (which became downright scary when the pain got so bad that I broke out in pajama-drenching sweat). The residual headache lasted a couple of days.

I had exactly one coughing spell.

But overall, I think I got off lucky.

Or blessed. Let's call it blessed.

For the loss of taste on that very first day, I am so very thankful. Had I discovered it a day later (or even four hours later), I would've dined with Mom, visited an aunt, and likely checked in on the mom-in-law. Because I was feeling fine (only allergies, right? Flu shot fatigue? Grumpy thyroid leftovers?). I'd have exposed my three gals for sure as I blamed my vague symptoms on a slew of other things.

A week later, and my taste buds have returned. Well, five or so of them. The five that are responsible for detecting vinegar. Vinegar in broccoli cheddar soup (which I won't have again for many, many, many years). Vinegar in plain toast. Vinegar in the pot roast. Vinegar in my cinnamon roll.

And the smell thing isn't much better. Mostly I smell burnt popcorn — though no one has burned anything nor has anyone popped popcorn. I still can't smell Stella.

Occasionally I smell the Lysol.

Often I smell vinegar.

But today, October 29th, I'm feeling a bit clearer headed. I'm much less weak. I've not had to collapse on the couch in a fit of exhaustion since waking up four hours ago. Yesterday I was on the couch after two hours of "up time" (though I haven't ventured outside in the rain to get the mail. That did me in yesterday for round three on the couch).

Today I will remain upright until the mail comes — and beyond!

It could happen! Baby steps here without the aid of a magic wand. Tiny goals...

I'm looking at my calendar (Go ahead and laugh. It's okay...) and tentatively planning in *very light and highly erasable pencil* some writing projects for November. If November and the people waiting in those days behave.

Hey, it could happen.

I'm excited about the projects. Some publishing stuff.

Some writing stuff.

A nice mix for my mixed-up, muddled mind. Tiny little tidbits that I can control no matter what the next few weeks hold.

I did get that collection up and running that I'd mentioned a few weeks ago. It's live in the Amazon shop and it's under the Book tab here on the blog: All the Feels Volume 3.

Slowly, slowly, I'm wrangling all those short stories into something that looks like progress.

And I started on the newsletter signup process. It's a work in progress that got stalled by, well, if you've read this far you know why it got stalled.

So, dear Reader, you're in November. November 9th or maybe a few days later depending when you stumbled onto this post. I'm back there on October 29th. I don't know what your world looks like yet. The one I've yet to catch up to.

Maybe it's tumultuous with election junk, virus junk, riots, blazes, or ice storms. Boy I sure hope not.

Maybe it's peaceful. Perhaps allowing a deep exhale from this wonky-donkey-butt year we've all had.

Hey, that could happen.

Because...

Perhaps you've found a way to unwind. To stay healthy and active and engaged in something positive. Perhaps you've discovered a quiet, soul-filling activity to ease your mind and heart.

Perhaps you've turned your back on the chaos and said "Stuff it," and refocused your energy on something you can control in your own little world.

And if you've been successful, when I catch up to you on November 9th, we can swap tips. At the very least we can swap some daydreams and gratitude lists and place our magic wand orders together from that new start-up I saw the other day.

I heard there's a discount if you buy the wands in bulk…

Looking Back: 765 days ago, I thought the world may rebound to "before."
Clearly, we've all learned that "before" only exists 1,067 days ago (prior to 1/1/20) and what we have now is, well, how it is.
On a positive note, 765 days later, I can eat broccoli occasionally, but I still pick up a hint of vinegar. Unfortunately, I am able to smell Stella Marie.
Little Miss Muse says she never gets sick with viruses, being a muse and all, and doesn't understand how something so tiny can cause such havoc.
Little Miss is about as tall as my knee, a chonky little imp. Small things can cause massive havoc, indeed.

107

THE SQUEAK

Anyone who knows me well understands how much I despise paying for "temperature." My little corner of heaven will be 67 degrees with a light breeze and zero—I mean zero—humidity.

In that wonky Indiana U.S.A. period between spring and summer (and likewise again between fall and winter), where the cycle goes from frost one day and 90-degree swelter the next—and where the open-all-the-windows period lasts long enough to open them all then run back through the house and close them all before the temp swings—I'll drag a box fan or a tiny space heater around from room to room to avoid "flipping the switch."

Flipping the switch: Turning on the main AC/Furnace to Cool/Heat the domicile. I may as well leave a window open—screen-less—and stand and toss money into the great outdoors. Fistfuls of dollars at a time. And we all know, once that switch has been good and flipped, it stays that way for months on end because we get spoiled.

Then, when the next temp change comes, I have to wean my peeps (humans and critters) back to my 67-degree happy place.

It's a struggle. (Yes, I know it's a first-world struggle, but we bloom and complain where we're planted.)

I despise paying for temperature.

Well, that wonky period happened while I was recovering from Covid. Me and my little space heater enjoying our cozy, isolated nest on the couch and me completely oblivious that the rest of the gang was freezing to death in the nether-regions of the house that I was trying to stay out of.

Waking up with blue lips and frostbitten toes.

Whining.

Complaining.

Until I finally gave the okay to flip the switch. Ah, well.

Poor Stella Marie *hates* the flipping of the switch. The growl of the furnace and the breeze from the floor vents freaks her all the way out. She cried and complained for three days, flipping her bushy tail in our faces and taking off down the hall like she'd been shot out of a rocket to escape the noise, only to find her favorite spot at the end of that hall also had a floor vent.

First-world cat problems.

As I started feeling better, I spent more time in the office. More time at the screen writing/plotting/dreaming of publishing—you know, what we all do when we have the time, right? Well, my office shares a wall with the utility room. Where the furnace is. The furnace that kicks on every quarter hour it seems...

And you know that squeak that happens when you're driving down the road and someone's water bottle or change holder or something in the dash starts rattling around? And you go berserk slamming the vents and rearranging items in cupholders to JUST GET IT TO STOP?

Something, on the office side of that shared wall, started that annoying squeak like Styrofoam against plastic.

I tried to ignore it. But that took too much away from my already depleted brain. I had better things to do with my energy than to force an ignore of a situation I could handle.

The next time the furnace kicked on, I smacked the wall. It didn't stop.

Twenty minutes later, on the next cycle, I moved all the items away from the wall. Secured the loose pens and paperclip jar and books that may have leaned too far off the bookshelf. It didn't stop.

I stomped the floor. It didn't stop.

I went in search of Amara's rogue cat toy springs behind the desk, but found none.

"Where's it coming from?" I yelled at my office full of cats and Little Miss who all four went scrambling down the hall. (I've always hated the sound of someone crunching ice or crackling plastic or clicking pens—my husband says I could hear a flea belch from across the room—but never have I been so enraged over the furnace. And I'm *paying* for that sound... urggg. It's like a spin-off from The Princess and the Pea, only with sound waves.)

So I stood and waited until the next furnace cycle. I put my ear to the wall next to my hanging gallery display of twenty-plus treasures sourced from multiple comic conventions, artwork from my kid, and a minuscule blue embroidered bunny patch that I found and framed after Grandma died (don't ask... that's a story for another day).

And I waited.

Bingo! One of my twenty-plus frames was jiggling against the wall.

The furnace kicked off before I could find which one. I only had enough time to rule out an Ewok, one unicorn, and Wonder Woman.

Back to the computer to wait until the next cycle. Got a few more words in. Then ear to the wall one last time to rule out Willy Wonka, that little blue bunny, and a *second* unicorn (yes, I know I have a problem, but it's a consistent problem, so there's that going for me...).

Then I found it.

At the very center of my gallery in the largest frame—a '70s molded plastic deal found at Goodwill and repurposed just for this wall to house one of my favorite characters.

Big Bird was the one complaining every time the furnace came on. I scored this print from a talented artist to commemorate the day I met Caroll Spinney, the puppeteer, at a comic convention. Now the yellow marvel hangs over my workspace, just squeaking away.

Ungrateful fowl. I secured the corner of the frame with sticky tack, and all is well once more.

You could see Kermit, E.T. and the whole Wizard of Oz gang, who hang just on the other side of Big Bird, reach up quickly to wipe the sweat from their brows as they narrowly escaped such serious accusation as to dare tinker with the sanity of the one not-quite-right-in-the-first-place.

Big Bird took his scolding like a man, the cats returned one by one as they realized their human wasn't going to blame them or set their tails ablaze, and Little Miss Muse floated in on a wave of lavender sparkles.

The writing resumed, the only sounds the clicking of the laptop keys and the ticking of the clock.

Until... the furnace kicked on again.

And...

"Where's that *COMING FROM*?!?!?"

Looking Back: I love my gallery wall of childhood favs. I've thought about rearranging my office or painting the walls-which would require taking down gobs of art. So, here I sit in the same spot, but the gang on the wall is happy. Very much looking forward to the Comicons starting up again to meet more artists. I seem to be missing Mr. Rogers, Indiana Jones, and the velociraptor from Jurassic Park.

I'll be sure to secure the frames against the wall with a few more Command hooks than I think necessary.

Little Miss Muse believes she will one day be so famous that artists from the world over will paint her likeness...

There's not enough purple paint in the universe to capture her ego.

108

WOULD YOU BE MY GUINEA PIG?

I f all things held strong and stable over the last couple of weeks (my recovery, the weather, the wifi and that blasted squeaky gallery wall) there should be a nifty new tab at the tip top of this blog. It should say Newsletter.

Under that tab should be a way to sign up with your email and get a free copy of my story "The Dragonfly."

Would you try it out?

Be my guinea pig? Pretty please?

Help me work out the kinks and knots and tangles.

Because, if you've followed the blog for any length of time, you know how I am with processes that require more than a couple of steps (or anything written in recipe format and requiring the application of heat).

And getting this newsletter thing set up required, well, about fifty steps.

Now I realize that there was probably a quicker, more direct way to upload the story manuscript into a delivery system, compose an email, comply with all the email regulations set for business dealings, get that email to send, make sure the story manuscript is in a file format my dear readers can enjoy on any device (pdf, mobi, epub) and get the links in the right spots.

Clickable, useable links, not ones leading to a dead end. And not ones that lead to Amazon's amazing daily deal on crockpots that you can sync to your phone (this product requires the application of heat AND employs digital setup, so that'd be a hard pass on my end...).

But I'm a novice at this publishing world stuff and apart from hiring someone to do it (and *that* taking hours upon hours to try to explain what I truly don't understand) or asking thirty different folks I met in the Vegas writing workshop how they did it and would they fly to Indiana mid-pandemic to help me out, I muddled through.

Fifty steps worth or so.

But hopefully, on your end, it's just a couple of clicks.

Click the button in the Newsletter menu.

Enter your email.

Check your inbox for a BookFunnel notification (if your inbox has strong filters, BookFunnel may have gone to spam). Open the BookFunnel email and follow the link to get your free download.

Four or five clicks for you. Fifty for me.

Pretty please be my guinea pig and let me know via bapaulwrites@comcast.net or on the Facebook message string for this blog announcement that it worked (Yay! Thank you very much). Or that it didn't work (Thank you for your patience, and I'll start the bug fixes).

Cheers! And thank you so much in advance.

Looking Back: The newsletter effort paid off and it still works. You can sign up on the website if you'd like and receive "The Dragonfly" for your efforts. Little Miss Muse is reminded of the electronic crock pot thingy and thinks that would be a nice Christmas gift for her to try making grape taffy with lavender—
Nope. Nope. And not a chance.

109

HOLD THAT THOUGHT

2020 has been a real gem, has it not?

Toilet paper shortages.

Travel bans.

Murder hornets.

Fires ablaze.

Cancelled plans.

And that blasted virus.

Which my mother picked up in the course of caring for others. Bless her heart. She's been hospitalized and is having a dastardly time of it.

Due to my limited thought capacity and lack of time and energy, this is a placeholder blog.

Why?

Because I've not missed a blog since I started this thing over 100 blog posts ago. And streaks are a powerful thing, I've been finding out.

Well over a year ago I wrote an "Emergency Blog" post that Web Guy had in his files in the case of an emergency. I almost pulled that card. But nope. I'm pounding this update out as I sit and wait on news from the hospital. Because that emergency blog would be like not writing a blog.

It felt like cheating.

And I like this corner of my writing world.

Even when my self-imposed goals and deadlines have gone to the wayside, this little spot keeps ticking along. It feels a normal part of life now. "Gotta get the blog done." "Gotta plan out the blog." "OOH! What a cool idea for a blog..." You get the idea.

And as I quarantine AGAIN, alone in Mom's house waiting for news, I needed this little corner. This tiny bit of normal.

So.

Next week, you'll get a free fiction short story. The following week another short update or I might be back at it. Time will tell.

If you haven't signed up for the newsletter, check the menu/tab bar and give it a shot...

But the streak continues. No missed posts. Blog 109.

Now, if we can just get mother on a streak with her breathing and energy levels, we'll show COVID who's boss...

Looking Back: That was a miserable time, for sure. I ate alone for Thanksgiving, watching Big Bird float along in the Macey's parade. But wow, was that awful. I did, though, with all that isolation time throw myself into a massive 1000-piece Star Wars jigsaw puzzle.
Little Miss Muse believes I should've thrown myself into our work-in-progress—
But sometimes, the CIRCUS doesn't allow for creative thought processes.

110

DECK THE DUCKS

I've written before about my duck problems. These never seem to go away. I guess ducks and the lines they do or do not form are inevitable. Like death and taxes.

Ducks not in rows.

Ducks swimming in the wrong ponds.

Distracted ducks.

Drunken ducks in daffodil patches.

And now, evidently, the calendar has dumped us in December where ducks must be decorated, shopped for, lit up, and hung over the mantel.

If you followed along a couple of weeks ago, you know our little family got hit with some long, drawn-out COVID chaos. Me in October. Then Mom in November (she didn't get it from me). Now Hubs in the merry month of holiday cheer (he didn't get it from me or Mom).

It appears we're doing a good job of staying away from each other's germs (or inhaling just the right amount of Lysol), just not the rest of the world's 'rona crud.

And now my back is squawking from chasing ducklings, ducks, geese and other uncooperative fowl that jump on the to-do list. I'm typing this standing up, waiting for the anti-inflammatory to kick in.

Threw the ice pack in the freezer and I'm scheduling some quality time with that chilly friend in an hour or so. Gonna be an interesting day...

So, another placeholder blog of sorts while I keep my blogging streak alive and while we figure out which ducks infiltrated our line without the proper paperwork, which ducks waddled off, and which ducks should be decorated.

A few ducks need to be paid off and shipped out of the country.

Until next week, here's wishing you health and peace and happiness while you deck your own ducks.

Looking Back: Holidays are hard for me—for some reasons I've made public and others I'll keep to myself. At any rate, I'm always very glad when the "jolly" passes and January arrives with its crisp, clean calendar pages and the world goes from reds and greens to whites and blues.
Little Miss Muse pats me on the shoulder (she understands my end-of-year struggles) and believes all holidays should simply wear purple.
She's probably not wrong.

111

FANCY FREAKOUT

"All writers without exception are scared to death. Some simply hide it better than others"—Richard Simon of Simon & Schuster

"The Art of War for Writers" by James Scott Bell has been my nighttime companion for a number of weeks now.

Nighttime companion defined: The book/author I'm currently reading before turning out the lights for the night.

(The hubs gets a little disturbed when I say I'm taking a specific author to bed with me. For example, "I'm sleeping with John Grisham tonight," or "Time to hit the sheets with Dean Koontz" just doesn't sit well. So "nighttime companion" it shall be until *that* doesn't register well, either, and I'll find a new way to freak him out.)

Bell covers mental acuity, practical tactics, and general publishing advice all in the style of the Chinese General Sun Tzu. Many of the ancient warrior's methods can be applied to all different aspects of life and business—not just war or writing.

Though sometimes sitting down to the keyboard or wrestling with an unruly character certainly feels like a battle.

I used to be scared to death and exhausted trying to hide it.

Writing for the short story challenges and submitting short story (after story after story) for editorial consideration got me over that fear. I don't mind getting rejection letters. I simply send the story out again or publish it myself. No fear. No worries.

But now, the worry's shifted.

After our round with the COVID chaos, the fear is getting back into the battle, so to speak. Will my Little Miss Muse keep showing up?

Will I remember where my InDesign buttons are when I go to create my next ebook?

Will I ever hit that glorious stride again, where fingers and brain have taken over and time stands still and the characters come alive and dance to their own tunes on the screen before my eyes? And I'm not "there" anymore? (Some call this a flow state, others call it insanity.)

Am I insane? (Please, for those of you who've signed up for the newsletter, don't email me about this point. I already know I'm a few clicks off normal.)

Have the real-life battles away from the writing created a mental chasm so wide between daytime drama and writing dreams that it can't be breached?

And oh. My. Word. I forgot I'd started a newsletter. Where'd I put the passwords to all of *that* stuff?

So, I freaked out a little last week. Well, okay. I had a complete and utter freakout. A black-tie-worthy, ball-gown donning fancy freakout.

Over the writing.

Over the buildup of stress of the last few months. Illness. Aging ones. Day job. Cats. Christmas. Writing.

And the writing should be fun, doggonit.

So, I did the unthinkable.

I bought calendars.

Plural.

Multiple.

They're everywhere. Dated ones. Blank ones.

Highlighters, pencils (with fresh, clean erasers), and pens of all colors litter my desktop. Post-It thanks me for my end-of-year contribution to their bottom line, as does White-Out.

All in an effort to control and create a fanciful structure on which to hang publishing and writing goals and dreams for the new year while maintaining balance and sanity with the real world.

Most of the calendars came from the Dollar Store, and at a buck apiece, I can afford to have further fancy and flamboyant freakouts and throw them across the room, into the garbage, out the window, or set them ablaze...

I'm taking this nugget from the book to put into practice today:

"If in the midst of difficulties, we are always ready to seize an advantage, we may extricate ourselves from misfortune." — *Sun Tzu*

James Scott Bell calls it "a snatcher of time."

And thus, the calendars. And the dream-planning. And the goal-setting. It all starts afresh with the new normal of "nothing is normal, not yet" mentality.

Snag a day here. An hour there. Fifteen minutes waiting on my boys to find their keys? Maybe that's enough time to forward-scoot the manuscript 200 words or so.

A slow day at work? Butt in chair, fingers on keyboard. 500 more words I didn't have before.

Raging ahead, freaking out and fearless all at the same time.

One specific fear, after having sold a handful of shorts to professional publications, is that the next story will be trite at best. At worst, a twisted jungle of cliches and low-hanging fruit presenting mere kindergarteners the opportunity to spin better yarns than B.A. Paul.

The Art of War for Writers helped sort these bits out.

And perhaps the book's re-quote that hit me in the gut the hardest comes from a man I'd only heard of here and there in writing courses when an instructor would refer to him as "prolific." I looked him up. And yes, one must scroll and scroll to get through Harlan Ellison's bibliography which spans novels, shorts and screen plays, not to mention wearing your index finger and a mouse out scrolling his awards.

And, from a cursory exploration of his Wikipedia page, the man was someone many thin-skinned folks would avoid due to his, well, cantankerous personality. Wiki even gave him a "Controversies and Disputes" section.

I digress to the quote, addressing my fancy freakout of future "bad" writing. The quote is as true for writers as it is for carpenters or cooks, golfers, or guitarists:

"If someone who writes that badly can become a writer, then even the dippiest of us can become a writer, chacma baboons can become writers, sludge and amoeba can become writers. The trick is not in becoming a writer. It is in staying a writer. Day after week after month after year. Staying in there for the long haul." — Harlan Ellison

So thanks, James Scott Bell, for accompanying me through many nighttime hours. Thanks for gleaning these quotes and offering practical tactics and a much-needed reset for my tired-out brain.

And, after a quick rabbit trail down the Google hole, I came across more quotes from Harlan. Most can't be re-quoted here due to the, ahem, adult ratings.

But I'll leave you with this one...

This quote is believed to be a Harlan Ellison original, though some may argue the origin. However, no one in their right mind—or even in the middle of their own version of a fancy freakout—would argue that it doesn't fit 2020 like a glove:

"The two most common elements in the universe are Hydrogen and stupidity."

Looking Back: The Art of War for Writers will need to be replaced soon. I've about worn the cover and the first few pages right out of the book. I visit it about once a year and I highly recommend it. I guess I do this because I still wrestle with the fears and issues it addresses. I'm likely to be crowned Queen of the Fancy Freakout if I don't find a Couch Guy (or Gal) soon. On a positive note, I did fire InDesign from my life and am now the happy, tear-free licensee of a program that doesn't make me want to cuss and fling the laptop through a window.

Little Miss Muse believes if I'd just listen to her, she possesses the answer that would address all my issues: Just sit down and write.

She's not wrong.

112

KISS IT GOODBYE

This past year's been a doozy, right?

Soon (if they haven't already) the major networks will start their year in review of photos and video clips of major happenings. Any other year, I'd likely watch a couple of those broadcasts. Sit on the couch with a cat and a fuzzy blanket and go, "Oh, yeah. I forgot about that" or "Wow. Did that happen this year? Seems so long ago..." and other such comments as are necessary when one reviews a whole year's content in a half-hour production.

I think I'll skip it this year, though. Kiss that tradition goodbye.

Then there's my own typical reflection time of "what did I accomplish in the last twelve months?" I had goals on 1/1/2020 that never materialized. Other goals took front-and-center. Goals like routine sanity-saving walks in the rain, watching over my "most vulnerable citizens," and generally surviving multiple COVID quarantines and still be married on the other end...

And being okay with only accomplishing that. That goal of watching and surviving and saving brain cells for the next battle.

I gave myself a huge gift and kissed the yearly routine of rehashing what did and didn't get accomplished in this year from Hades goodbye.

Kissed it real hard.

And we all know down deep in our knowers that 2021 will hold no more or less magic than we all thought 2020 held on December 31, 2019. The virus, political upheaval, and social injustices won't vanish because the ball drops just right, the clock strikes a certain tone, or the fireworks crackle and pop just so. 1/1/2021 will not be much different than 5/2/2020 or 9/23/2020, or any other random day we could choose from the calendar.

Unless we choose it to be different, that is.

We can choose productivity instead of procrastination.

We can choose joy over growling about how bad things are.

We can choose new adventures in new directions in new hobbies (or resurrect old loves).

We can choose. Despite what the media shows us. Despite what the forecast says. Despite the numbers and graphs and charts that have been thrust in our faces every time we see a screen.

We can choose. In our own little corners.

We can choose how we respond.

By the time this blog posts, we'll spend only four more days in 2020, give or take. We get to choose how we spend these last moments of this "unprecedented, uncertain, tumultuous" year. Backward-bemoaning or forward-reaching.

Then, at 11:59 on 12/31/2020 or thereabouts, we can choose to say adios to 2020 in joyful remembrance or raging regret, in angst or exhilaration, in flamboyant hilarity or in despair. We can choose.

Good riddance.

Sayonara.

Bonjour.

Ciao.

And then kiss it goodbye.

Looking Back: It's funny how God or the universe or mere coincidence show up. I needed these words I wrote to myself 705 days ago (Yes, my inner geek is adoring that "how many days since _____" Google search). Our raging

CIRCUS can throw me off-kilter and I temporarily forget that I do have a
choice to stay in the ring or leave the Big Top for a breather.
I can choose.
Little Miss Muse says that I choose poorly most times. During those
breathing breaks (she says this with air quotes, her lavender nail polish
glittering in the office light) I should choose writing instead. Who needs to
breathe? Breathing is overrated—
I point out she's not entirely wrong, but could I please have her permission
to multitask writing and breathing.
She's thinking on it.

113

COUNTDOWN TIME!

M any of you know over the last few months I've been working on getting a handle on my short stories. They were everywhere. Deep in cyberspace. Waiting on submissions. Waiting on acceptance or rejection answers from publishers. In drawers and files galore.

Everywhere.

The result of my grand short-story wrangling is a handful of books organized by genre and now available on Amazon in ebook and paperback form.

The good news?

I've placed six of the different ebook collections on a countdown sale that will end one week from today. After that?

I'm seriously leaning toward "going wide" with these collections. They'll go back to the $4.99 price point and be available not just on Amazon, but also on other marketplaces like Kobo, Apple, and Barnes & Noble.

Or maybe not.

I've not decided.

Time will tell, as 2021 has started me on another kind of countdown—one that has more to do with life events than writing, but all life events affect the writing. If I have time to send them wide, I will. If the next three months look shady (and, let's be real, 2020 is still casting a long, deep shadow on the start of this year, so lots and lots of shade to be found), then I'll keep these ebooks exclusive on Amazon for another three months and there would be another promotion in the future.

But for right now, here's the deal: These six will be on sale for an incremental sale, starting with 99 cents today (1/11/21), then gradually increasing in price over the next seven days until they reach their $4.99 price point once again.

Here are the ones in the sale:

Out There: Sci-Fi

Just a Tick of Whimsy Volume 2: Fantasy

Mystery Minutes: Mysteries

All the Feels Volumes 1 and 2: Feel-good general fiction

Spunk and Spice: A bit of feel-good, a bit of mystery, all showcasing some spunky senior citizenry

And, until at least mid-February, if you have a Kindle Unlimited subscription, you can read them for free! But hurry. If 2021 loosens the noose around my neck and I can shake free the minutes, these titles will be sent to other ebook distributors and will no longer be KU options.

I hope the start of your New Year was gloriously peaceful. I hope the rest of the year will be, too.

If not, find a good book—or six—hunker down, and wait out the shadiness!

Looking Back: Those titles went wide, meaning they're available in multiple locations like Barnes & Noble, Apple, Google, and on my own site. I just finished formatting five new ones, which will start on Amazon and also "go wide." And the fun thing is, stories never spoil. So no matter what shade you're dealing with, you can always grab a book or four—no matter when it was published—and escape from your current conundrums.

Little Miss Muse believes I should hire someone to format and publish things so she and I can simply write new words.
I inform her that would require a reduction in the amount of grape bubble gum, purple soda, and lavender glitter I purchase through the year.
She's okay with me doing this "grunt" work for the time being...

114

TANGLED

Have you ever dealt with Christmas tree lights that "someone" threw haphazardly into storage the year before? Even if those lights weren't ripped from the branches of your tree in the throes of cleanup, and even if those lights had been carefully wound back up, even being next to one another can cause the bulbs and wires to make, well, connections.

I've done that. And sometimes I needed a trash bin and a trip to Dollar General for new strands. I don't have the patience.

Have you ever dealt with a drawer full of old necklaces? The delicate chains intertwining and doubling back on themselves in hopeless knots?

I've done this, too, sometimes requiring toothpicks or tweezers to tease apart the tangles.

How about a fishing line? When the reel spits out great gobs and chunks of line for no good reason other than to turn what should be a peaceful outing into a frustrating restringing fiasco. Or when your fishing buddy casts their line over the top of yours and the lines tangle mid-pond?

I've experienced this. Many times. Out comes the pocketknife for a well-placed slice just above the knotted mess. Restart.

Likewise when a child decides to "curl" their own hair with a rounded brush. Or with the tires of a Hot Wheels car (why???). Lord, help me, I've dealt with the screaming demons these events produce. Bring out the scissors and peanut butter and place a phone call to the salon.

(In case you aren't aware, peanut butter supposedly smooths out knots and help the strands of hair slide easily out of the tangle. Supposedly. I have two children who may disagree with this at-home remedy and whose noggins smelled of nuts for days.)

Knitting yarn? Sewing machine gobbles? I can't say that I've dealt with the sewing world so much, but I've heard stories. And I also heard that cats like to help.

Well, Little Miss Muse handed me a complicated, tangled mess of a short story. Never before have I had one come to me in such chunks intermingled with fishing line-like knots. Here a chunk, there a knot, another chunk.

Then she'd bounce back into the room and declare "I've got the perfect ending!" And I'd type it out for her. Never you mind that she'd not supplied me with an appropriate beginning, let alone the makings of a middle.

The next thing I'd hear is a paragraph—not an entire scene, mind you, just a paragraph—of the middle of the middle.

Then, she'd startle cats and throw purple glitter, yelling, "Hey! Whaddya think of this?" Then out would spill the end of the beginning. Or some tiny sentence fragment.

And, then, out of the clear blue sky (well, at the time I was writing the story in question the skies had remained dull winter gray for days, but you get the idea), Little Miss Muse would stroll into the office, her chubby little finger scratching her chin and say, "Do you think we should cut that bit about..." and she'd proceed to tell me which bits to clip, poke toothpicks at, or smear peanut butter on.

I want to like this story. But I don't yet.

I want to connect with the character in the scene, but Little Miss just exploded the set and wants to do a re-cast.

Sitting down to the computer for this tale feels like being handed a jigsaw puzzle by an excited three-year-old and you know good and well that puzzle's missing a third of the pieces and, likely, there's peanut butter smeared on the rest.

I must admit this has shown me just how addicted I am to that "flow state" where somehow the story goes from my brain, out the fingers, and onto the screen without so much as a thought about the black-and-white marks required to communicate the adventure. That glorious dance between muse and mind. Effortless.

But this is not that day. This wee fib of a tale is not effortless.

This tale, I fear, will require a visit to my thinking couch with my fuzzy unicorn blanket, a yarn-free cat, and a giant jar of peanut butter for good measure.

And as soon as my delete and backspace keys stop smoldering, I'll summon Little Miss. She and I will have a stern staff meeting, and then I'll get back at it.

I will finish this dastardly short if it's the only thing I get done this week!

UPDATE: The above was written mid-writing of "Just Enough." Now, I'm a few days removed from the trauma of it all, and here's the outcome:

I had just about enough of writing "Just Enough."

I like the beginning paragraph. I like the ending four lines. Exactly four—no more. A total of about 300 words. I'm not a fan of the 4303 words in the middle.

I like one out of the five characters. One. The snarky one. The one that could cause mayhem and spill blood. But it wasn't that type of a story.

Should the story be rejected out of its current market, that one paragraph, four lines and one character may get their own show. We'll have grand fun.

But the rest of it may be stuck in a drawer to be seen no more, no more, no more, no more. A hit-the-road-Jack sort of thing.

And don'tcha come back no more.

In the end, some doors were slammed. Some "do not disturb" signs were hung. But it's done. Submitted on time. Finished.

Overall, though, Little Miss seems no worse for the wear. She's still prancing and dancing. And I'm simply proud that I managed to refrain from smearing Jiffy on my laptop monitor.

Looking Back: It was rejected. That fool of a tale. But, it made it into Spunk and Spice Volume 2, given the role the grandparents play. It fits well there, even though it gave me fits to write.
Little Miss Muse declares she knew that was its destiny all along. "It gave us another title, didn't it? Without it you'd be one story short for Spunk." Without it, I'd have had the brain cells to have finished two or three other things, but I digress...

115

IN THE FLAP OF A WING

E ver heard of the butterfly effect? Where something as simple as the flap of a delicate wing can change the course of something much bigger, say, the weather?

I have a true-to-life tale of a butterfly effect. Where a few tiny decisions cumulated in a much different outcome of an event than would not have otherwise happened.

Or maybe I was simply playing a cosmic game of dominos in which the last one fell in my tiny town's library parking lot on a dreary winter day just this month...

Or perhaps it's a case of apophenia—forcing meaningful connections between unrelated events.

I'll let you decide:

Picture It: Illinois, 1958.

A company called Enesco was born, destined to bring high-quality giftware to the United States and beyond. Precious Moments was their head-of-the-pack line, but they branded other figurines for all seasons and all tastes. For clarity, giftware refers to knick-knacks, what-nots and other dust-collecting items that would sit on shelves in the '70s, rest in curio cabinets in the '80s, hide in attics in the '90s, and eventually end up as Goodwill treasures or estate sale finds.

Meanwhile, in Pennsylvania, author Dean Koontz writes and writes. And has his first bestseller in 1973. And keeps writing them, and writing them, and writing...

In the late '70s, Beth is born in a tiny hospital in Indiana. No one would call her B.A. Paul for many decades, but there you have it.

On some unknown day in some unknown year, someone, likely a lady (we shall call her Mrs. Collector), purchased a set of four Enesco figurines. The knick-knacks, ahem. Excuse me. Giftware. The giftware featured tiny children in various playful scenes such as on a seesaw and playing with puppies. You get the idea. No idea when or where or who Mrs. Collector might have been. But she/he/they keep these tiny bisque pieces in great shape. Likely stored in bubble wrap in an attic somewhere east of the Mississippi River.

Lincoln City, Oregon, unknown year: Dean Wesley Smith records a writing class which tells aspiring authors to read best-selling books.

Indiana, 2017: Beth gets hit hard with the writing bug. Dreaming and goals take shape. Beth takes a writing class from Dean Wesley Smith. Who tells her that if she's to be a decent writer, she must read the bestsellers.

Beth starts reading the bestsellers.

(Hang with me now, I really am going somewhere with this... you're about to see the butterfly flap its wings and all the tiny dominos fall into place...)

Indiana, 2018: Beth and the Hubs attend an auction. We bid on and win a box of "giftware" with the sole purpose of putting the pieces on eBay to make a few bucks. Mrs. Collector's group of four playing children figurines were tucked inside this auction box. Sometime that next week, Beth lists these little people for sale on eBay.

Indiana, Summer 2019: We adopt a street kitten named Malachi Maxwell. He can't use his toes properly.

California 2020: Dean Koontz now has hundreds of pieces of work and remains on the bestseller list.

Indiana, December 26, 2020: Lockdowns have driven Beth nuts, coupled with the holiday chaos, and, at the first available opportunity, Beth goes to the library. Dean Koontz has a book in the "New" section, a bestseller, which means she needs to read it and remember to turn it back in in less than two weeks. (She read it in two days).

The lockdowns also mean that the Paul family has spent lots of time at home with Malachi Maxwell—who still cannot use his toes properly. He's destroyed the left leg on most of Beth's pants with little snags here, pulls of thread there. But alas, he can't help it...

Colorado, January 4, 2021: Mrs. Collector's figurines on Beth's eBay account tickle the interest of someone west of the Mississippi. The auction sells to a Denver buyer after all this time.

Indiana, January 5, 2021: Beth packs up the figurines and remembers she's finished the Dean Koontz book, which needs to be returned. Since the post office and the library in her tiny town are nestled right next to each other, the combined trip makes sense. Otherwise, she'd return the book on the 6th.

And since she'll be out anyway, she may as well see about a new pair of pants. But the clothing store doesn't open until 10.

So she waits. And writes. And writes some more (but not as much as Dean Koontz) until the clock strikes ten and it's time to leave. She loads up her book, her package and her wallet and drives downtown.

She approaches the turn to the library parking lot, intent on crossing the lot to return the hardback book in the outdoor dropbox. Other than the staff vehicles, no one is at the library yet.

Except one lone guy.

Another patron, an elderly gentleman from what Beth can tell under his jacket and mask, parks a tiny pickup truck and exits the vehicle as she pulls into the lot. He has a little stack of books tucked under his arm.

Then she sees it.

His pickup truck is moving. Very slowly. Barely inching.

She looks closer, applying a full stop to her own vehicle. Heart beating faster, peering through the glass of his pickup from the glass of her own vehicle to see if someone perhaps slid into the driver's seat after he exited.

She sees no one. Her heart beats faster. The truck picks up speed —if only by a few inches at a time.

The man is halfway to the library door, and his pickup truck is gaining on him.

Beth honks. Honks again and again. Her palms begin to sweat.

The man turns, clearly perturbed, and still does not see the truck.

Beth points frantically, about to exit her own vehicle to scream at him, because there's no way she can run that fast that far and stop the truck. Or even push the old guy out of the way.

Then he sees it.

His books fall from his arm to the ground. And, thank goodness he's spry for his age, he quickly covers the mere four steps needed to reach the driver's side door, jumps in and slams the brakes, stopping the truck at the very spot where he'd have been run over by it.

He waves his thanks after he re-parks the truck and gathers his books. Beth waves back, glad to not have witnessed a catastrophe of contusions and broken bones. Glad to not have needed to call 911.

Just glad.

Glad that she likes auctions and eBay and that someone founded Enesco. Glad that Mr. Koontz wrote and wrote and wrote. And that there are wonderful Mrs. Collectors out there. Glad she started taking writing courses from Mr. Smith and not someone else who may not have pounded home that she needed to read bestsellers. Glad that the week before that very Dean Koontz bestseller was available for borrowing and had to be returned sooner than is standard. Glad someone in Colorado prompted her to leave the house in the first place to mail a package—right next to the library. Glad, at least for this moment, that Malachi Maxwell's toes don't work quite right and that the clothing store doesn't open until ten.

If any one of those factors were missing or different??

Well.

You can use your imagination on how the dominos may have otherwise fallen...

Looking Back: I must say, when I reread this blog, I had no idea where it was going. After reading it, I remember that day, of course. But if I had stopped halfway through, I couldn't have told you about the little old guy and the rolling pickup truck. It was as if I was reading someone else's work there for a second.

Isn't it amazing how memories become buried then resurrected with a few lines of text?

At this stage of the game, it's amazing that I can remember stuff that happened at breakfast, let alone 677 days ago.

Little Miss Muse says I was reading someone else's work because it was she who gave me the idea for the sequence of butterfly flaps to begin with.

Thanks, Little Miss. What would I do without you?

116

LIFE ALONG THE WAY

The blog site was getting "heavy." Or at least it felt like it. A few months back I was trying to link to a previous post and had to dig and dig through the Blog Archive in the menu. Lots and lots of blogs. Over 100 to be precise.

This entry makes 116, not counting all the free fiction pieces...

So Web Guy and I (well, mostly Web Guy because I've no clue...) decided to put the blog on a diet and purge those first 100 blogs.

Actually, I really was going to purge the blogs, then Web Guy said, "Hey, I think you should purge the blogs." Right about the time that I was wrestling *Life Along the Way* through InDesign.

So it worked out well regardless.

Through this process, I went down memory lane from June of 2018 to September of the "year that shall not be named." I reread all 100 blogs, made notes for myself on lessons learned. I laughed a little at some of my stupidity-ridden thinking. Cringed a lot at typos that slipped by. And cried some over the "in memory" posts.

I think the hardest part of the project was coming up with a title. I noticed a pattern throughout the blogs — one that pervades every step of the writing journey: Life. Getting in the way. Life along the side. Life. Life keeps happening no matter what goals or dreams or hopes or disasters dash in and out of our way.

The second-hardest part was watching Little Miss Muse gloat from the corner of the office and take credit for EVERY GOOD THING since the dawn of time.

But I digress...

Life Along the Way will be free for Kindle Unlimited readers in e-book form. Paperback is available, and I'll run a free promotion every now and then as long as the book is exclusive to Amazon.

Thanks to all who have hung with me through this incredible ride so far. Thanks to those who are fairly new to the site. You are all appreciated!

P.S. The short story collections (Out There, Spice and Spunk, All the Feels, and Just a Tick of Whimsy volumes) will be going wide this spring. They'll remain in Kindle Unlimited until 2/16, so hurry and download if you've not already.

Looking Back: Life Along the Way has done pretty well for a newbie author-ish memoir thingy. You're actually reading its sequel right now. Isn't that cool?
I enjoy the blog quite a lot. Little Miss enjoys the blog. We'll keep doing it until it's not fun anymore. Then we'll do something else.
Little Miss Muse believes we will be writing the blog from beyond the grave.
Perhaps she's right. Or, someone else can ghost write it for us when we've crossed the veil...

117

ENOUGH!

I remember spending the weeks at a time with my grandparents as I was growing up. There was a rhythm to their day, honed out over decades of domesticated life. Rise with the sun in the summer—or before first rays in the winter, coffee pot on. Gas cooktop lit. Something sizzling in the cast iron skillet.

Breakfast at the tiny table in their small eat-in kitchen.

Reading time—mostly the remnants of the prior day's newspaper.

And then morning news, local and world.

Work in the garden. Lunch. Clean. Visit neighbors.

Coffee pot percolating again. Something boiling on the stove.

Lunch at the tiny table in the small eat-in kitchen.

And then the news at noon with (insert the name of the middle-aged anchorman or woman here).

Back to the garden, tending yard. More neighbors. Start supper. The peeling, chopping, basting, what have you.

Something baking in the oven. Coffee pot on its last shift of the day, eager to be cleaned and reset for the morning.

Supper at the tiny table in the small eat-in kitchen.

Pie. Always pie in the evening. Mostly raspberry. Sometimes apple or peach. Sometimes sugar cream for a change with a perfectly toasted meringue topping. Sometimes chocolate pudding. Raspberry, hands-down, was my favorite.

Then dishes. Another reset for the next morning.

And the evening news. Which included an hour on the local station, then Grandpa rising from his special chair to "turn the antennae" to better pick up a station from the west (or it could have been the east or any other cardinal direction—I'm directionally dyslexic). And then another hour of world news from one of the national broadcast stations.

And then the newspaper for that day. As much as they could.

And then discussion of all things "going on in the world."

All day. Each day. Every day.

As a young kid, it turned me off from current events, all but the "nutshell" versions at any rate. That grandmother was my main source of news headlines until she died at age 91. I didn't have to turn on the broadcast stations for years.

That was nice.

Enter 2020.

And now 2021.

Enough. I can't watch anymore. Just a rundown of the headlines gives me indigestion and 20-minute stretches of hiccups. Even "good news" stresses me out with questions like "will it last?" or "is this spun content?" Because my cynical answer to those questions is: No, it won't last and yes, it's probably not the truth, the whole truth, and nothing but the truth.

So, help us all, dear Lord...

I just can't. And please don't read that as I don't *care* anymore. I like to be an informed citizen, I just don't need to hook myself up to a steady diet of media cuisine.

Too much.

On the Facebook feed, too much. I scroll to the writing groups and fly past the current-eventish type drama.

Email, too much. Any subject line there with a hint of world goings-on gets deleted without a second thought.

Casual conversation with the Walmart clerk. Too much. I hang tight behind my mask and just smile. No small talk. Small talk leads to, well, current-eventish type drama.

Enough.

So, what to do?

Shut off the screens. No earbuds, either, lest my Pandora be interrupted with a public service announcement.

Go outside. Raining? That's okay, I'm not made of sugar; I know I won't melt. Snowing? No issues. I bought new gloves for my Christmas gift to me. And I have extra socks to wear down deep in my not-so-great boots. I won't freeze to death.

I'm blessed to not live in a big city where the outdoors is much smaller than it is here. I'm blessed to have a quiet backyard. I'll be making even more use of that as 2021 barrels on.

If a screen is to be on, it'll be streaming writing classes, publishing podcasts, or ideally, the cursor will be dancing across the white page, barely enough time to blink, as Little Miss Muse flits and flaps over the monitor, directing me and my (or her) characters on their next adventure.

I'll create worlds that are far, far worse than the one we're living in —making our reality seem a cakewalk. I'll create worlds that are far, far better. Characters that transport us to a place of escape and ease...

But at least it won't be the here and now that gives me the hiccups. It'll be the "somewhere out there" that gives me chills and hopes and dreams, and...

Well, you get the picture.

And because I've had enough, perhaps my word count for 2021 will blow the roof off my house.

Perhaps batches and snippets and chunks of those words will transport you away from the reality that we have into a different one. An escape from the chaos.

Because, perhaps, you've had enough, too.

Looking Back: We really are blessed to have ridden out the Pandemic in a rural area. I can't even imagine the chaos in the bigger cities—and not just from the virus. The habit of avoiding the news at all costs continues. I just can't even. I did write a fair number of shorts in 2021, but the general atmosphere in the world and within our walls with our own drama sucked most of my brain cells away.

Little Miss Muse reminds me once again that I should just listen to her, and I won't need all of my brain cells. All I need to do is type fast.

Well, sometimes her ideas are discombobulated and gobbledygook-ish. So.

Brain cells on board is a good thing.

118

BERNIE BURNOUT

Ok. It was cute at first. Perhaps too cute, no matter which side of the political spectrum you land on (and in our country at the moment, it feels like there are spectrums on top of spectrums on top of, well, you get it).

Bernie in Mittens.

All over social media.

All up and down and through my Facebook feed.

After a bit, the memes saturated all the feeds, and I began seeing the same ones over and over. Bernie in outer space. Bernie on the Friends couch. Bernie with the Beverly Hillbillies. Bernie on the bench with Forrest Gump.

And my favorite—if I were forced to pick one—Bernie with Julie Andrews, uh, excuse me, not-quite-a-nun-yet Maria, and all the Von Trapp children high up in the mountains singing "Raindrops on roses and Bernie in mittens." I had to wonder for a moment which of those children lugged his folding chair up the foothills—or did they take turns? I'd have made him sit in the grass with the children.

Then it happened. Bernie, in his folding chair and cozy mittens, started creeping into the photos of family and friends. Apparently,

Bernie gets around to our local high school basketball games. He's traveled back to pre-pandemic world and accompanied some good friends of mine on their Walt Disney World vacation.

And he's eaten at every restaurant on this side of the Mississippi with someone I know.

EVERYONE was photoshopping Bernie. I'd be reading along, thinking I was catching up on a family member's recent adventure, and there he'd be.

Good grief.

Over and over again.

I'd reached Bernie Burnout. And this came about the same time as my "Enough" rant last week. Forever and always trying to avoid news and upheaval and then I had to contend with this old man in mittens clogging up the real family news with the photoshopped/bombed family news.

But, alas, as with all things Internet, something else bumped Bernie memes for a run in the social media feed spotlight.

Enter the Lawyer Cat. Oh, my word, was I ever so glad this distraught kitten took the place of Bernie's mittens—even if for a little bit.

If you've been under a rock (or have taken a much-needed social media fast), you can find the video lurking over on YouTube.

And, even better, if you Google "Lawyer Cat Merchandise" you can order your very own t-shirt, mug, mouse pad, painted rocks, buttons, cross stitch, or magnet featuring the famous line: "I'm here live. I'm not a cat."

And maybe even better, a piece of history blazed with "I'm prepared to go forward with it."

Now, to be fair, there's Bernie merchandise, too. And bless the teacher that knitted those mittens and did some good in her corner of the world. The funds from official merchandise (pushing 2 million, I believe) were donated to food banks in the Vermont area.

I can't say the same thing for Mr. Lawyer Cat's items. I don't know if there's official merchandise—to me it looks like independent creators cashing in on the mishap, but I'm seriously tempted to splurge on a shirt from an independent Etsy artist. I've not decided on a design yet, though.

(I did find a seller with a pack of two stickers—one Not-a-Cat and one Bernie in Mittens. I think I'll pass on that deal, but you may want such souvenirs of this grand Internet Meme time we live in.)

At any rate, it gave a massive laugh and a cure for my grumpy current-event hatred and brown-mitten burnout.

And, in researching the links for this article, I came across another filter mishap from March of last year. I likely missed this one the first time around because I was obsessed with Darth Vader and Tom and Jerry memes of the Coronavirus. Murder Hornets had their five-second fame somewhere in there, too. (Don't judge me — you know you also caught a wave or two of relief from someone's dark and twisted mind). This one, an Italian priest attempting a video of mass (I think, I don't speak Italian).

Attorney Rod Ponton, thank you so much, sir, for that much-needed chuckle break. If only for an internet-meme moment. I'm printing out your phrase and putting it above my computer. Quite motivational if you think about it: "I'm prepared to go forward with it."

Forward with what?

The work in progress (update on that soon).

The continued ban on the news cycle.

Planning for the next mental health break.

The next step in all the things I've been putting off.

Onward. Forward.

Live.

And not a cat...

Looking Back: You can find the links to the videos in the appendix. I had to sit back and think about the last meme that made an impression on me. Actually Googled "most popular meme right now." The ones that came up I wasn't familiar with, many to do with Elon Musk and the World Cup (but not Musk at the Cup, so...)

Little Miss Muse believes one day she'll achieve viral meme status.
She's probably not wrong.

119

SLICED

I do believe I am, at heart, a dog person. But the circumstances of life over the last few years have precluded our home from adopting a high-maintenance pup. So we opted for cats. Well, I opted for ONE cat. Somehow, cats attract more cats and now we have three in the house. And those three have sent out some hive-mind message to the neighborhood and now several cats—not our cats—patrol the perimeter of our property. And leave footprints on the garbage can lid. And sleep in the landscaping bushes. And serenade the two lady cats through the sliding glass doors. A song of their people...

But prior to our current round of furry companions, I was definitely a dog person. Dogs. Always happy to see you. Don't know how to hold a grudge. Always ready to play with very little—if any—begging or coaxing required on the part of the owner. And human/canine playtime never required much forethought or preplanning. Tug? Grab a rope. Fetch? Just grab the ball and toss. Chase? Run.

With a cat? Well, one must think this through. Perhaps the cat is angry because their Fancy Feast Turkey Florentine was fifteen minutes late. Don't play with an angry cat.

Perhaps the cat is birdwatching in the breakfast nook. They've no time for you.

Perhaps the cat is napping on the back of the couch (their couch —not your couch, just FYI). Don't bother.

Perhaps the hands on the clock have swung within fifteen minutes of Fancy Feast time once again. Again, don't bother.

Perhaps the cat is already in solo-play mode, and you, dear owner, believe you can simply stroll over and join in, only to be greeted with a flick of the tail and the rear-view of the feline derriere walking away in a huff. Oh, the intrusion!

But when the stars align and the cat, perhaps, has decided to schedule you, dear owner, in for a few moments of quality time, then you, dear owner, must now THINK IT THROUGH. The toy of choice should be of the cat's choice, not yours. And you, dear owner, must sign the contract that states if the tinkle ball rolls down the hallway, and the cat chooses to give chase, the cat may or may not be seen again for four hours, or until Fancy Feast Time. This counts against your allotted playtime minutes and you, dear owner, must live with the fact that quality time with your kitty will leave you unfulfilled.

Perhaps you should've buckled down and bought that English bulldog.

However, if engaged playtime continues and the cat bores of the tinkle ball chase, you must once again THINK IT THROUGH. Toys, for the enjoyment of the feline and the protection of the human, should be attached firmly to long strings or twenty-four-inch sticks. The sharper the claws, the longer the front leg reach, the longer the string or stick needs to be.

A couple months ago while playing with Stella Marie (my long-haired, mini-Maine Coon-like lady with razors for toes), she got a little bitty bit excited.

Like really excited.

Like, "Hey, I feel good today. I was abandoned, shot in the back with a pellet gun, had a litter of kids under a porch, was fostered, someone took my kids away, I was put up for adoption, and now this lady who says she loves me wants to play fuzzy-catnip-mouse-on-a-string toy with me. Why not? I've put in my hard knocks. It's time to let loose and live a little."

We'd played quite a while—I was thrilled and honored to have been included in Stella's very busy schedule. Her good vibes were still in high swing when I laid down the teaser toy on a string at the end of a very long stick. (See what I did there? A string AND a stick because, well, razors for toes.)

Then I made a grave error in judgment. I did not THINK IT THROUGH.

I patted the couch—her couch, not my couch—and instead of joining me on the cushion, she swiped up with one paw, claws out ready to grab the fuzzy catnip mouse, but instead got two of my fingers.

I didn't even feel it at first.

The first thing I noticed was the blood oozing from under both sides of two fingernails. Both sides.

Then the burn.

Then the blood decided oozing wasn't sufficient and, quick as a flash, blood everywhere. I squawked and jumped from the couch—still her couch, not mine—and sped to the kitchen. Stella was unhappy with this commotion and canceled quality time with me for three days. See? She holds a grudge.

From oozing to burning to gushing. Then the throb. Then the red and swollen fingers when I'd planned on writing. Hard to type with pressure-dressed fingertips dripping peroxide and Neosporin onto the keyboard.

She sliced me good. Weeks later, I still have a hairline scar from the edges of the fingernails. I truly thought Stella may have surgically dissected one nail from its bed, but alas, all parts are accounted for.

While my hand was bandaged up and I waited for the oozing to subside, I turned my attention from typing new words to working out an error in judgment in my work in progress.

Next to my keyboard, I have a legal pad where I jot down chapter-by-chapter notes as I write. This keeps me from losing track of my characters and prevents me from creating accidental magical pickup trucks (it happens, folks). As I was going back through the manuscript notes, I realized I had not THOUGHT IT THROUGH. (I'm sensing a theme, here…)

I had an information flow issue and needed to divide up chapters and rearrange things a bit.

I also realized I'm old. And how things worked in middle school when I was in middle school is no longer how things work in middle school. I had not THOUGHT THIS THROUGH.

So, I grabbed a pair of scissors—not nearly as sharp as Stella's implements—and sliced. I sliced and sliced each chapter's notes into little strips. I spread them all out all over the place to rearrange the scenes in a more logical order. Then, with a pen housing ink the color of my oozing blood, I made notes and sliced some more.

A productive session to re-start a stalled project.

And now, as I type this, I'm sitting on Stella's couch. She sat next to me for a few quick seconds, long enough for a quick scratch under the chin. She jumped to the back of the couch and stretched out behind my shoulders. I hear her purring in my right ear. My left ear is full of her "fur feathers" as she swings her bushy tail back and forth across my shoulder and up the side of my cheek. One of her paws reaches out and touches my other shoulder. I see the very tips of her little razor toes.

She presses down with that one paw, letting me know I'm right where she wants me to be.

And that it's her couch.

I sit very, very still. I type a little slower, a little softer, with my still-scarred fingers so as not to disturb her slumber. I push all thoughts about English Bulldogs and Great Danes and sad-eyed pound puppies far, far away, lest she read my mind.

Because I'm thinking this one through…

Looking Back: That stalled project is still, to this day, stalled. The CIRCUS decided to add an extra ring, and on top of that, my characters don't want to do what I've told them to do. Instead, they're giving me a thousand and one options to readjust the plot line (which I guess I'll have to do, since hey, the characters are in charge of their own destinies in this particular project).

Little Miss Muse says she's gonna sic Stella Marie on me if I don't get that fictional gang out of the ditch on the side of the road and on to their final destination.

Shoot. I'll sic Stella Marie on me if I don't get going on that one soon...

120

THE GREAT 2021 PROCRASTINATION PURGE

A hh, spring. The first day of spring in this just-as-rocky-as-2020-ever-was year is Saturday. From the time this goes live, we've only four full more days of "official" winter.

But I bet the good folks in portions of Colorado will beg to differ. As the weekend approaches, they'll likely still be digging out from around, under, and alongside of massive wintery piles. Winter can still happen here in Indiana, too. I've seen my share of Easter Bunnies hopping through two-foot drifts back in the day. (I've also walked to and from school in the snow—uphill.)

But, hey. The calendar says spring is happening. So we'll go with that and hope for the best.

And, as I'm toiling away at revamping (uggg... I'm so sick of revamping, restarting, re-anything-ing that I'm about to put myself into timeout—where still nothing will get done but my brain might rest) the current work in progress, that notification of *Spring Begins* on my calendar prompted me to clean things that didn't need cleaned: the inside bottom of the Mason Jar that holds my paperclips, the metal teeth of the tape dispenser. I even lint-rolled the cats' fuzzy mice toys.

But with everything I cleaned and tidied, I felt my mind clearing a little bit as well. So I kept on using this as an excuse to justify my solid track record of procrastination.

I cleaned some more and decluttered and generally purged through all the rooms with reckless abandon. I took away an SUV packed full of junk (and I do mean not one square inch of room was left, I was driving half-sitting off the seat) to an auction house. Another back-end full to Goodwill. And the garage and the south side of the house is piled high, waiting for the right day when the transfer station is open for recycling and general dumping of broken and marred things.

The garage is the last stronghold, and for good reason. If I applied my purging skills to that space unsupervised, my poor hubs would be left with exactly one golf ball (stop losing them, and you'll always have one, right?) and exactly one golf club (a stick is a stick, yes?). So to keep the marriage intact, I've left the garage for a day when he can be home and stop me from tossing his toys all away.

Massive, massive amounts of procrastination purging. But, hey. It had to be done, right?

Then came the office filing cabinet. I filed our taxes and cleaned out that uninteresting but much-needed "adult life" drawer. Got a black trash bag of papers to burn in our firepit as no Walmart-grade personal paper shredder could keep up with all that. I had taxes all the way back to 2003. IRS says three years, so adios to well over a decade of manilla-stuffed folders.*

But the drawers under the "adult life" drawer? Those are fun drawers stuffed with writing classes and writing notes and story idea notebooks (started and abandoned), bits and pieces of manuscripts, Little Miss Muse's greatest hits... and, and (you'll be proud of me) a more recent filing system of contracts, payments, and rejection letters set up right in front of all that old stuff (okay, maybe not so proud. Should've purged those drawers a bit before slapping a brand new system in there).

My purple little imp, wings aflutter and glitter flying everywhere, became overjoyed about these drawers. If she can't get me to write her new words down, we can walk down memory lane and bow to her ever-present genius. "Ooh. Look what we did way back in 2015. Wasn't that fun?"

And "Eeeek! That was so cool. That notebook I started and didn't finish. Well, I started it and you never finished it."

And lots of, "See, I told you that idea would work. You should listen to me more."

I admit I rather enjoyed walking down this path with her for a while. Little Miss really did drop some amazing ideas here and there. Little Miss Muse bombs—or rather Baby Little Miss Muse bombs, as the idea of her wasn't fully formed, but there she was the whole time.

Like a parent walking back through baby albums and past report cards. Ahhh. Those were the days.

But the feeling was short lived...

And now she grins and glitters the walls and the floor over the simple memory of the purge we did together last week. I just swept this floor.

She prances with pride and gloats that she's the only reason I ever have a bright idea.

Not the hours of work put in studying story form and structure and characterization.

Not hours upon hours of practicing scene beats and setting, and

—

And now she's drug out her lavender lute from her ever-growing pile of bribes and gifts. I knew when I gave it to her for Christmas that it would come back to haunt me, but 2020 was such a rough year, she needed a little cheer...

She's strumming and humming and... and now bellowing at the top of her tiny lungs.

Reveling in her own accomplishments.

I and my efforts, clearly, are chopped liver next to Little Miss in all her glory.

"Hey." I say to her. "Hey!" A little louder. She can't hear me over her plucking and prancing. She's donned one amethyst high heel and one violet Ugg boot and is clopping around like a two-legged horse.

All three cats flee the office, tails bushed and eyes bulging, in a single-minded herd.

"HEY!!!" Loud enough to rattle the windows, but it gets her attention.

She pauses mid-pluck and mid-stomp, the Ugg boot midair.

"If I promise to go back to writing, will you come with me—quietly, like a good little muse?"

She lowers her foot, the boot barely making a sound on the hardwood.

Little Miss lowers her lute, one chubby finger accidentally plucking the highest note on the neck of the instrument.

She grins. Glitter flutters from her wings. She tips her head sideways—which has become code for "What will you give me for my time and trouble?"

I tilt my head back in response. "One can of grape soda and three pieces of grape bubblegum."

She tilts her head the other way and drops the lute with a hollow twang and puts her hands on her chunky hips. "Two sodas. Four gums. And I'm almost out of glitter."

I almost snark back that if she'd stop spraying it EVERYWHERE and ALL THE TIME that she'd not be out of glitter.

But I bite my tongue. I've an entire chest full of all shades of purple glitter just for situations like these. The soda. The gum. The glitter. Always buy in bulk for your creative muses, folks. It saves gobs of dough over the months.

The deal struck, we abandon Memory Lane and take a north-bound turn onto Get-R-Done Drive.

Next year, 2022, I'm scheduling in this time of great purge. A time of taking off a day or two of the day job and planning on a no-writing stretch. Just sheer elbow grease, a hefty supply of trash bags and donation boxes at the ready. A fresh stock of grape gum, glitter, and sodas.

Perhaps if I control my organizational system, it won't take nearly as long or be nearly as complicated. And maybe it won't trigger Little

Miss into a fit of overjoyment that it takes a week to unbury us from the glitter...

Perhaps the blog title this time next year will be something like: The Simple 2022 Spring Tidy-Up. And perhaps I won't be procrastinating anything.

One can hope.

*I AM NOT a tax professional nor am I an accountant. So if you, based on the reading of this blog, decide to likewise purge, shred, or burn your own personal financial records, please seek advice from someone who knows more than Google or I do. Little Miss Muse and I absolve ourselves from any of your resulting legal matters...

Looking Back: Current procrastination projects include creating a reading nook complete with a fun circular orange rug that the cats have claimed as their own, a thorough reordering of the pantry shelves, flipping mattresses, and yes, this very Life All Over Again *project—because, yet again, I've characters that are refusing to do as told.*

Little Miss Muse says she'd forgotten about her lute. But, thanks to my procrastination, she's had the time to dig it out and is now flittering about again.

I sense another deal is about to be struck... Double the first offer if I get back to my original work in progress...

BABY GROOT AND THE WRONG ANSWER

Fair warning: This blog post contains scene spoilers (but not those oh-great-now-it's-ruined kind of spoilers) for Guardians of the Galaxy Vol. 2.

Don't you just love it when your ignorance is highlighted in neon? I mean, you could be the most reasonably intelligent person on the planet. You can dress yourself and hold a job and at least pretend to have a clue.

At least you think you are. Reasonably intelligent, that is.

Then out of the clear blue sky—or out of the invisible atmosphere that is cyberspace—someone or something points out just how dumb you are. Even if it's a sliver of dumbness—there it is. On display.

Like for my birthday last year when my grown-ish Gen Z kids attempted to "gift" me with the keys to their language. A language that uses English, but not the English I taught them. I hear familiar words coming out of their mouths, but none of it makes sense. My brow furrows until I have just one eyebrow and my head hurts from thinking through the phraseology. Like trying to pick out a full sentence in Alpha-Bits cereal but missing all the vowels and having only Xs and broken Cs to work with. They talk in text-speech and code. They tried to let me in. To "school" me on this new and better language. But alas, I'm from a different era, I guess.

And then there's anything culinary. Again, I'm using recipes in ENGLISH. My one and only language. But still...ignorance on display, boiling over, slopping messes, and setting ovens on fire.

But this past month? Oh my. Computer speak. Uggg...

Let me explain it with an analogy that you Marvel fans will enjoy. For those non-Marvel people (what even in the world??), I'll try my best to explain.

In Guardians of the Galaxy Vol. 2, we have prisoners trying to get free after a mutiny on board a spaceship. Baby Groot (a small, tree-like creature with super strong little limbs) wants to help our heroes, Yondu and Rocket, out of their jail jam.

But Yondu needs a piece of tech from the bad guy's lair to make his weapon—and the escape plan—work. Rocket (a cyber-punked talking raccoon) plays translator between Yondu and Baby Groot. Yondu explains exactly where the piece of technology is. What it looks like. The color...

Yondu, satisfied with this explanation smiles. Rocket, knowing little Baby Groot's ignorance so well, grimaces.

Baby Groot, happy to help and eager to leave behind all things awful, infiltrates the evil captain's quarters while the enemy sleeps and snores all around—but he doesn't bring back the right piece of tech to our jailed heroes. He brings back:

Underwear. With a smile on his face.

Another explanation from our heroes, and Baby Groot brings back:

An alien rat. Baby Groot gleams with joy.

A third explanation, and a super excited Baby Groot brings back:

A prosthetic eyeball. The only one happy about this is Rocket (the raccoon has a prosthetic fetish—don't judge me, I didn't write the script).

The next try results in a desk. The next? A severed toe. (He really *is* trying. He's giving it all he's got. Wholeheartedly.)

Even on his final attempt, Groot just can't get it right, and a third party must step in and help the little guy out.

So... here's why all this matters. I am Baby Groot in this real-life, kill-me-now-please scenario...

My Web Guy says, "We need to update your security certificate on bapaul.com."

I say, "Okay." I smile dumbly. I've no clue, but I'm up for whatever. He's speaking English. I know this. I just don't *know* this.

And since neither Web Guy nor I possess a cyber-punked talking raccoon with a prosthetic fetish to translate, Web Guy sends me to my domain host with THE EXACT instructions to tell someone over there what I need.

It's in another language. I can't make heads or tails of it. Total and complete ignorance. I just know Web Guy is grimacing as he gives me these instructions. He knows me well. I'm bound to screw it up.

So I copy and paste exactly what Web Guy says into a chat with the folks over at GoDaddy. They give me an answer, which I copy and paste back to Web Guy, and I'm so excited. It was so easy.

Until...

Web Guy says I brought him back what amounts to... underwear.

Let's try again. Perhaps the next chat will open with a different technician that will be able to help me in just the right way. The next tech barely types in broken English.

I bring back a prosthetic eyeball to Web Guy. He's not impressed and sends me back with more copy-and-paste work.

Then I get an artificially-intelligent-but-smarter-than-me chatbot who gives me... a giant metal desk. Surely this is what Web Guy needs?

No. In fact, Web Guy is as equally unimpressed with the giant metal desk as he was with the underwear and spare optical orb. This goes on and on, through alien rats and severed toes.

I'd rather sever my own toes than deal with tech stuff. Or cook. Or learn a new language that's even still in English...

I gave up.

My "third-party" saving grace was to hand Web Guy a set of my passwords and logins so he can maneuver without my ignorance getting in the way.

And way back, several paragraphs, some of you may have gasped and thought "Oh, my, bapaul.com isn't secure?"

Let me explain, in very basic terms because I assure you, basic terms are all I know.

When you type in bapaul.com the tiny little icon in your web browser shows that the site is not secure. What this means is that if I try to collect information from you (your name, address, email, etc.) that my site could potentially be hacked and your information stolen.

The good news? I'm not collecting anything from you unless you sign up for the newsletter. You're visiting here, reading along and that's it. You're fine. I'm fine. No hackers. No severed toes. No strange pairs of rogue underwear.

But wait! There's more! If you type in www.bapaul.com (you know, actually typing in the three Ws) the site shows secure and everything is fine and dandy.

Likewise, if you got here through the Facebook link, it should show secure, because I've been wasting precious seconds typing in all those extra Ws when I post about a new blog—at least the last several since I found out about this glitch.

I've not a clue why this is. Web Guy does. GoDaddy might. But they're speaking plain English and I can't translate what they're saying... There aren't enough letters left whole in my cereal to figure it out.

In the meantime, if you do want to sign up for the newsletter? That goes through a third party who is secure, and your information is protected. The emails collected for the newsletter signup are submitted through a service called BookFunnel. Their page and site are totally secure, so no worries.

And, if you haven't yet, go ahead and get that Newsletter (link up in the menu bar) into your repertoire of things to check periodically. Because periodically, I'll be updating that with publishing news and new releases.

You also get a cool free short story for your trouble.

And I promise I wrote it in plain English.

Looking Back: My toes curled re-reading this one. But alas, the problem was solved and life moves on.
Little Miss Muse was aghast with the amount of time we spent typing things that weren't fiction words while trying to work this stuff out. If I'd listen to her, the money-making bestseller would've hit the charts by now and we could hire a team of folks to do this without bugging us (her) with such unimportant details.
I can't argue that. But I'd hire a cook first.

CIRCLE THE WAGONS

I need a Reese's Cup. Maybe lots of them. Frozen ones. Oh, my goodness. And a long, long walk to cool down.

As I write this the week of March 24, I've gotten notice (personal notices, mind you, from real people in my life, not just read-it-online notice) of another gigantic uptick in spammers, scammers, and generally sadistic people who prey on the elderly or anyone who dares to answer the phone from an unknown number.

It all ticks me off on even the best day. Many were the times I had to talk my elderly grandmother out of doing something stupid over the phone with her bank account.

Many were the times I've had to sort through loved ones' emails and snail mail to help navigate what looks like a good idea from what was a definite snake-in-the-grass evil plot to drain bank accounts.

And now, now? Now I'm ticked. Because I was working on my novel. And I got so fed up I had to stop and rant. Little Miss Muse and all three cats scattered from the office when I tossed the phone across the desk in exasperation. News of another poor soul fallen victim to thieves.

(Side note: Don't you miss the days when you could slam down the phone? Now to end a call, we press a polite little button. We don't even have anything to "hang up." I truly believe some situations call for a handheld receiver to be slammed down. Hard. No more, though, so a-tossing-we-will-go. Then the retrieval of the phone to ensure the screen isn't cracked.)

Then I got mad all over again. Because I already had this scammer rant back at the beginning of the lockdowns. And here we go again. (The scammers never go away... they just multiply, change their game, employ new technology, and attack afresh).

I can hear Little Miss trying to console the cats after my rage explosion. The cats are having none of it and may very well be self-soothing by climbing onto the kitchen counter and having a taste of my turkey that I laid out for my lunch. Which now I have no appetite for, so I peeked into the kitchen and told them to go ahead. Have at it.

Take all the turkey, you little thieves.

These monsters (like a herd of cats to unsupervised turkey) know when the stimulus checks hit the bank. They know the time of the month you get your Social Security deposits. They know you or a loved one is waiting for a vaccine. They know people of a certain age group are likely to have grandchildren, and that these folks would do anything for those kiddos. They know the chances are high you shop online or at Walmart and might have a package on the way that needs "just a bit more information."

These Blood Thirsty Ingrates just won't quit.

So, the following is from a personal Facebook post back on March 20, 2020. I'm gonna leave it right here, it's all still applicable. It's all still happening.

Circle your wagons, blow your whistles, and watch out for your loved ones.

If you're in the "target" demographic, especially elderly widowed ladies (sorry gals, that's the cold, hard truth), gather your girlfriends and turn up the grump!

"Miss Bethany's about to blow a gasket... Please allow me my *hope-fully* one-and-only pandemic-induced Facebook rant:

While taking such great care to protect at-risk demographics from the virus spread, we've created fish-in-a-barrel scenarios. Seems that's the rule of the day: Fix one problem, five more problems grow big ugly heads.

Blood-Thirsty Ingrates (BTIs) have stepped up their scams—especially toward seniors.

BTIs are bad news on a good week, let alone now with the virus fear fodder. Isolation and panic can cause even otherwise rational humans to grab onto any bit of attention or hope, and the BTIs know it.

The following came across my screen in some form or fashion in the last 24 hours. I didn't go looking for examples—they're everywhere:

-The Red Cross is NOT going door to door in Gramma Hettie's neighborhood with Covid-19 test kits for the low, low price of $29.95 and verification of the last four of her SSN.

-Great Aunt Irene is NOT wanted for drug trafficking and overdue speeding tickets in three states. And Medicare will NOT reinstate her insurance NOR clear up outstanding warrants for the low, low price of $99.99, the last four of her SSN, and her dearly departed mother's maiden name.

-Your gregarious 85-year-old Grampa Walter does NOT have a long-lost, sweet-talking, great-great niece named Martha Lou who happens to be trapped in an overseas hot zone and needs $5,999.99—or whatever he can spare via Western Union—to get back to the States.

Look out for your loved ones—not just their health, but their whole wellbeing. Have a conversation with them about this. Be proactive. Be diligent.

It seems we're walking around in a real-time movie script co-written by King, Koontz and The Gang. Watch for those plot twists. Not everyone is who they claim to be—from the voice on the phone, the knock at the door, or the family member who just showed up out of the blue...

And if you happen to be one of those BTIs, and you're reading this... Hmmm. I'm gonna stop there because I've already had to tell Jesus that I'm sorry FOUR TIMES this morning for glorious glittering visions of electric chairs, woodchippers, and industrial meat slicers."

My phone was ringing as I wrote this post. Today. March 24, 2021. I didn't answer as it came up as an unknown number.

But they were kind enough to leave a voicemail.

Apparently, I'm wanted for a felony in California and possibly

Alaska. But for the low, low price of my Social and a credit card number, they can clear that right up for me.

Gee. Thanks.

And now back to the novel if I can get the cats out of the turkey and Little Miss Muse out of the freezer. I've no idea what's she's doing in the freezer.

Likely looking for a Reese's Cup.

P.S. Yes, yes. I did apologize to Jesus for dancing visions of all those BTIs taking long walks off short piers into shark-infested waters, slipping into great vats of lye, and generally tripping into highway traffic.

And I've made an appointment with him to apologize again tomorrow.

Looking Back: The BTIs are the bane of my existence some days.
It never ends.
Little Miss Muse says she had a perfectly good reason for being in the freezer and it wasn't for a Reese's Cup. And that I shouldn't be surprised to find her in there more often...
She won't tell me why. Which aggravates me. Quite a bit. So now, I must apologize to Jesus all over again.

123

BIFOCALS

A few weeks ago, I mentioned the difficulty I was having bringing my Web Guy back the right answer for updating this website.

Turns out, he had to do the footwork on that because I'm technologically illiterate.

Good news is, though, that the security certificate for bapaul.com is all good now. You should see a little padlock up in the browser bar from here on out. If that thing ever comes unlocked or you get an exclamation point, or perhaps a baboon hyped up on caffeine, shoot me a message, and I'll forward it to Web Guy...

Now, onto the problem-of-the-moment.

Eye Guy.

Well, he's not the problem. I'm the problem. Just like Web Guy wasn't the problem before. I was the problem. Just like dear Hubs is NEVER the problem. Ever.

Tag, I'm it.

Always... (can you tell I'm mini-ranting?)

For the last couple of years, I've been holding reading material further and further away from my face. Even my computer setup consists of a peripheral monitor waaay far from my nose. With enlarged print.

It got so bad in January, I thought about hiring that caffeinated baboon to hold my reading material ten feet away—I'd have had just as much luck deciding between it, is, and I'm. They all looked the same. So I guessed words... eeek.

Seriously though, in January, my arms could extend no more and reading and work on the laptop became more difficult. By February, I figured all hope was lost and called the Eye Guy. Who made me wait six weeks for an exam.

And it finally happened.

"You're old," Eye Guy says.

"I know this."

"No. I mean, you're gonna need help now."

"Yes."

"Lots of help. More than a few clicks of help."

(Eye Guy is actually very kind and would never say those exact words. Even with my trouble reading, I could read between the lines —or behind his eyes—and know this is exactly what he meant.)

And we're good buds. He's kept my family legal to drive and operate heavy machinery—at least from a visual standpoint—for as long as I can remember. So if he says I'm old... Well, that's that.

Bifocals, here I come.

So he measured my face. Then I paid him my salary for the year.

And I waited. For eight days. I waited in jubilant expectation. Because he held a page of text up for me to read in the exam. He showed me the text with my plain, single-vision prescription. Then he showed me what it would look like with bifocals.

Oh. My. Word.

I could actually see things!

Like periods, and commas, and dashes... Oh My!

And words said what they said, not what I had to imagine they said. Wow. (How I've remained employed or wrote anything that made any sense since this whole vision thing started is beyond me.)

"Ahem." It's Little Miss. *"I don't need glasses."*

She's taking the credit for me not getting fired, so I'm ignoring her because she could care less about commas, and periods, and dashes...

The morning I got the text that my new eyeballs had arrived at the Eye Place, I dropped everything and went to snatch them up, sure that by nightfall I could pick a pimple off an ant's butt three counties away.

The Eye Gal fitted the frames to my face. She gave me some pointers on how to adjust. And, as I was still seated there, she gave me a page of print. I could see!

Then I stood up. To go back to my life with my 20/20 enhanced old-person eyeballs.

Well.

Have ya'll ever watched "Dr. Strange"? Remember how the universe turned in on itself? The floors and walls and ceiling all bending and collapsing? Amazing special effects in that movie.

Not so amazing in real life.

I'm telling you, when I stood up, the walls of the Eye Place did what no computer-generated imagery could ever master.

The wallpaper wobbled.

The floor grew a staircase right in front of me.

The checkout counter ballooned then shrank.

And that was before I ever walked across the parking lot (I'll not tell you what happened *out there* or what I must've looked like to passerby).

I sat in the car for a moment and wondered if I should call someone to drive me home. My jubilant expectation turned to jaded aggravation.

I had it in my mind that I would adjust to my new glasses in a matter of seconds. That all would be well with my visual world.

Hahaha.

It's been more awkward than learning to drive a stick-shift on an icy road with an overbearing parent (a story for another day and the reason why I still don't drive a stick-shift).

One minute I'm fine. The next, I've got my arms out like I'm walking a tightrope, sure the ground beneath my feet will swallow me whole.

I don't know where to hold my book to get the best view (the print is crystal clear, there's just a tiny window in my frames where this effect takes place). I don't know where to hold my phone, where to place my laptop on the desk...

Once in a while, I step on a cat. Apparently, I've developed blind spots where I can't tell the difference between floor and tails.

I could be cohabitating with a baboon, and if said ape were to stay in that cat-swallowing blind spot, who knows how long he'll be here?

On the plus side, Little Miss is thrilled that my frames are purple. A few times she's landed on my shoulder with a chubby thud and tried to see through my lenses from my point of view.

She doesn't understand what the problem is.

Purple frames should be all I need. Purple anything solves all kinds of problems.

Who cares about the lenses?

Now, she's smudged them up with her grimy, grape-soda hands.

Now she's chasing the cat.

Or maybe it's the baboon—they're all off in that part of the room where the wall and the floor are doing jumping jacks.

It's time to wrap this up.

Clean off the bifocals.

And hope when I stand up to check on the cat that I don't fall down the non-existent stairsteps in my office...

Looking Back: I now have pink frames and have adjusted. Somewhat. I also get run through the mill on the vision tests now that Glaucoma has been detected in my mother. I love my genes. The Hubs got an old, but new-to-him midlife-crisis/bucket list, Jeep that's a stick shift. He'll probably teach me how to drive it in an icy parking lot for putting up with my jabs...
Little Miss Muse believes purple frames would've been better and reminds me she already knows how to operate a stick-shift.
Since the Hubs has a touch of OCD, I'll have to refrain from letting her grape-gum crusted hands touch the gears.

124

AND THE STORY GROWS

Oh, how I wanted to introduce you all to a new friend (well, not new, but newly materialized in a touchable, tangible form). But I'm traveling, and the photo I snapped of this wonder-filled character doesn't do it justice, so we'll have to wait another week or so until I can do a proper photo shoot.

But now?

I'm in Tennessee. Morel hunting with my Uncle. For those who may not know what a morel is, it's a wild mushroom that only pops up in springtime here in the Midwest. It's the only type of mushroom I care to eat (those button-top things are clones and are nowhere near the delicacy that people think they are. Hold all mushrooms of the clone varieties off my pizza and out of my omelets, please).

Anyway, I grew up hunting morels with my grandparents and parents, aunts and uncles, and we've all but lost our private hunting spots in Indiana. Those sweet, sweet honey holes (or glory holes as they're known to the serious 'shroom hunters), now belong to others. I hope they see the value of their properties, the magic hiding under the debris on the forest floor and at the field edges...

But I digress.

The bad thing is morels are picky little buggers. They require just the right soil composition. Just the right soil temp. Has the sun shone at just the right angle for just the right number of hours? Have the nights been warm and the days been rainy? As you scan and grid out your search area, are you holding your tongue between your right top and bottom molars while your nose twitches to the left? Is your truffle pig ready, primed, and bribed?

In spite of all this, there are springs where we found them by the pound, and oh, the joy! And we've never, ever sold them, though they could bring up to $75 per pound depending on the year and who's desperate enough for a taste of the earthy gems. We've always fried them up or given them away to those who appreciate the flavor experience and can no longer traverse the terrain themselves.

This year, Tennessee seemed our best bet, and we could visit family at the same time. Uncle has a couple of private property spots where he found them last year.

But that was last year.

This year? The weather hasn't been ideal by anyone's standards. A week or two before we were to visit, Uncle sends a video of a flash flood stream/creek/river rising through his yard in a matter of seconds. It's now the middle of April, and frost still tickles the grass tips.

To complicate matters, evidence of the brown, round biological excrement pointed to a heavy presence of deer, wild turkeys, and goats?? These discoveries caused phones to emerge from many a back pocket, LCD screens glowing in the dusky forest light, and frantic Google searches for "Do [fill in the blank here with mammal name] eat morel mushrooms?"

Of course, the answers always returned in the affirmative—and who could blame the creatures? They know high-end dining when they sniff it.

The only good news is that these critters' digestive tracks don't necessarily digest the spores, and they're passed along somewhere else. Another property. Another county. For another season. One can only hope that all the droppings we saw contained spores from other parts of Tennessee, and one year soon, a new colony of mycelium and up will spring the wondrous treasures.

Come to think of it, I wonder if that's how *shiitake* mushrooms are propagated? (Can't take credit for this dad joke — that's all Uncle...)

We trampled and stomped and traipsed through acres and acres of forest, finding nothing of the edible mushroom sort, but all the while enjoying the other finds. Dogwood blooms, bright blue birds, impressive rock formations, and babbling streams.

Then we explored a few more acres.

And more.

And more.

It was great to be outside and unplugged.

Then it happened. Finally.

"Found one!" Uncle spotted the first one.

I look up from my spot in knee-deep briars, still struggling with the bifocal issue, and there he stood above a ravine twenty feet high —the ravine, not the Uncle or the mushroom.

Then he wasn't there anymore, but his echo of "Here I go" bounced off the cedars and elms and ash.

Yup. There he went. Toppled right down the side of the ravine.

"Did you fall on that mushroom?" (Don't judge. I have my priorities: rare fungi status first, amazing Uncle status next.)

"No. Don't think so." I rushed to the sound of his voice, careful of my footing lest I step on the only mushroom south of the Ohio River and lest I, too, skid down the side of the cliff.

I mean ravine.

"Are *you* okay?" (See, I asked and would've gladly sat next to him until the EMS could fish him out from the bottom of this forty-foot crevice if the need should have presented itself.)

When I reached the edge, Uncle was standing and the bottom of the ravine, grinning. "I tripped over it."

"I can see that." This 'shroom was growing sideways out of the bank about three feet down. Three inches tall and dried up, clearly many days past its prime—the mushroom, not the Uncle.

"Pretty strong mushroom to do that."

"Grabbed my ankle." He bent and rubbed his leg. "Threw me right over the edge."

"I see that."

I eased my way toward the mushroom and waited. That's what you do; you don't pick the first one. You let all members of the hunting party see the fungus in its natural surroundings so their eyes can pick up on the pattern and the colors... I called over the Kid. (19, but he'll always be a kid). Kid came close and—tripped and rolled right down the side of the sixty-foot cliff.

"Hey, don't land on the mushroom!" I warn as Kid slid sideways through leaf debris and briars, landing at the base of a cedar tree.

"No worries." Kid said. Uncle went to help Kid up but became distracted by a rogue bass fishing boat stuck out of the side of the ravine just down from where the guys landed.

I took a step back, lest the mushroom sense what's about to happen. My fingers reached for the base of its stem to pluck it from its perch high above the ravine and high above my two guys down in the valley, but as I bend, Kid shouted, "Hey! Look what I found!"

Temporarily blindness paralyzed me for a moment.

Turns out, Kid found a tactical flashlight at the base of the cedar. Despite years of being in the elements, the light still worked, obviously, and my new bifocals magnified the beam, searing my retinas. Eye Guy would be proud of him. Evil devil lights...

The mushroom saw its chance. Its fungus-y fingers gripped my wrist—and down it threw me, a hundred feet to the bottom of the canyon. But not before I plucked its cheeky stem from the bank.

"Don't roll on the mushroom!" the boys yelled in unison. (See? Everyone in the party had perfectly positioned priorities.)

And I didn't roll on it. Held it up above my head as I went skidding to the bottom.

"Look! It's still in one piece!" I stood proudly at the base of the cliff, amazed as I looked up at the edge that none of us had broken bones from that hundred-foot fall.

The guys cheered. While I was busy fighting the morel out of the ground and rolling down the hill (it took forever to reach the bottom

— two-hundred-feet worth of territory to cover), they had busied themselves securing that aluminum bass boat. It's best to have reliable transportation when exiting canyons of such magnitude.

I situated the mighty mean mushroom in my front shirt pocket. Then Uncle with his walking stick and Kid with his new-old flashlight helped me aboard, and we sailed off into the wild blue yonder with a single morel and not a care in the world.

Mother Nature may not have grown the mushrooms in them thar woods, but, boy, can we grow a story! I'll leave it to you, dear reader, to untangle reality from fantasy...

Looking Back: Okay, Uncle was the only one that slid down the hill. The Kid did find a flashlight and there was (and still is) an old aluminum fishing boat stuck in the woods. We found one more that year in another forest, and that was the extent of our grand hunt. But we had a great visit.

Little Miss Muse looks forward to another trip to Tennessee—next time it will likely be to Killer Nashville where she and I will learn the ins and outs of writing crime fighting scenes from industry pros.

125

MANIFESTATION

I have amazing fans. I really do.

Some of them point out the stupid mistakes I make, saving me from eternal embarrassment and career-killing moves. I love them for it.

Some of them shower me with compliments like, "Wow, that made me cry." Or, "Gosh, wouldn't I love to see that on Netflix." Or my favorite, "Are you okay? I mean, that was creepy. Are you okay?"

And I love them for it.

Some of them buy what I write. What a gift! I love them for it. Each and every one.

And a few folks gift me with the tangible. Notebooks. Pens. Unicorns... I love them for it. So much fun to grow the collections!

My aunt read *Life Along the Way*, and as she came across anything that I mentioned I was fond of (and that could be safely sourced in a global pandemic), she stuck it in a box. She surprised me with Kraft brand macaroni (really, folks, don't get the generic on that one). Reese's, Lindt, and Ghirardelli were also gleefully unpacked and hidden around in various hidey holes. Bubble Wrap and Saran Wrap (seriously, head on over and grab a copy of the book, and you'll understand). A yogurt container full of dimes also made its way into the box. What fun manifestations of ideas mentioned in that silly blog book.

This same aunt keeps me in full supply of copy paper and printer ink. What joy! (I have an office supply fetish, and I'm not ashamed of it.)

Now, friends, here's where I'm gonna get in real big trouble. You see, I can only have one Number One Fan. With the capital letters and all. Just one.

This title was officially grabbed early on, a couple of years ago.

My dear Hubs wanted that title, reading all my stuff and encouraging and putting up with me. But he's not my Number One Fan. Love him. Bless his heart.

My dear mother would like that title, seeing as she's known me the longest of anyone on earth, like when I was only two cells old. Supportive and encouraging as she is through thick and thin, she was a bit too late to claim the capitalized version of the title. Love her. Bless her heart.

That dear aunt, encouraging and supportive as she is, missed it by inches. Love her. Bless her heart.

And let's not bring Gma Lois into the mix, God rest her soul. I can only write this now because she's passed, or she'd have gotten into a fistfight over the whole idea. Bless her heart.

The Number One Fan title goes to a dear friend who I've known for over twenty years. We'll call her Miss L for short.

Miss L sent me with luggage tags, notebooks, heart scarf, and lots of love and prayers to Vegas, though the love and prayers would've been enough. Bless her heart. Miss L also snuck hankies and encouraging notes into my suitcase. Just in case my heart was to be broken into a million pieces while facing a panel of professional editors scrutinizing my short stories.

I'm surprised I didn't open my case to find Miss L had stowed away.

And, just weeks before my dear aunt gifted me with that giant box of goodies, Miss L chases me down with a package and a shy little smile. Gobstoppers and Ghirardelli!

Miss L accidentally spilled a glass of water on her copy of *Life Along the Way*. I told her no worries — I'd gladly give her another copy.

No. No.

This lady dried the pages, stuffing socks between the pages to soak up the moisture. She then smoothed the book out and put a dresser on top of it to flatten it. A dresser. "Good as new."

I don't think I have any book in my possession that I'd be that dedicated to when Amazon is just a click away...

One day a few weeks ago, I got a couple of texts and what seemed to me like a frantic phone call from Miss L. "I need to see you tonight." My heart dropped a little. Usually when one of our family ladies calls like that, it's bad news. After Miss L assured me she was fine, I relaxed and kept my hind end home that evening to see what was up.

She brought in a package all wrapped up. About the size of a six-month-old, but lighter (the package, not Miss L). Grinning from ear to ear.

We sat at the table as I unwrapped it.

And out popped Little Miss Muse. In all her purple glory. Hair everywhere. Cape.

Magic wand.

Eeek!

"Miss L, what have you done?" I was totally gobsmacked. There she was, my muse. Manifested in tangible form. Sitting in my lap like a small child.

"Well, I woke up at midnight and decided to make Little Miss." She said this as if it was nothing. Just like that. Idea in head to idea in real, touchable form.

I sew even worse than I cook, so this was a mighty feat in my eyes. She sewed the doll's body and clothing. She fashioned the magic wand. She put each individual strand of hair on Little Miss Muse's head. An artist friend of hers painted on the facial features.

What a gift!

The whole time, the spirit of Little Miss Muse bopped around the table, flopping from one of my shoulders to the other. Balancing on my head, her toes digging into my scalp. "Let me see, let me touch. Let me taaaakkeee."

We struck a deal that she'd keep her sticky mitts off my doll for six packs of grape bubble gum, a new pair of heels, and a cape. Now she wants a cape that glitters as brightly as the doll's does. Little Miss swears her original cape is starting to dull. Muses are such fickle and picky creatures.

The doll of Little Miss sets on the mantel up out of reach of curious kitty claws and the actual Little Miss Muse's rants and rampages. The photo doesn't do her justice at all. She's simply stunning.

Never would I have dreamed that anything I wrote would bring folks to laughter. To tears. To insomnia. To the stores. To the craft table. It's a huge blessing to me. So whether I have only the handful of fans I do now, or whether that number grows to the thousands, that properly capitalized Number One Fan title can only be held by one Miss L.

Love her big.

Bless her heart!

Looking Back: Miss L continues to (and forever will) hold the title of Number One Fan, remembering National Author's Day and showing up at my local author events.

Hubs and I purchased the doll an acrylic case because I was terrified the cats would not be able to resist her yarn hair. Miss L also upgraded her with a purse full of purple glitter vials. Too fun! I imagine if Little Miss Muse ever attempts to grow up, this doll would be the teenage version of her. Check out the photo in the back of the book.

Little Miss believes growing up is overrated and would not allow her the freedom from accountability that she currently enjoys.

I don't disagree.

126

THE CASE OF THE MISSING EYEBALLS

It's been a long couple of weeks around here. As I write this, all three cats are sacked out in the office, their faces smushed flat down into their preferred slumber surfaces. They only lift their heads when the crows outside caw a little too loudly, but the felines are too tuckered to approach the window for a round of bird watching.

After all, they "helped" all over the house with my latest freak-out escapade and just can't cat anymore.

Even Little Miss Muse has slumped a bit through these last few days. I've found trails of not-so-shimmery glitter and half a dozen half-drunk grape sodas. She's just as tuckered as I am.

Everything's a tiny bit—or a whole gob of a bit—discombobulated.

Last night (and many nights previous), I sat my alarm for six a.m. with the best of intentions. And this morning (and many mornings previous), I woke up at one a.m., three a.m., and five a.m.

For the seventh or eighth day in a row, I turned the alarm off.

All. The. Way. Off.

You see, Hubs has a bad case of insomnia. Like, a consume-all-life-as-we-know-it kind of case. So when he's up pacing from room to room trying to find a spot to slumber, I'm awake listening. Or herding cats. Or trying to get Little Miss to simmer down, because really, three a.m. isn't the time for the clicking of keys and lights all on for creative play. Not when someone else is desperately trying to sleep.

So, my sleep schedule (fragile on a good day, thanks to the evil thyroid gland's temper tantrums) has been turned on its head. Which means my mental clarity (fragile as it is on a good day) is also discombobulated. None of my ducks are in any kind of a row. Lost them all.

Every single cotton-picking one of them.

The goose and emu are likewise missing.

This morning (at nine a.m., not six a.m.), I'm stumbling around doing that mental to-do list thing. Breakfast. Shower. Laundry. Litter Box Duty. Two sink-fulls of dishes (as that's another thing that can't be done in the evening when Hubs is finally dozing. No noise from the kitchen is to be had).

And I needed to find my glasses. They were on my nightstand with my phone. I picked them up. I know I did. And then... Poof! Gone.

The searching ensued, and I, trying not to panic in my sleep-deprived and over-worked state, performed a few menial housekeeping chores along the way so as to not be even more behind on things.

Think. Think. I just had them in my hands...

And I know you're all going, "Oh! She was probably already wearing them." Nope. I checked my face first. Because I've done that before—looked for a half hour for glasses that I was wearing. They also were not perched atop my head, nor were they hanging by one earpiece from the neck of my t-shirt. I checked those three spots five times each. Pat face. Pat Head. Check shirt. Check down the shirt. Check pants pockets. Repeat. Like a panicked version of The Macarena.

Under the bed? The nightstand again. The drawers of the nightstand—though I know I didn't open those. Hub's nightstand. Bathroom. Shower. Sink. The toilet basin...

I'm going crazy.

I retraced my steps. I think that first absentminded chore I performed was litterbox duty. I was relieved to find nothing but litter in the litter box.

But what if I'd put them on my head and they'd fallen into the litter as I was scooping? Out to the garage to dig in the dirty litter bag.

No glasses. Thank goodness, but not really, because I was getting a headache. The day-job jobs had piled up from yesterday, the chores continue to mount, and this blog wasn't going to write itself. I needed those glasses.

Think, Beth.

What else?

I'd started laundry. I dug through a pile of yet-to-be-folded clothes and towels. Nothing. I dug through the yet-to-be-washed mountain of blankets and jeans. Nope. I stopped the washing machine, pulling out sopping wet, dirty clothes and feeling deep into the freezing cold water. No luck. I hadn't tumble-dried them, either.

Little Miss kept trying to chime in. She'd started to wake up from her slump, the glitter shining a tick more brightly. And she started in with the snark. "Someone call a detective. Any detective. Nancy Drew. Matlock. Sherlock..." As she mentioned Sherlock, her little eyebrows rode way up her forehead and her impish grin filled the room. I knew what she was thinking. Either Sherlock would do — Mr. Downey Jr.

Mr. Cumberbatch.

Especially Mr. Cumberbatch...

No. Wait. I'd really like to have my glasses on for that.

Garbage can was next. I went through the first four layers before I figured they could've have fallen past the horde of leftover food I'd cleaned out of the fridge.

The fridge! They're in the fridge...

No.

They were likewise not under the table or counters. They were not under Malachi, who was sunning himself on the table or trailing behind Amara, who was singing to a spring. Stella "helped" by following me around. I believe she told the other two cats that "the filler of the dishes needs help," and by this time, I had a miffed Muse and three cats trailing me all over the house trying to find my eyeballs. I wondered if Stella "helped" by hauling them off and sticking them in the box springs. (Their favorite place to hide things. I kid you not).

I sunk down on the spare bed to think. Dialog at the Eye Place ran through my head. "I lost them. Yes, I know I've not had them long. Yes. I know it will cost big. They're in the house, but I can't find them, make me another pair, please." I could see the look on Eye Guy's face at my discombobulated story and mental capacity. No. Wait. I couldn't see the look — no glasses.

The cats joined me. Little Miss plopped herself down on the pillow, her chunky butt cheeks sinking deep into the spot where I'd love to lay my head down and go back to sleep. I was almost in tears. Tiredness. To-do lists growing by the microsecond. Missing feathered fowl.

Little Miss wiggled. And wiggled again. Shifting and grimacing.

I jumped up, scattering cats, pulling covers, and throwing pillows. In glorious flair, my bifocals came flying out from a pillowcase, tumbled through the air, and landed in Little Miss's chunky hands. I don't remember even making the bed. Not *that* bed.

I'm losing my mind.

But I've found my glasses.

Ahem. Little Miss found my glasses. And now the day-job jobs are under control. The blog is almost written. The cats are conked out.

And Little Miss is ready to rock and roll on our current work in progress.

Now.

Where'd I put my manuscript?

Looking Back: I don't wish insomnia on anyone. I also don't wish anyone to live with someone experiencing a debilitating lack of sleep. Those were dark times where visions of cast iron skillets and sledgehammers pranced through my head until Hub's Doc Man straightened him out. And then I had to apologize to Jesus for the hammers and skillets. Little Miss Muse believes if we'd been writing for the same amount of time we've spent looking for lost items that we'd have four more novels in the bank.

I don't disagree, but I also pointed out that she's the reason some of those things were lost to begin with. Need I remind her of the fresh batch of grape soda that went "missing." Only it wasn't missing, was it Little Miss?

It was consumed.

She digresses and hands me another idea for a short story.

127

STASH AND REPEAT

A few months back, my Number One Fan and my Number One Aunt gifted me glorious surprises based on the book *Life Along the Way*. Many of those surprises were of the chocolate variety.

Reese's Cups. Ghirardelli. Lindt.

You get the idea.

After opening the first package from Number One, I showed the Hubs and the Adult-ish Male Child my gifts. My heart swelled from the act of kindness, and my sweet tooth was temporarily satisfied as I partook of a few dark chocolate squares. Then I made a grave mistake: I put the rest away in the kitchen.

For the next time when my sweet tooth should overtake my good sensibilities.

And then... *poof*

Gone.

Stressed as though I may have been at the time of her gift, I *know* that I did not consume ALL THAT CHOCOLATE from my Number One Fan.

Not that quickly.

I also know, stressed as he was at the time, that Dear Hubs did not consume ANY of the chocolate—he's a cocoa hater, that one, and was cleared by default.

Little Miss Muse? I lay many a blame on her shimmering wings, but the disappearance of tangible treats is not one I can toss in her court. Anyway, she prefers grape gum and blowing giant purple bubbles in gleeful celebration to melty chocolate misery-tonic.

Likewise the cats. Missing chicken? Stolen raw turkey burger right out of the skillet? The occasional tax receipt? Nail clippers and paperclips (Stella Marie has a serious issue with tiny metal things). Absolutely.

Chocolate? Not so much.

That left one suspect. The Adult-ish Male Child of mine. Love him, but he's a sweet treat thief. I know this about him, but somehow, in the course of busy and stressful days, I forget this.

I'll put Hubby's lunch treats in the cabinet after a grocery store run.

Poof Then Hubby has no lunch treats.

I'll leave an Edwards Chocolate Cream Pie in the freezer for an upcoming get-together lest I have to *gasp* cook something.

Poof There is no Edwards Chocolate Cream Pie in the freezer.

I'll make Hubs or Mom-in-Law a strawberry pie (a pie that requires only heating a crust and slicing berries, lest any of you believe my culinary skills have improved since my last kitchen disaster).

Anyway. I bet you can guess. *Poof*

After several rounds of this, we started hiding nonperishable sweets in the underwear drawers, in the spare suitcases, and in the bottom of the closet. Pies, not so much – I'm a disaster of a cook, but I do understand certain things can't withstand the climate in an underwear drawer.

I should've done the same with that bag of chocolate heaven. Put it with the socks or on the top shelf out in the garage behind the half-used buckets of paint.

But I didn't. Instead, I found irrefutable evidence littering the floor under Adult-ish Child's desk. Those shimmering blue Ghirardelli wrappers tossed to and fro without a care in the world.

The semi-weekly grand disappearance of sweet treats seems to happen in the wee hours of the night when the Adult-ish Child indulges in gaming while his hard-working parents sleep.

Well.

Learned my lesson.

After the Number One Aunt gifted me with very similar goodies as the Number One Fan, I got wise to him. This time, I would keep tight control over the chocolate cache. I refrained from opening the Reese's bag. I tethered the urge to slice into the box of Lindt truffles. I likewise denied myself even the slightest whiff of Ghirardelli caramel squares.

All packages remained closed and sealed, lest the scent draw the Adult-ish Male from hiding, drool escaping down his chin.

For fear that he may be on to the underwear drawer thing, I found new spots. And, since we've had one round of stressful chaos after the next (thus depleting my goodies to dangerously low levels), and since I doubt this particular child reads my blog, I feel secure in sharing with you, dear reader, where I stashed my stash.

And, the next time I should be gifted glorious stress-reducing (or celebratory) chocolate, I'll not reuse these spots... Should you need to hide your stress-reducing (or celebratory) sweets from those who claim to love you dearly, feel free to steal my thunder.

I flipped the box of truffles on its side and slid it onto the book-case between Webster's Dictionary and *Life Along the Way*. Blended right in.

For the bag of Reese's Cups... I ate frozen broccoli for lunch. Well. I cooked it. Sort of—it was a chew-and-swallow and get-on-with-it kind of lunch. But I saved the broccoli bag. I stuffed the Reese's bag inside the broccoli bag and secured it with a clip. I slid this into the very back of the freezer, no one the wiser.

These tactics even worked on me. Out of sight, out of mind until, well...

The truffles met their match after a particularly bad three days in the trenches with work and the insomniac Hubs.

The broccoli-floret covered Reese's bag was opened on a likewise particularly bad day. Replaced into the freezer. Repeat. Several days of this.

But I reminded myself chocolate therapy in tiny, secret bits sure does the soul good.

And now I'm down to just one more stash...

The IRS says to keep your tax returns for three years. I keep mine for about five. Somewhere in the middle of those five years, the Ghirardelli Dark Chocolate Sea Salt Caramel Squares await their turn for consumption.

Yes, I've got the expiration date memorized. No, they won't live to see that day. Whether celebration or stress relief, that bag of Ghirardelli will be my pal quite soon.

Little Miss reminds me we've made some short story sales. So even in the middle of stressful minutes, we do have reason to celebrate.

She winks, lavender mascara dripping down her chubby cheeks.

I get the point. I'll stock her up on her grape bubble gum, and I'll save the caramel squares to celebrate the upcoming announcements.

Giddy little jump-and-squeal chocolate caramel moments...

Complete with sticky, purple bubbles.

Looking Back: Stashes are still important for humans and Muses. Cats, also, appreciate a good stash of springs and fuzzy mice—usually tucked away under the couches and fridge.
Little Miss Muse says the space between the walls and deep inside the air ducts are the best places to store already-chewed grape bubblegum.
I sense a long, detailed discussion is needed.

128

WOBBLES AND TOPPLES

It's been another long week.

It started off as if someone had wound me up tight—like one of those old-fashioned tin toys. At first, I could conquer the world. Buzzing along, one foot in front of the other.

But then wobbling ensued.

Then more wobbling.

Then toppling.

Slowly, slowly, the week became longer and longer.

And now my Great Chocolate Hideaway stash is nearly depleted. Even the dark caramel chocolate squares hidden in the 2018 tax return.

Since my last entry, we've realized the Hubs and I will no longer need to hide his stash of white powdered doughnuts and honey buns in the underwear drawer. I could bring out the chocolate squares from the filing cabinet and leave them in the open if I so desired.

Because Adult-ish Male Child, the reason for all the hiding, has moved out.

Flew the coop.

The last of our little birdies out in the wide, wide world.

It came as a semi-surprise to us, but not to him. This child thinks things through, assumes we've read his mind, then announces with great flair his grand plans.

This time the grand plan included an apartment that was available right now. Now. NOW.

This very second and not a second later, and all moving activities must happen in the next five minutes or disaster would ensue.

Well, who am I to argue with Adult-ish Male Child? In his adult-ish wisdom and 19 years of experience on this planet, he had a rock-solid plan. And a seemingly unlimited supply of energy.

However, those of us who've moved anything more than a trunk full of belongings from Point A to Point B know that nothing happens in five minutes—and if things can go wrong, go missing, or get broken, they will.

Go wrong.

Go missing.

Get broken.

My more than 40+ years on the planet tell me these things. My 40+ also means that I do NOT have an unlimited supply of energy.

It was an exhausting week. Poor Hubs is still struggling with a myriad of health issues, waiting on the next test and the next doc appt. My routine is on its head. Ducks are out of rows. Cats are off schedule and missing key pieces of "their" furniture throughout the house. Their confused cries echo in empty rooms.

Little Miss Muse has run amok. Messes of epic proportions in every room.

My self-control is waning fast.

So.

Out came the chocolate from deep inside the 2018 deductions and proof of income.

One square.

Two squares.

Three squares.

I still have some left. Chocolate, that is. Self-control and the ability to reason, not so much.

Web Guy asked me how empty-nesting was going at the EXACT

same time Adult-ish Male Child was calling. The kid has a gas stove in his apartment. He smelled gas. What should he do?

"Turn on the vent, crack a window, and hope for the best." Some mom I am, right? (I did know that the oven hadn't been used for quite some time and there was a 98.4% chance that it was just that first-turned-on smell. My more than 40+ years on the planet tell me these things.)

Lest you think I'm totally cold hearted and that I would dare risk his safety with that 1.6% chance (and yes, I had to pull out the calculator—I'm exhausted, and simple math eludes me at the moment), I did lay awake for a long while waiting for the news that Adult-ish Male Child wasn't asphyxiated and that the apartment was still standing.

He didn't asphyxiate. The apartment is still intact.

I texted Web Guy back: Empty nest. Busy phone.

Ask me in two months once we've all adapted to this newfound strangeness. When the health issues are on track with some sort of plan.

When the ducks have returned to some kind of rows—or at least paddling in the same pond, that'd be nice.

When the kitties stop glaring at us over empty-five-minutes-too-long food bowls, razors showing from their piggie toes.

When Miss Muse has cleaned up the glittery mess she's left EVERYWHERE and is ready to put her head back in the writing game. (Soon, Little Miss, soon... I promise.)

That's the thing about excited Adult-ish Males and Muses (and cats when the sun goes down): Unlimited ideas. Unlimited energy.

I, on the other hand, find the energy levels during times of great stress deeply tied to having one hand in the Ghirardelli bag and the other with a death grip on a Diet Coke—the equivalent to someone sticking the tin-toy key in my back and giving me a good wind-up.

Here's hoping for one-quarter of a "new normal" week this week. Then one-half the next. Weeks with fewer wobbles and topples.

Then, well. We'll see how the supplies of chocolate squares, Diet Coke, and tin keys hold up.

Looking Back: Adult-ish male child has done quite well out in the world. Even learning to cook on his own, since I failed him in that regard. However, I do believe this was when the Powers That Be built the rings for our CIRCUS. The Hubs and I are still hoping the next (insert some future unit of time here) will prove to be calm/normal/peaceful.

But the CIRCUS came to town and shows no signs of leaving.

Little Miss Muse says we should embrace it. Dress in lavender leotards and install a tight rope from the trees in the front yard to the trees in the backyard and purchase a couple of lions from the dark web—
I stop her idea factory here. No tightropes or lions for me.

And I'll be a hundred years dead before anyone spots me in a lavender leotard.

Little Miss Muse says she can see to those arrangements, since Muses are eternal. She's writing a note in her calendar.

129

THE FIRST TIME

Firsts. They're super special, right? (Some of you just got a dirty-minded image—keep it rated PG, please. Don't go all TMI on me...)

Your first elementary school teacher. (Mrs. Back, Kindergarten circa 1980-something.)

Your first crush. (A little blond-haired boy in first grade, circa 1980-something-plus-one-year, who gave me a grape-scented scratch-n-sniff sticker off of his A+ math paper. And Little Miss goes WILD! Grape is her favorite.)

Your first car. (A gold Nova that my mom had painted teal green for me, circa 1990-something, totaled by an old woman pulling out from Kentucky Fried Chicken with a drumstick hanging out of her mouth—I kid you not. She stepped out of her smoking car, clutching the greasy boxed dinner to her chest with one hand, dangling the finger-lickin'-good drumstick in the other.)

Maybe your first car *was* your first crush... (Not quite a car person, but if that little Nova hadn't been wrecked beyond redemption, I'd still be driving it around.)

Next week for Free Fiction Monday, you get to experience one of my firsts.

My first "yes" on a professional sale.

Which brought the first giddy-little-jump-and-squeal of my career—followed by weeping.

Yes. I wept. But only for a few seconds. I'm not a crier by nature.

Then a second giddy-little-jump-and-squeal as I dried the snot and eye drips.

Though I sold another story that made its way into an anthology chronologically faster, "Leftovers" was still my first *yes*.

The main character, Scripture Jennings, was the first character born from my imagination (or that of Little Miss Muse) who stuck in my head long after I wrote him.

This sale was validation and a huge boost to that wonky, wobbly, trembling low self-esteem that most creatives suffer from, especially at the beginning of new endeavors.

"Leftovers" was proof I could string a few words together and make someone smile. Or think. Or pause. Or dream. If only for a moment.

That lovable, quirky character pulled his weight and pulled on the imagination of Dean Wesley Smith and walked right into Issue #8, Fall 2019 of Pulphouse Fiction Magazine. B.A. Paul was in a table of contents! (Check out the link and check out the back cover. There I am. First one in the author list—only because my pen name has fewer characters than anyone else's, but still. And an even cooler thing? I met nine or so of the other authors out in Vegas. Next time, I'll take the magazine with me, and they can all sign it. EEEK!)

Little Miss Muse wants you to know that she also pulled her weight and dropped every good morsel of that story into my subconscious.

And what glorious morsels they were.

"Leftovers" is quirky. It's tender. And then it's twisted. It won't be everyone's cup of tea, but hey. Neither is Star Wars (I don't understand why this wouldn't be everyone's favorite...) or Iron Man (Seriously, though. What's wrong with some folks?).

When the short story posts next week, just be forewarned — pure innocence can bring about some fascinating consequences. You may just be tempted to curl your toes, pull your glasses down for a better look, and then glare at me over the screen.

But it's all in fun. And that first sale sure was glorious fun!

And now, since it's been a long, long few weeks, I'm heading off to the next item on my to-do list. Before all the ice melts in my Diet Coke. And before I run out of those little chocolate caramel squares that keep me going in times like these, lest I'm forced to resort to a lowly banana to calm my emotions.

Bananas.

For emotional turmoil...

Now that'd be a first.

Looking Back: Scripture Jennings is still one of my favorite characters. The story is now in the collection All the Feels Volume 3.
As for the crying bit, the CIRCUS is in full swing and I accidentally cry in the cat food aisle or random hallways with no warning. An appointment with a Couch Person is forthcoming.
Little Miss Muse wants to point out that every good morsel in All the Feels came from her. And that I should take her with me to see the Couch Person because she'd like some skills to cope with her author that won't just SIT DOWN AND WRITE THE BOOK ALREADY.
I believe Miss Muse needs a Couch Person well versed in anger management.

130

BIG-NAME BORDER BATTLE

You know those jobs that you figure will take a couple of hours? Tops? Then you can get on with what you really want to do? Like take a walk, or fish, or binge-watch mermaids or spaceships.

Or, hey! I know!

Write some new words already!!!

One of those jobs where that still, small voice in the back of your head nags you and says it's probably not gonna time out the way you think...?

This is one of those times...

We moved into our current home about ten years ago. We're painting the main living spaces for the first time since moving in. We were happy with what the previous owners had picked, so much so that we purchased from them and left much of the décor they had hanging in our new-to-us "Game Room."

This room was at one point a garage, and those owners converted it into livable square footage and wired it for sound—quite literally. Half of the room held a pool table and later swapped that for a ping pong table. Both tables mostly housed clutter or some ongoing project. You know, like a treadmill often turns into a closet of sorts.

The other half of the Game Room boasted an enormous wall of built-in shelves holding archaic video and sound equipment left as a "housewarming" by the previous owners. Surround sound speakers hung high in all the corners, wired to the main system. We didn't use this equipment, and it mostly housed spiders.

We enjoyed most of the art left on the walls—old-time movie prints and artwork of movie reels and old-fashioned popcorn containers. We added our own Marvel and DC movie-themed items. The ceiling was even painted black to absorb extra light for those all-fun movie nights.

We weren't a fan of the wallpaper border, however. Bette Davis, James Cagney, and Rita Hayworth depicted on old movie posters. Fred Astaire and Ginger Rogers also adorned this vintage-ish border. In fact, this border, I said, was the first thing we'd change when we moved in. It just wasn't to my taste.

Ten years later, Rita and her cleavage are still hanging all around that black ceiling.

And now it's time to paint since the Adult-ish Male Child moved out and since the Hubs would like to change the name of this room from "Game Room" to "Man Cave."

Currently, the walls are dark hunter green and marred beyond reason.

Time for a refresh.

We (the Hubs and the lady cats) spent the better part of one evening removing gallery-style wall art hung with screws, nails, sticky tack and who-knows-what-*that*-was and puttying the holes closed. The felines would stand on the desk or a shelf and stretch along the walls, picking at nails we missed. They were quite the help (insert huge eye roll here).

I removed all the outlet covers—gobs and gobs of outlets. Amara helped with this task. She'd stick her toe beans into the areas around the exposed wall sockets and scoop out loose drywall. I scatted her away with a broom lest she blow her tail off her fanny.

I unscrewed the brackets holding up the speakers. Took wire

cutters, prayed these were truly sound system wires and not live electrical wires, held my breath, and snipped the speakers free. Exhaled, glad these were indeed dead speaker wires and not something fishy running to one of those outlets.

I didn't blow myself off the ladder. My cardiac output seems fine. My right eye is twitching, but I'm calling that one a stress reaction to general life circumstances and not electrocution by stupidity.

Time to remove the wallpaper.

Climb the ladder with the putty knife. Nick a corner free, aaannd... nothing. James Cagney gloats.

Try a little harder with the knife. Aaannd... dug a hole into the drywall. Bette Davis blinks those smokey eyes at me. I ignore her. No big deal. I'll putty it later.

Go to the store. Buy fabric softener and a spray bottle. This is supposed to dissolve the glue.

Now the Game Room smells good. Really good. Enough to give Fred Astaire and Ginger Rogers a new kind of high-step to their dance along the rim of the ceiling.

Wait 15 minutes. Climb the ladder with the putty knife. Nick another corner.

Aaannd... nothing. Yet another hole in the wall to putty closed later and a gleaming smirk from Ginger. Nothing can stop this woman.

I soak another dose and wait another 15 and up the ladder again. This time I applied more muscle, earning me an even larger spot to putty. Rita Hayworth has an iron-clad cleavage. She seems quite proud of herself.

Descend the ladder, leave the house covered in fabric softener, blue paint (from the touch-ups I did in the utility room), and teeny-weeny bits of wallpaper. And lots of sweat.

Sherwin-Williams will help me. And they won't judge me for my disheveled appearance.

I spent some money there on a new tool and a new bottle of wallpaper removal solution.

Drive back home. Back up the ladder. Score the wallpaper with my new tool so the new solution will soak through. Spray the border. Again. Wait 15. Again.

Back up the ladder. Again.

Aaannd...

Yup. You guessed it.

To-be-puttied spot #3.

I could've fed a small army of toddlers some excellent Happy Meals for what I spent there. Set them loose in the Game Room and let their shrill shrieks peel the wallpaper off the wall. It would've been more effective.

I gave up. The border wins. I do believe this star-studded cast was adhered to that hunter-green wall with Gorilla Glue tainted by whatever they use to hold rocket ships together.

Congrats Rita and Ginger. Congrats Cagney. You too, Bette and Fred. Have the wall. Have the nooks and crannies around the black ceiling. Dance, sing, and act forevermore.

But, you'll be doing it under a layer of beige paint, Sherwin-Williams CC 19 Curio Gray SW0024 to be exact. Eggshell. Paint *and* primer even.

And for the final performance, you can walk the red carpet under the Hub's new golf club or football field or otherwise Man-Cave-appropriate border.

Because it'd take me a hundred years to remove you guys in all your movie star glory.

Because I know when I've been beaten. (I wonder if the movies depicted on the border had anything to do with this — a kind of forewarning: *Hard to Handle, Dark Victory...* I'm sensing a gang-up-on-Beth theme, now that I think about it.)

At any rate, I certainly know when I'd be better off writing instead of trying to scrape Academy-Award-winning cleavage from my walls.

Looking Back: We did, indeed, paint right over those award-winners. We have not, however, hung up a new border. We move very slooowly in the decorating department.
Little Miss Muse thinks the Hubs should've painted the room purple.

I point out that she's my Muse and he'll have to get his own with its very own favorite color. Now she's pouting in the corner, hoping the Hubs doesn't get the writing bug. There's only room for one Muse around here...

131

THE CASE OF THE GLOATING SWINE

S hort and sweet this week.

Because I cooked porkchops.

(That was my first mistake. Thinking I could cook.)

I made enough to feed us empty-nesters for several meals, as a matter of fact.

(That was my second mistake. Trying to plan ahead.)

Purchased those chops fresh, baked them thoroughly. Sides of steaming mashed potatoes and rolls. Fresh salad and...

The gloating swine took its revenge.

Ten bites in, and I'm doubled over in the bathroom.

A few hours later, poor Hubs had the same general symptoms, the cats didn't know why I was running up and down the hallway ALL NIGHT LONG, and Little Miss Muse had lost some of her sparkle. She even refused her latest shipment of grape soda.

Some things just don't settle well with food poisoning, even for a muse.

It was bad.

And that "I swallowed a lead balloon" feeling has persisted for days, worse with movement, better when lying flat on my back.

So... while I recover and purge the fridge of all possible offending foods (I'm not a betting woman, but I'd gamble it all on the gloating swine), try to hold down my toast, and figure out if we can afford a live-in chef, here's a quick update:

I've got several professional sales coming to publication this summer. Keep a watch here for those cool announcements.

Check out "Leftovers" in the Free Fiction section—that was my first "real" sale — and one of the most fun characters to write. It'll be replaced with a new story on July 5, so you've got until then.

If you haven't already, you can sign up for the newsletter and get a free short mystery, either through the NEWSLETTER tab here on the blog or through this link. If you've already signed up and think something is "broken" because you've not gotten a newsletter. Well, I'm the broken cog in that wheel. Hoping to get the newsletter updates going soon, but in the meantime, get your name on the list and enjoy "Dragonfly."

Web Guy helped me rearrange the BOOKS section on the website. Each book now has updated links where you can find my work. Click the cover images for retailer options. *Life Along the Way* is only available on Amazon and is still free to read if you have a Kindle Unlimited plan.

So, as I down four more Alka-Seltzer berry chews, I wish you well. Happy reading, happy summer, and may all the meals you consume be free of the gloating swine.

Looking Back: As I reread these blogs, I'm shocked at how much has transpired that I'd totally forgotten about. This was a three-day stretch gladly pushed into the nether regions of my mind.
I've also taken to keeping a running list by my keyboard as I review. Newsletter keeps making the list, working its way into the #1 spot of things to do for 2023.
Little Miss Muse reminds me once again that a bestseller could, in fact, pay for a live-in chef. Especially if we sold the cats.
I offer that we could afford the chef now if I stopped the steady influx of bottle rockets, lighter fluid, purple glitter and grape gum.

Little Miss is now off giving the cats their morning catnip treats and whispering sweet nothings in their ears.

132

SUMMERTIME DREAMIN'

Short and sweet this week. Again.

But not because I cooked porkchops.

As a matter of fact, after that disaster, I've done very little cooking. And we've been running to and fro from one doc appointment to the next as fast as we can to get poor dear Hubs in line.

Turns out that the medical universe is as behind on scheduling procedures as I am on my writing goals.

I'm also quite disoriented (doesn't take much) as to the calendar. The last time it was this bad was when my grandmother passed away, and I remember seeing holiday items on clearance but not recalling the holiday at all. Oh, and it was bad during that stretch last fall when COVID hit and time rolled off the calendar like water off a duck's back and went I know not where.

Strange sensations, those.

Life rolls, some folks call them. Big emotional events when every ounce of brainpower goes to only the most necessary tasks at hand— and the muses and the kitty cuddles and the general fun and dreamy parts of living go by the wayside for the time being.

And where did June go? If it weren't for this blog, I'd have gotten no words down at all this month.

At the time of this writing, I've got three days left in this summer month. Three days.

I'd planned on starting a great big writing challenge in June.

Plans. Hahaha.

However...

Now that we have a semi-shaky plan (as compared to no plan and nothing but sheer terror) for the Hubs, and the Adult-ish Male Child has settled (as well as the dust that had kicked up in our home from his move-out) I can finally see itty bitty sparkles of hope.

Hope that Hubs will feel better soon (come on docs, we're on a roll... don't fail us now).

Hope that I'll be able to keep up with the laundry (or at least have time to get to Walmart to buy extra underwear and effectively push the laundry problem for another week).

Hope that the paint colors we picked will STAY ON THE WALL and not slide off in withered desperation while we sleep (I've been having vivid nightmares, can you tell?).

Since a few of those hope-ish sparkles are purple, I have hope that Little Miss Muse hasn't packed her purse and plum stilettos to head for another author's office. She's still hanging in there with me. I swear, sometimes she's got the patience of Job, and other times, well, she's like a kitten on caffeine pills.

Those little purple shimmers of light have sparked some dreaming.

And, another bit of good news? Those red-eyed, drunkard cicadas have finally stopped SCREAMING! Ahhh. Once the stench of their rotting carcasses clears the yard, it could be a pleasant summer.

So, I've got three days left in June. (So do you if you're catching this on Monday morning).

Three.

And the inklings of a plan. I know the dangers of outlining plans in public. I also know it tends to give me a bit of a jump start after mucking about in the doldrums. So, here goes.

June Goals (a whopping two goals—start simple, they say, right?)

1. One short story to clear the cobwebs and allow Little Miss to stretch her wings and shake out her tutu.
2. Make it to July.

July Goals: (This is scary. This month has all of its days left. So much can happen in so many days. Or so little, depending on how you look at it...)

1. Four shorts.
2. Three blogs and a free fiction for you guys.
3. Novel 2 reread to figure out where I left my characters and what they were wearing when I ditched them (hopefully I did *their* laundry and their wardrobes are stocked for a few more chapters). I also believe my last several chapters in the WIP (work in progress) actually belong in Book 3. We shall see. Sometimes Little Miss likes to work ahead. Waaaay ahead. Only she doesn't tell me that's what she's up to until I'm massively confused by what we produce in our joint endeavors.
4. Make it to August.

August Goals: (August? What's August? A month with five Mondays. FIVE. Mondays.)

1. Four shorts.
2. Four blogs and a free fiction (did I mention this month has FIVE Mondays?)
3. WIP novel done.
4. Start dreaming of fall.

There it is. A summertime plan. Whether goals or wishes or pie in the sky, I've no idea, as all of this must be worked around the current life roll and a dozen or so unknown factors.

Factors like laundry. And food poisoning. And temperamental thyroids.

And moody muses...

So, here's to dreamin'.

Here's to summer.

Happy Fourth to you all...

May your laundry be caught up, may your thyroid glands glisten with health, and may you avoid porkchop food poisoning at your Independence Day picnic!

Looking Back: That novel mentioned here isn't done—it's a bit longer than it was, but not done. All those other goals were met by the end of August, late but done.

Another thing? That novel project was interrupted by a totally different novel. I can procrastinate writing by writing like no one's business...

And the cicadas? We had thousands and thousands in the trees around our house. I couldn't be outside much longer than it took to go to the mailbox. They were awful. This year, we had a dozen or so that I noticed. A few guys that were simply late to the party.

I feel like that sometimes. I missed the party boat and am frantically paddling to catch up. With goals. With life. With sleep...

Little Miss Muse says she didn't mind the cicadas and actually befriended their leader.

I'm not surprised.

133

SNOT EVERYWHERE

This was going to be a complete and thorough update on those self-imposed deadlines and goals I outlined in the last blog. A completely honest assessment. Thorough, with adjustments, tweaks, and more self-inflicted restrictions and rules. Totally writing-focused.

But now there's just the following snarky recap.

Because there's snot.

Everywhere.

I. Mean. Everywhere.

Last week, Stella Marie contracted some sort of feline upper respiratory thing. Snotty, sneezing, drooling (I think her throat hurt). But because of the holiday, I held off rushing her to the vet. By the time the office was open for non-emergent issues, she was better. Still a little sneezy, but better.

As of last night, she began singing the song of her homeland at the top of her lungs and dancing to and fro with EVERY chirpy-bird toy she could find. The wee hours of the night were filled with her happy howls and the fading electronic squeaks of a pale blue narwhal, red cardinal, and mouse-on-pumpkin.

I planned on stripping out the near-dead batteries from those toys today. But she sensed my aggravation, and she's hidden them.

Likely in the recesses of the box springs or in some other unknown-to-me-even-though-I-lived-here-first part of the house.

Little Miss Muse probably helped her.

And there's nothing I can do about Stella's singing voice. Or her choice of two a.m. through three-thirty a.m. for choir practice. Little Miss, however, thrives on a bit of chaos now and again and enjoyed Stella's recovery howling.

As of two days ago, Amara and Malachi started with the same head cold symptoms. Amara is still stomping around here like a boss, chasing springs, and keeping sharp eyes on the perimeter. All the while she's sneezing and spraying violent fountains of snot everywhere that Stella missed. Sliding glass doors, walls (freshly painted walls, mind you), floors, television screens, and my style guides for the day job. Nothing like needing to look something up and grabbing a booger-crusted reference book.

Poor Malachi, though. He's not so hot. Mouth breathing, fever and very, very needy. Like "Hold me, Mom, I'm dying" kind of needy. Now *I'm* covered in snot. Shirt. Pants. Arms. Hair. Glasses (I've cleaned the lenses four times and it's not noon yet). The laptop screen has not escaped his aim, either.

This poor guy's status prompted a call to the vet. And a trip to the vet in a too-small carrier. (The irony is not lost on me that the free fiction story for the month is based on this very cat and a trip to the vet. If you've not read it yet, you can check it out until the end of the month).

He came out with a shot in the butt and oral antibiotics. Also, Amara is not fond of the fresh-from-the-vet smell he now carries and has slapped even more snot out of him three times. Literally.

She's now howling in time-out, interspersing hissing with sneezing.

It's been real around here. And the above only addressed our feline fiasco and not the long strings of human happenings.

So.

Here goes the recap:

June :

1. One short story to clear the cobwebs and allow Little Miss to stretch her wings and shake out her tutu. UPDATE: *Miss Muse has spread her wings with 2K words on this particular task, then... sick cats and other human ailments from various and sundry sources. Missed it, but at least I got it started. And the cat snot has permanently cemented the purple glitter she's been spreading about to every.surface.in.the.house. So yeah. Snot and glitter.*
2. Make it to July. *Check. I've got skid marks and road rash on my soul, but hey. We made it to July.*

July:

1. Four shorts. *Hahaha. Not started, but it's just the 9th. Plenty of time.*
2. Three blogs and a free fiction. *One blog down after I spell check this one; the free fiction will be from last year's efforts. Two blogs to go.*
3. Novel 2 reread to figure out where I left my characters and what they were wearing when I ditched them. *Not yet. Packing it for a weekend away, and we'll see what happens.*
4. Make it to August. *Hopefully with no skid marks or road rash. Or snot. Glitter, I can deal with.*

August goals not reposted here because, well, too much life to live to think that far ahead. I'd be thrilled to knock out the ones above.

And stay snot-free.

All the way to August.

I've got to leave a good day or two to clean.all.the.snot. But not until all three cats are done blowing out boogies.

Aannnd...

I hear hissing.

And thumping.

Likely Amara.

Removing more snot from Malachi...

Here's hoping the rest of your July is bright and shiny and you hit all of your self-imposed deadlines with glee!

Looking Back: The fantasy short story based on Malachi can be found in Just a Tick of Whimsy Volume 1. The jury's out on whether posting goals in public is a good thing or not. At any rate, I'll carefully consider the CIRCUS status before setting deadlines, or hopes. Or dreams.
Little Miss Muse reminds me Stella told her of the jealousy brewing between the lady cats that Malachi got his own story already and the girls are still waiting for theirs.
They'll have to wait a bit longer
Three novels in progress. Three.
It's an awful thing when the Muse and the felines gang up on you.

134

BLACK CATS ARE LUCKY!

Time for a quick giddy-little-jump-and-squeal moment!

Back in March of "The Year That Shall Remain Unnamed," the world turned upside down. I'd just returned home from the Vegas writing workshop where several of my stories managed to make their way into professional publications. I was on a high, and Little Miss Muse was equally squeal-filled.

But "The Year that Shall Remain Unnamed" hit hard.

Everywhere.

Everyone.

Including the little group of pro editors from the workshop. A couple of the projects had to be canceled. The market was too unsure. The funds were unsure.

Everything was... unsure.

I understood. I, too, was unsure.

Then an email hit my inbox from Mr. Michael Bracken. I'd submitted a mystery short story prior to that trip and—even amid COVID—he accepted my submission to Black Cat Mystery Magazine.

Now, I'm not a superstitious person, but I know folks who are (I'm related to a few of them). I believe, for those of you who happen to be of that skittish persuasion, y'all can relax about those black cats.

At least in magazine form.

Because this Black Cat was pretty lucky for me...

One of my creepy mystery shorts, "Coral Cove," was picked up by Black Cat Mystery Magazine. The editor, Michael Bracken, was a joy to work with, and I so appreciate the opportunity to be tucked into the pages (or float along on the digital data stream, as the case may be) with other talented authors.

You can find Black Cat's full lineup of mystery offerings and browse other genres from Wildside Press. Issue #9 is the newest release. At some point, I believe the magazine will be available in print form, but I'm not seeing that option live just yet.

The setting of "Coral Cove" had bobbed around in my head for a long time. I'd always found coastal neighborhoods with their cookie-cutter structures and brightly colored siding intriguing. Were the people inside mirrors of their domiciles—cookie-cutter personalities, nearly robotic in their daily journeys? Were these simply vacation rentals, or do families make the coast their permanent place?

How many happy memories were shared by the inhabitants?

How many terrors?

How many tokens hang on their walls to ward off superstitious lore?

And, if my own family's vacations are anything to compare with, how many knock-down, drag-out fights occur within those walls over the classic "Where do you want to eat" debate?

Little Miss Muse, however, wants you all to know that she'd *never* let me put anything so mundane as the McDonald's versus downtown diner duel in "Coral Cove." Unless, of course, it ended in someone losing an eye. *Wink*

"Coral Cove" won't appear anywhere on the blog or in any of my personal collections for quite some time. So, you mystery lovers, go check it out. Perhaps you'll get lucky and find another author or two who scratches your mystery itch in this issue of Black Cat Mystery Magazine.

Looking Back: Coral Cove is available in Dark Minds. I chose to stick this mystery in the "horror" collection because of the slick deviousness of the protagonist.

Even with an empty nest, the "Where do you want to eat" debate can send thoughts of divorce court lawyers dancing through our heads. And since my cooking is so bad, we have this conversation often...

Little Miss Muse is still vying for the live-in chef.

I'm not against it. The Hubs isn't either if we could get him/her to sweep up the never-ending cat fur and glitter as part of the deal.

135

ALL I WANTED WAS CINNAMON

Those who know me best know I adore dumb T-shirts.

Let me rephrase that: Those who know me best believe my T-shirts are dumb. My closest friends cringe when I show up to a brunch or dinner out. Some folks I warn: "I'm wearing the Ewok today" or "You'll have to excuse my lucky gnome shirt." I do this to get the eye-rolls out of the way.

My friends, ever practical, roll their eyes anyway and get over it because they love me. A few close buddies have tried to "redress" me multiple times, pointing out more respectable options hanging from thrift store racks or glistening in department store windows. I cringe at the uncomfortableness of such garments and the not-me-ness.

They cringe at me cringing.

And I keep on wearing what I wear.

I'm sure I'd be the ultimate fashion-disaster fodder for that show "What Not to Wear."

But I love my corny shirts. They're comfortable. They're geeky, nerdy, and off-the-wall, often inspired by pop culture and all things I loved as a kid (and still let my inner child gloat over), or things I find tongue-in-cheek hilarious as an adult. Or things that tickle Little Miss Muse in all her glittery purple glory.

I do draw the line at wearing actual glitter, though. That's Little Miss. And she spreads enough glitter around here that I'm positive my lower lung lobes are 83% metallic. No MRIs for me...

If I ever have to go to a black-tie event, I'll die a thousand deaths, call my fashionista gang to dress me, then head home to change out of the "monkey suit" and into my happy, baggy 100% cotton "Thanks, Science" shirt, which sarcastically laments the fate of alchemy, Pluto, and the brontosaurus.

Often, I'm not even aware I've donned comical or quirky attire. It's the clean garment on top of the laundry pile. Often, strangers will stare at me, make a comment or smile, and I have to look down to remember what I'm wearing.

I'm always thankful in these moments that I am, indeed, wearing something, and that I didn't escape my home in a half-dressed state.

I was running errands the other day and went into a discount store to pick up a single item: A jar of cinnamon. That's it. That's all I needed from this place.

It's 9 a.m. The only other folks out at that early hour shopping in our small town are elderly folks. And two white-haired sisters (or best friends, or fellow escapees from the nursing facility) each with her own cart are in the aisle. With the cinnamon. The ladies are dressed like, well, ladies. Button-up blouses, crisp and neat. Mid-shin-length skirts with dainty floral prints. Reminded me of how my grandmother used to dress to "go to town."

Clearly, I didn't get that gene. The "dress up to go to town" gene.

I give them their space, waiting patiently for them to pass. Lady #1 smiles at me, nods, then looks at me a little longer. "I like your pocketbook."

Well, that's not what I was expecting. I thanked her and told her I liked it as well, reminded again of my grandmothers who called their purses pocketbooks.

"Where'd ya git it?"

"I bought it online."

That, dear readers, was the wrong answer. Remember, all I wanted was some cinnamon. To fix dear Hubs French toast. That's it.

(And yes, for those who know me well, I ended up butchering the French toast anyway, so what happens next is all icing...)

I proceed to stand there as Lady #1 gives me the firmest tongue-lashing I've had in quite some time on the dangers of online shopping. How punks and predators lurk there, and "they'll git you every time." She continues her scolding as she rounds the corner out of sight. I just stand there, head hung, not out of shame of my online purchasing habits, but because why fight or defend? She'd made up her mind, and at least she cleared the cinnamon aisle.

Lady #2 moves her cart up to Lady #1's now-empty space at the end of the cinnamon aisle. I can see the jars of spices from where I stand. But, again, I'm giving them space and allowing them time to pass. I'm so close...

Lady #2 moves in closer. And squints at my chest. Clearly, she wasn't fixated on my owl-print pocketbook. Purse. Bag. Whatever.

Clearly, she's looking at my T-shirt. (I hope, or else this gets really, really weird...). And as is customary, I look down at my shirt, too.

Here. We. Go.

Lady #2 asks in a long, southern drawl, "Is that Big Foot ridin' a uni-corn?" Emphasis on *Foot* and *uni*.

I look down at my shirt again, wishing that it was the antique typewriter shirt, but nope. Fantasy, all the way, baby.

I muster a timid "Yes, ma'am."

She continues to stare. At my chest/shirt. It's awkward. She tilts her head this way and that, giving me a silent tongue lashing with her eyeballs. A lashing that would rival that of her partner in crime (who was still complaining two aisles over about the generations that are too dependent on technology).

This lady hates, I mean *hates,* my shirt. But she's more reserved than her cohort.

Lady #2 finally says, with all the love in her heart (because at this point, it would be rude to just walk away?), "Well. I guess he's gotta ride on somethin', don't he now?" And she takes her cart and leaves the cinnamon aisle.

As she passes me, I hung my head again, not to hide shame in the shirt, but to hide the fact I'm about to bust a gut laughing at her obvious disgust and meager attempt at hiding it. "Yes, ma'am."

Best reaction I've ever gotten from any piece of clothing I've ever worn in my entire life. Hands down.

But I got my cinnamon. Well, Hub's cinnamon.

Made it to the car.

Laughed all the way home.

I'm sure I gave those old gals something to rant and discuss all the way back to wherever they came from. Especially Lady #2, who clearly didn't state her entire mind.

These gals have inspired another short story, as a matter of fact. The characters will have names and massive personalities much like my fellow shoppers.

I rather like those women. Speaking their minds. Doing their thing. Being themselves with no fear of judgment. White heads held high and proud. Go for it, grannies!

I hope one day, when I'm old and tired and white-haired (or bald, I'll more than likely be bald), that my kids (or my keepers) have kept me supplied with unicorn-riding sasquatch shirts. Or Ewok shirts. Or lucky gnome shirts.

I hope they don't dress me like a "proper" lady, in button-up blouses or skirts or eeeyikes—pantyhose (kill me now!).

I hope I'm still me.

I'll escape my nursing home (hopefully wearing one of these shirts, or things would get really, really weird...).

I'll push my shopping cart down the discount store's cinnamon aisle.

And I'll scold some young shopper on spending habits and choice of attire.

The young shopper will try not to bust a gut laughing at me.

And maybe my character might end up in someone else's novel...

Looking Back: I cannot go into that store or use cinnamon on anything without thinking about those ladies. I still have that shirt. The graphics are so worn that I actually looked up where to buy a replacement. Thank

goodness they still make it. You can Google for yourself if you want your
own Big Foot Riding a Unicorn shirt.
Little Miss Muse wonders if she'll ever be featured on a shirt.
I told her if she were to accomplish fame enough to warrant it, I'd be the
first to wear it in public. So long as she's riding a unicorn.

136

NOTHING LIKE IT

Unboxing Day!

These aren't brand new titles, but rather copies of ones I've already done that I ran out of.

I ran out of!

Because folks are asking for copies of this or that. "And do you have any more, please?" And I'm happy to scatter the paperbacks into my minuscule corner of the wide, wide world.

My dear aunt wanted "one of everything, please," to give my *great* aunt for her birthday. So I had to place an order. Because I was out of "one of everything."

But even with this small print run of not-new-to-me titles, this wave of "unnamed" emotion came over me. (If you would even dare to call it a print run— a traditional publisher's "small" print run for a new author may be around 10,000 copies. I printed five each. Five. No zeros.)

I can't quite capture the feeling in a word. To see something once only alive in my imagination show up in tangible manifestation on my doorstep in an Amazon box all holdable. Touchable. Feelable.

These words don't work: Thrilling. Sensational. Gripping. Magnificent. Fabulous. Rip-roaring wild. Those words only work for me during the writing process when Little Miss Muse stands tap dancing on my head and my fingers won't fly fast enough over the keys. Like trying to control a wild, bucking bronco—bareback and with one rein.

Joy? Happiness? Love? Those strong connotations I tend to reserve for family, friends, and faith. And it didn't feel the same.

My thesaurus fails me. Little Miss nods in agreement as she sits on the edge of the desk sucking on her grape lollipop, her chunky legs swinging her new lilac stilettos (five sizes too big, all the better to clonk around the house in). She knows the word. She's not giving it to me, though.

She's also silently taking all the credit as she peeks over the edge of the box, running a sticky finger along the spines of the books.

I like the term *giddy-little-jump-and-squeal* moment. I've used it quite a lot when a story sells or when Little Miss Muse gives me that plotting breakthrough I was looking for. But I didn't do that when this box came. I didn't cry or laugh or shout for joy.

My reaction was something more internal, the emotion staying centered somewhere under my rib cage.

Satisfaction? Contentment? Pride? Nope. These don't work either. I'm never satisfied or content with any of my creations, and my temptation is to tweak and re-do and re-vamp, etc., etc. In my mind, no story or cover or blurb is ever "right" or "good enough."

But at some point, you've gotta call the thing done and move on.

And so, until Little Miss coughs up the vocabulary, I'm declaring this line of thought done and moving on. There's simply no word for it. (Dopamine and endorphins probably have quite a bit to do with it, but let's say there's "no word for it" and not get too science-y.)

What that shiny new pile of paperbacks did do, though, was spur me over to Amazon to place a fresh order for grape lollipops. In bulk.

With Little Miss fully restocked, we're knocking out some of those Summertime Dreamin' goals. Update coming next week...

Looking Back: I recently placed another order—ten each this time, and the feeling was no less intense when I opened the box and scattered them on the table than what I described in this blog.

Life Along the Way *sold out at my first signing. Who knew?* Mystery Minutes *is also a big hit. I ordered more copies ahead of Christmas and in anticipation of heading out to another local signing or two if I can find ones geared toward general audiences.*

Little Miss Muse thinks we should aim big and do a print run of 10,000 per title.

I remind her again of the finite grape soda funds and she now believes runs of five or ten are just fine for right now.

SOMEONE STOP ME

I've been cleaning house lately—not just the sweeping up of a dozen "extra cats" every other day or scouring the kitchen sink on the rare occasion (I hate the kitchen).

I'm talking about the purge-it-real-good kind of cleaning. We painted, updated *very* outdated (or non-existent) décor, and generally gave the interior a facelift. Most of the main living spaces are done. We finally have a display case for an ever-growing collection of vintage tropical bird figurines (more about those on another day) and have a coffee table for the first time since wee little ones. (And NOW they make coffee tables with the corners all rounded off and soft. Now. Not when my kids were wee little. Now. But I shall be happy because I also am about as coordinated as a wee toddler, and I'm sure those rounded-down corners will be a blessing to my clumsy self going forward.)

With all the things we've hung and assembled, I'm very proud to stay the Hubs and I are still married. Nothing brings out the snark like interpreting directions after long days at work and 110-degree heat indices that seep through the air conditioning.

Many folks seemed to start *and* complete this purge-and-cleanse process during the Spring 2020 lockdowns.

I can't exactly remember Spring 2020. I know we got one room painted, intending to do all this extra work, but then, well. Something happened.

Something always happens to derail the plans.

So, here we are, doing the purge-it-real-good clean (which turns out is much easier when the adultish-children are out of the house).

And I'm ashamed of myself.

I'm a bit of a squirrel.

Like one of those squirrels who bought into the conspiracy news around the birdbath that the acorn crop this fall will be meager and you'd better get ready or starve. Said squirrel in a half-rabid panic begins strategically—or haphazardly—placing caches of acorns all over the neighborhood.

My acorns? Notebooks.

How long have I been "collecting" them?

Years.

Decades.

I've always had an office supply fetish, but this is out of hand. When my kids finished their school years, I thought I'd done a good job paring down the paper products to only the things I'll use.

But somehow, I'm still wading in notebooks.

Anytime I'm in a store, any store, my just-in-case-a-notebook-apocalypse sixth sense kicks in, and I find the stationery aisle. Or, say it's a hardware store, I can find that one rogue end-cap displaying some random handyman special to-do list notepad. And I'm tempted.

I'm not a handyman. I'm not married to a handyman.

I *know* I do not need a handyman to-do-list pad with the measuring tape border and a convenient magnet on the back to affix to my toolbox. But I can't help myself. I'll pick that pad up. Turn it over. Imagine all the wonderful ideas and lists to make on it.

And I put it in the cart. And in the cart, too, goes a pack of those flattened-out pencils that won't roll off your lumber as you're measuring and cutting. (I don't have lumber. If I did, I wouldn't know how to measure or cut it. I don't need these pencils, but they do match the handyman to-do list notepad soooo well...)

Sometimes, good sense kicks in and I'll stick the notebook back on the shelf, even as I worry I may never find another paper product of that sort again.

When we're at garage sales or auctions, and dear Hubs isn't with me, the office supplies are mine. Reams of paper, old school boxes full of pens (there may be a vintage one in there, don't ya know?), and crates of return address sticker labels (I seriously don't even know—it's a sickness). Even when the dear Hubs is with me, I often make him cart my finds around like a pack mule. He doesn't try to stop me. It's not worth the fight.

August is hard for me. When the school supplies come out in giant aisles all to themselves? Bins of pencil sharpeners, dry erase markers, index cards, and binder clips. And rows and rows of folders and notebooks and paper...

Jail me now. I'm gonna go broke.

The photo doesn't even show the notebooks I'm truly using (I lost count at eleven), the ones I've piled to give away (two-feet tall pile), nor the half-dozen that slipped behind the dresser as a cat came galloping through the room just before I snapped the picture and the pile shifted.

I have squirreled away, stored, stashed, hid on purpose, hid on accident, and generally "placed" notebooks all over the house.

All. Over. The. House.

Notebooks everywhere.

A few weeks ago, I wrote about how there was snot everywhere. I don't know how I even got all the cat snot cleaned away without breaking an ankle on All. These. Notebooks.

I must stop. I have enough.

Please, pretty please. If any of my local peeps catch sight of me out in the wild, and should I have in my hands or in my shopping cart notebooks, journals, calendars, planners, paper pads, or folders, please stop me. Likewise, I don't need any more mechanical pencils, highlighters, eraser tops, paperclips, or Post-It notes.

I don't.

Stop me.

And don't believe my lies when I tell you I'm shopping for someone else. Or that I'm truly out of the thing in my cart. No way, not even in an office supply apocalypse, will I ever be "out" of any of the above-mentioned items.

Pay no attention to my tears or trembling hands or beads of forehead sweat when you insist that I put these items back on the shelves. To leave them for someone else.

Someone else who will *not* appreciate their worth, mind you.

Just ignore these baseless pleas. Get nasty. Be bossy. Stomp your foot and wave your arms around and call me a fool.

If I run, chase me.

I'll take you to lunch for your trouble and to make up for the scene I caused in the office supply aisle. It'll actually save me money —you can even order dessert.

Then after, maybe we can run over to OfficeMax.

Because I'm out of index cards.

Looking Back: Let's not discuss the fact that my freshly purged notebook stack has swollen just a bit since this original post.
Let's not discuss the fact that I have, indeed, purchased more Post-It Notes (but it was a kind I didn't have, all very sticky and lined and nicely sized to plot out plots and stuff...).
Little Miss stands judging me with her hands on her hips, about to tell me the money would be better off spent on glitter or gum. Or thrown into our "PERSONAL CHEF" savings jar.
I reach behind my new stack of manilla folders, and pull out a sheet of grape scratch-n-sniff award stickers that I scored during the back to school sale. I put the sheet into her chonky hands.
She softens a bit.
Scratches.
Sniffs.
And grins.

138

EVERLASTING BUBBLE WRAP

Five Mondays, yes? August has five of these buggers to wrestle through. It's the month that wouldn't end. Five Mondays of crisp fall-ness or fresh spring-ness, now those I could handle with no attitude.

Okay, not nearly *as much* attitude.

But August? Who declared summer to be glorious and magical? The bugs. The heat. The heat index. No thanks.

And, since none of you would let me buy a new notebook, it just made the scalding, swampy middle of August that much more unbearable. Even Little Miss Muse is looking a little like a mannequin in a wax museum with a bum HVAC system.

I've had to get up from the desk twice already to break up frenzied feline fights in the hallway. It's the heat. And the humidity. Or they got in a tiff over a rogue bug. Bugs. Heat. Humidity.

August is awful. Sorry, summer lovers. It just is.

Perhaps to ease the stress I shall drive five towns over to where no one knows me and fill a cart to the brim with all things paper goods...

Or. Or. Or.

I could go to the nearest gas station or the nearest virtual Amazon shopping cart and load up on those new-fangled sensory bobbles.

They're like everlasting bubble wrap, y'all. (I stole the one in the picture from a child. I gave it back, I promise. But I didn't want to...)

I think Pop It! might be the original brand name of this little goody. Not sure, though, as the article I was trying to read blocked me. Apparently, I "reached the article limit" with this publication and need to subscribe to their newsletter, pay a fee, or auction off a blood relative to keep reading.

At any rate, here are some other titles/descriptions of this stress-relieving, anxiety-squelching, no-batteries-needed gizmo:

Push Pop

Pop Push

Big Pop

Krazy Popper

Silicone Popper

Bubble Fidget

Sensory Bubble Popper

And I'm gonna stop right there because as I read back over those names all listed out like that, it's starting to sound like I'm running an ad for a "pop"ular R- to X-rated genre of fiction. But I don't write in *that* genre, so let's change directions.

(And you, dear reader, just went back and reread that list, didn't you? Tsk, tsk, tsk...)

I think a more appropriate name is Everlasting Bubble Wrap.

You pop, push, or squish those little bubbles. Then, you flip it over, and pop them again.

And again and again.

Seriously, I don't write in that genre.

I need to stop.

Some manufacturers have even paired these silicone bubbles with the fidget spinner design. Now you can spin and pop, and flip and pop, and twirl and pop...

I really, really need to stop. It's got to be the heat. Or the heat index. Or that there's still ANOTHER MONDAY after this one.

Back to PG ratings now.

They come in all sizes and shapes and colors, from simple square grids, to unicorns, Yodas, and dinosaurs. Santas, pineapples, and game controllers.

Crabs too.

(Now, I didn't mean anything by that mention of crabs... See how dirty your mind is? I'm running on PG ratings, here people.)

Little Miss believes the only way Pop It! could be improved upon is with an accompanying poof of purple glitter.

Or a smoky, purple haze.

I told her she couldn't call it purple haze. She grinned. Then winked. Then fluttered off sideways, bumping into the hall walls.

Had to pause writing this so Little Miss Muse and I could have a conversation. She swears to me her grape soda was left in the hot garage too long and went sour. She drank it anyway. She swears this is the reason for the sideways flying — that, and dodging the stupid bug the cats were after. And the heat. And the heat index. And that she's got to inspire yet another blog NEXT MONDAY.

"Five Mondays. It's all too much," she cries as she spreads her chonky self over my desk in dramatic flair. Hurry up, autumn. My muse is malfunctioning.

Perhaps to make it to the end of August de-stressed and ready to enjoy the glorious fall season, I should replace the notebooks in each room (and drawers, and closets, and cabinets) with a Pop It! And maybe the stress will go down.

On second thought, maybe several of each in each room with brand new pens! I'll take a unicorn in sherbet colors, Yoda, and a giant square grid.

And a King Kong and Godzilla Pop It! for those really, really stressful days.

Little Miss raises her head off the desk to request half of them to be in shades of purple.

"All the shades of purple!"

And she's off, fluttering and flitting down the hall. Stirring up the cats again, crying "Bug! Bug!" and generally wreaking havoc all over the house.

"All the shades of purple." She's made a groovy jingle from that phrase to the tune of "Mary Had A Little Lamb."

I have to go now.

She's got the cats squalling and wailing. Malachi especially hates her shrill voice.

I really need to save this document and be done—

"All the shades of purr-rrrple, purr-rrrple, pur-rrrple..."

On second thought, there aren't enough Pop It!s on the planet for this summertime stress.

"...shades of puuuurrrple!" Dining room chairs crashing to the floor in the next room.

I gotta go.

I suppose I should simply be happy her favorite color isn't gray.

Looking Back: Now, those pop-it designs do come on the sides of purses. And, glory be, on the covers of notebooks and the caps of markers... And the price point has come down as well.

Little Miss Muse, reviewing this blog over my shoulder, starts to twitch a bit. She doesn't fully remember that day of bouncing off the hallway walls. And she admits it wasn't the warm grape soda, but she had, indeed, found an old stash of 100% grape juice in the warm garage and that may have been the reason for the sideways sauntering.

That explains a lot...

139

IS IT SAFE YET?

Is it over yet? August, I mean. Is it over? Five Mondays of sweat, heat, bugs, humidity...

Is this it? Did we make it?

I think so. I think by the time this posts, and by the time any of you read it, we'll be well on our way through the last August-y Monday in the Eastern Daylight time zone, 2021.

The next month with five Mondays is November. That'll be more tolerable unless the Indiana weather elves churn out another wave of evil heat in the middle of fall. It's been known to happen.

There. I'm done whining about that.

But Little Miss Muse? She's not done whining about anything.

And I've retreated into this hole of safety with a fuzzy blanket and whichever cat wants to hide from her frazzled fury.

Little Miss is not a happy camper, and she's not done whining. As a matter of fact, I think she's on the fritz. A purple-glittery glitz of a fritz.

She's been helping me fire up the short stories. That's been great.

She's been helping me fire up plot ideas for the novel work-in-progress, and that's been great.

She's been helping me fire up ideas about novels that won't be written for another ten years. And that's great. Sort of.

She's just fired up.

Possibly due to that bad batch of grape soda from last week, or possibly from the heat, or possibly that she and I have been in this hidey-hole of safety for way too long, isolating from drama and family disasters of all sorts.

And now that we're poking our heads out and getting some fresh air and fresh plans, she's malfunctioning. Stories go from sweet Hallmark-ish tales to twisted, dark webs of horror in a matter of five sentences. Plots for the now-novel intertwine with plots for novels-to-be. I cleaned up four piles of grape soda burp-ups. Those are not fun, people. Not fun. Especially when the cats track through it...

Then I find out she's been watching the news. A steady diet of gloom, doom, terror, and torment. I caught her last night with the remote, flipping between one bad news story to the next. I told her it was time to go write, think about something else. Change our focus. And she told me to go glitter myself as she unwrapped three grape bubblegum pieces and crammed them into her already full jowls.

Well then.

Bad idea. News of any sort from any media outlet is a bad idea for heat-weary creative types with art to manufacture. Bad for logic-ish types with tasks to manage. Bad for those combination folks who swing from creative to logic with each passing hour. Bad for us all.

Just don't. With the news. Limit consumption to the headlines at most. Perhaps just a single headline at that. Protect your malfunctioning muses, your peace, and your sanity from the state of the universe at large.

Perhaps dig a safe little hidey-hole.

Throw in a fuzzy blanket, a good book, and a critter of your choosing and ride out the insanity.

Looking Back: That last line about the blanket, book and critter? That's my go-to coping mechanism. And I still am not watching the news 465 days later.

And it was exactly 465 days later that I realize it wasn't a bad batch of grape soda. Was it, Little Miss?

She's still sulking at her loss of memory from that time. She worries she may have missed some glorious bits to throw into our next tale during her, ahem, episode.

I suggest perhaps she needs to find a Couch Person for muses that she can schedule while I do time with my Couch Person. She promises to think on it, and I'm glad seeing that true therapy sessions and purple imps probably don't mix...

140

WRAPPED AROUND THE AXEL

I'm late.

Half the time I write these blogs at least a day or two ahead of time. The other half, I've gotten several weeks ahead, and Web Guy dishes them out to the wide world each Monday.

But I'm late. I was supposed to have this written and off to Web Guy by last night.

It's four a.m. The cats are confused, so I fed them early to stop their swarming. Which means they'll demand their tuna delight gravy edition dinner an hour earlier this evening.

The Hubs is about to wake up for work, and he'll also be confused as to why I'm at the desk. Bless his heart, he'll probably start talking to me. Which is a dangerous undertaking even in the eight-a.m. range, let alone four hours earlier.

I'm not a four-o'clock-in-the-morning kind of writer. I'm a two-o'clock-in-the-morning middle insomniac who can mentally wrap herself around all sorts of axels of unimportance until six a.m. Then I'll write about it later.

I like that phrase: Wrapped around the axel. Implying that one can get hung up like an untied shoelace during a bicycle ride and wreck forward progress. When I was a kid, my mom didn't want me wearing flip-flops to ride my bike because I'd sliced my foot on those evil grippy pedal grip thingies. (It's 4:15 a.m., please bear with me. The vocabulary part of my brain is still in silent mode). So I wore tennis shoes and managed to throw myself over the handlebars when the axel ate my shoelace so completely that I became one with the bike.

Lately, I seemed to be wrapped around all kinds of axels — real and imagined. If I'm not careful, I can get hung up on the minutest of details and not deal with big problems.

Especially when thyrodic brain fog sets in. And when life stressors pile up, demanding attention all at once (how dare they not wait in line patiently?). And my internet has been on the fritz, making all of the day-job duties take four times as long.

And now it's 5:24 a.m. Something happened. I went to look up a word and may have gone through a Google wormhole. Then I laid my head down on my desk for just a second. Or many seconds. I awoke to a cat checking my pulse —Stella Marie sitting next to my head with her razor pigs on my neck. I told her I wasn't dead yet. And please do not call the other two cats in for carcass removal.

I can get wrapped around current event axels – not one thing to control there. I can get wrapped around "what if" axels. What-if axels are great for story construction and plotting, not so much for peaceful sleeping.

A couple of weeks ago, my first-world axel problem was the disappearance of my favorite beverage from every single store in our town. In all forms. Cans, bottles, two-liters. All gone. I ranted about this quite a bit to the Hubs, who tried to find some a town over with not much luck. So he brought me a new brand to try.

Gag me now. It's Canada Dry or bust.

I got grumpy. I complained. I could've spent that energy on something productive, but nope. Let's spin on this issue for waaaay longer than necessary.

I mentioned this to my mom and my aunt as a point of conversation. And they rescued me. Bless their hearts, I now have enough Canada Dry Zero Ginger Ale to last until spring.

Another axel? We have an "End Construction" sign at the end of our road. It's a lie. As a matter of fact, all "End Construction" signs in the state of Indiana are all lies. I got grumpy. I complained way too hard and way too long about this slip of ethics on the part of construction crews.

Bless their hearts, working in this awful heat. I don't envy their jobs, and they seem to be doing a good job. But stop with the lying signs already. We Hoosiers know it will never end...

Devil's-front-porch level of heat can send me axel spinning, twisting, and cartwheeling. I struggle to concentrate or breathe in triple-digit indices. I got grumpy. I complained.

Thankfully the weather has eased up to tolerable and, dare I say it, enjoyable, especially in the evenings. Nice, cool weather and an ice-cold Canada Dry work wonders to unwind my hang-ups.

And now I'm wrapping myself around the axel of whether or not bicycles have axels. They have spokes. Those shoelaces get caught in spokes. Not axels. At least I think, at 5:38 a.m. that that's how it is.

And I was right. The Hubs is talking to me. Telling me he didn't sleep until two a.m. because he "couldn't shut off his brain."

Twisted around some axel, too, he was.

5:49. He leaves in fifteen minutes. At which time the cats will settle back down, and I will attempt to sneak another 90 minutes of sleep before the day job starts.

I will likely require a midday coma to replenish a few brain cells the off-yet-again thyroid has claimed. Hopefully, Stella can palpate a pulse, holding off the feline forensics crew one more day...

Looking Back: I confess about half-way through the rereading of this, I Googled bike axels. Because I'm still unsure. I was happy to see as I read further, that I am at least consistent with my past self in the fact that neither of us knows anything of bike anatomy.
But the analogy holds.
And Canada Dry has been on the shelf for quite some time. I now save the caffeinated Diet Coke for extreme writing emergencies in an attempt to tell myself I'm making wise decisions.

Little Miss Muse reminds me that my choice of artificially sweetened
beverages is not making up for the fact that I—
I stop her there. The world need not know ALL of my hang-ups. They
already know about my chocolate stashes. Thank you very much.

141

STRESS-INDUCED

Over my four-plus decades on the planet, my body has come up with various responses to stressors –whether I give it permission for such responses or not. Hives, insomnia, and loss of verbal filters come to mind.

I had my first stress-induced nosebleed during an organic chemistry final at college. And, no. I don't remember anything from organic chemistry except that carbon seemed to be a big deal, and my professor wrote the textbook, so he expected us to know that material and all the extra stuff he "forgot" to put in the book.

It also occurs to me there may have been more pages to the final exam than in the textbook.

The professor was kind-ish, though. Or so I thought. He allowed us to make notes on one five-by-seven-inch index card and bring it to the final.

One card. Front and back.

Do you have any idea how small I can write when properly motivated? Pretty darn small.

The kids filed into the auditorium, one of those stadium-seating deals. We scattered across the room, leaving one seat open on either side of us to avoid cheating. Like any of us could see anyone else's index cards. All of them written in font size -24. I chose an aisle seat, figuring it wouldn't take me long to fill in and/or flunk this particular exam.

And the professor paced. Up and down the stairs. Across the back of the room. Across the front near the stage.

I scanned the test. Answered what I could from what I knew. Then started the agonizing process of attempting to answer twelve-part questions with my wimpy notecard, realizing quickly that nothing I wrote on that card was of any use. I could hear the flipping of pages all over the auditorium—likely my compatriots realizing the same thing.

Then, on one of his laps up my aisle, the professor stopped. And yelled. Loudly. In my direction.

"What the &%$# do you think you're doing?" He was staring right at me. I thought.

He climbed a few more stairs until he was even with my shoulder and continued yelling. At the girl seated behind me.

But it was too late at that time for me to relax and concentrate with the drama unfolding behind me. His booming voice continued, accusing the girl of cheating. Apparently, she'd taken her one five-by-seven card and added micro flaps to it. Still one card, but like quadruple the surface area.

She begged and cried for mercy, explaining it really was just one card. He threatened expulsion, ripped up her exam, confiscated her little flappy notecard, and sent her bawling from the auditorium. He yelled so loud my desktop shook. My hand shook as I laid my single, non-flappy notecard on the desk so he could see I was a virtuous student.

Some bozo snickered from the other side of the room and, still standing directly behind me, the professor started in on another rant. The room went silent except for the scratching of pencils across paper and a few muddled coughs.

Prof went back to his pacing and scrutinizing, and I went back to the test.

Then it happened.

Drip. Drip. Drip. Directly on page three of the exam. With one hand I squeezed my nostrils tight, with the other I signaled for the professor.

And then he accused me of cheating with the girl behind me. "You just want to go to the bathroom to talk about the test."

I showed him the test and unclenched the nostrils, blood flowing freely. I asked if he could bring a Kleenex if I wasn't allowed to leave.

The answer was no. No one was leaving the room without a failing grade. "I'll grade your bloody test, but you won't be leaving that chair." No one laughed this time. I think a couple of girls cried.

So I handed in a bloody test with bloody hands — and a bloody shirt by that time. I think I got a C after the curve, which means I and more than half of the auditorium flunked it anyway.

Some folks complained to the administration about the event. I don't know what became of the professor. Probably nothing—this was many, many years ago. I don't know what became of the girl with the flappy notes. I suppose she never tried that method again, though.

Little Miss Muse catches me having another stress-induced issue, much like the overworked gal in the photo. "You need a vacation. From your troubles," she advises, as she flits around the desk, generally making a glittery mess and toppling over piles of notebooks and to-do lists.

I pause this blog construction to rub my temples. "Will you be accompanying me on this vacation?"

She grins. "Of course."

"Then I don't see what good it will do. You're keeping me awake from two a.m. on."

"But my bestest ideas come at two a.m. You should know that by now." She pulls a long, sticky string of purple gum from her mouth and twirls it around her chunky fingers.

"I'd have better luck vacationing with the organic chemistry professor."

"He was old back then. He's probably dead now." She blows a grape-flavored bubble in my face.

"Better yet. The ghost of the organic chemistry professor won't chew bubble gum."

She doesn't seem phased. "You wouldn't do well with a ghost muse. They're a high maintenance variety." I don't point out the cases of grape soda, the closet full of purple high heels and bottles of glitter strewn all over the house. Bribes to keep the story ideas coming.

Albeit at two a.m.

I think I have hives now.

Until next week, may your sleep be sound, may your stressors be few, and may your muses fall silent during your peak hours of rest.

Looking Back: You can add tremors to the list of things my body does under stress. I'm not a fan of any of them, but the handshakes and under-the-rib shivers may be the worst yet.
Little Miss Muse still believes that a vacation from my problems is in order. I still believe that if she comes, we still won't get any rest.

142

EYES ON YOUR OWN PAPER

Not sure why my latest journey down memory lane is taking me back to school days. Last week it was the organic chemistry final. This week, it's the day I knew Didn't Study Guy was cheating off my papers in high school.

Blatantly stealing my answers.

I told the teacher about it after class, and he told me the next time to write down the most ridiculously wrong answers I could think of.

And the teacher would pass me.

It worked. No more cheating from Didn't Study Guy, and the teacher moved him to the front of the class.

Soon after, several teachers started using two versions of their tests.

Lately, I've been writing marketing and web articles for the day job. Every one of those firms requires a plagiarism check before submitting. And though I've attributed quotes and gave credit where credit is due, I still get a little twitchy as I watch that checker circle spin and spin, its AI bots scouring the internet for instances where I may have "copied off someone's paper."

Plagiarism is a huge deal these days, and it's much easier to do than sneaking a peek over someone's shoulder during an English test.

In a few online writing groups I frequent, authors are losing their collective minds – and sometimes their collective body of fiction – over the plagiarism issue.

One author discovered her books listed for free on a foreign website. Without her permission, clearly.

Another found that entire chapters of content had been lifted and pasted onto blogs and read aloud in podcasts. Without his permission, clearly.

Stolen content.

Back in 2019, Nora Roberts lashed out against this. You can read her reactions to someone lifting her work by following the link in the back of the book.

Sometimes, someone infringes on another's copyright in innocence – after all, you don't know what you don't know. Like a local artisan painting Hello Kitty on a canvas and making a profit at a craft fair. Seems innocent.

Perhaps the same artist also painted Mickey, SpongeBob, and R2D2. But, if money changes hands, that's a huge no-no unless the crafter has purchased a limited license through some sort of pattern (sewing comes to mind) or obtained expressed written permission. And Disney, Sanrio, and Nickelodeon don't give out those permissions to us regular folks.

And most regular folks I know don't have enough set back for legal fees should one of their powerhouse IP lawyers come after them for making a buck off a trademarked image.

If you're a consumer of entertainment, be mindful of where your money goes – payment should reach the creator (Yes, even if that creator is a billionaire. Don't be a jerk...).

Pay for your subscriptions. Avoid pirated music and videos.

Make sure the paperbacks you buy have covers...

If you're a creative, first, understand copyright law. It's the best way to protect your intellectual property. Nolo Guides are clear and easy to digest on this matter.

Second, if you're tempted to use poetry, song lyrics, or characters that another creative dreamt up, beware. You'd better have ten lifetimes of lawyer fees saved up...

And last, Be Original!

For example, Little Miss Muse with the chunky attitude, purple glitter jars, and lavender stilettos is mine. You can't have her.

Eyes on your own paper.

In other words, go get your own muse.

Looking Back: I'm thrilled to have a manifested Muse in doll form. Equally thrilled to have partnered with a friend to commission digital likeness to use on the blog and on the occasional book cover.

Little Miss Muse gets excited about this too. She wonders if she'll ever be pirated or plagiarized or stolen to make someone else money.

She's got quite the ego, but there's no chance of that unless we get back to writing the novel...

143

CONCENTRATION QUIRKS

Twirling hair.

Fiddling with a necklace charm.

Cracking knuckles.

Twisting a ring around and around on your finger.

Gnawing on your lip.

Clicking a pen (Save me now! you people who click and tap and clack!! *I* can click and tap and clack, but if you do it near me, game on, buster!)

Concentration quirks. We all have them. Well, I guess we all do. Perhaps some folks don't need to concentrate like others, but that's a blog for another day.

Some folks just can't concentrate without their noise-canceling headphones. I tried that in the last couple of weeks, and though I appreciate that they help with the ringing in my ears when all is quiet, I'm not a fan yet. My headphones aren't entirely comfortable, and I ended up with a headache – or what felt like a weird earache – every time.

And Little Miss wasn't a fan. She kept pulling one of the earpieces away from my head and letting it snap back into place, fearing I'd not be able to hear her fabulous plot twists if I canceled out the noise.

Come to think of it, this may be why I was in pain every time I donned the set.

When I was in elementary school (here we go again, down memory lane...), a kid in my class always had his tongue hanging out whenever he did his worksheets. He'd write away, all the while that tongue flapping this way and that. He did it on the playground and in gym when we'd have relay races or basketball drills. In the cold weather months, he had a permanent circle of chapped skin all around his lips from all that licking and concentrating. Poor thing.

I remember the PE teacher warning him that if he didn't keep his tongue in his mouth when he was running, he'd end up biting the tip of it clean off.

I thought about that boy the other day when I was on the lawnmower. The zero-turn mower that I've tried to master over the course of the summer. It's taken a bit of practice, as I grew up using a mower with a round steering wheel. Right, left. And foot pedal brake. Stop. Go. Simple.

Zero-turns are a whole 'nother beast. Levers. No pedals. Like steering a rabid horse more than steering a car.

Mowing is usually soothing for me, seeing the progress down the lawn, strip by strip. The hum of the mower drowning out all other sound. The smell of the fresh-cut grass. The world just... melting away.

But just about the time I think I've gotten the hang of the levers and those tight turns, I get tripped up and there goes the soothe...

Anytime I get near the road – and especially if traffic is heavy – I forget everything I've learned. I see myself landing the mower in the middle of the street, causing a massive pileup.

It's much better now than at the very beginning of the summer. But this last week, I evidently forgot everything I'd mastered.

And then I noticed it.

My tongue.

Hanging out.

Especially when I'd get near the road and need to make a tight turn.

Concentrating way too hard on something that should just... flow.

And I thought about that little boy. With his tongue hanging out. And specifically the warning the PE teacher gave him. So I'd reset my mouth, readjust on the mower seat and try again. I'd be okay through the main part of the strip, then, near the road again, out the tongue would come, thereby increasing my concentration on the gears as I neared another turn and tried to keep the mower in the grass and out of the street—or out of a tree.

Then it happened.

On one particularly difficult strip filled with telephone poles, tie downs, and a street sign, I forgot to replace my tongue thoroughly behind my teeth. I concentrated a little too long...

I think I still have all of my tongue, but not all of my blood.

I need a new concentration quirk, especially for the mower, I suppose.

That feeling of forgetting everything I once mastered? It's showing up during writing times. I find my tongue hanging out, begging my brain to connect and find that "flow" state where productivity flies out of my fingertips... and the world melts away.

Little Miss offers me grape bubblegum and some of her soda stash. I tell her those are likely more addictions rather than concentration quirks. She begs to differ, and pops bubbles and twirls her gum waaaay out of her mouth to prove her point, sticky everywhere.

I become frustrated. I'm losing control of my muse — again. It's like trying to reign in a rabid horse, or a wonky zero-turn.

"Yeah, but my quirks are better than *that*," she says, as she points to my face.

Where my tongue is hanging out the side of my mouth as I try to concentrate on writing this post.

I replace it behind my teeth.

Crack my knuckles, click my pen a few times, and reach for a wad of Little Miss's gum...

Looking Back: I've taken on a new quirk. Instead of sticking out my tongue,

I'm chewing the inside of my lip. I'll be able to hang a full-sized lantern from the hole in my lip by the time the current work in progress is done... Little Miss Muse believes I shouldn't have to concentrate so hard since she's giving me all the material anyway, and all I have to do is type.
She might not be wrong...

144

PUFFED, POOFED, AND HACKLED

We have three resident cats.

Three.

Each entirely different in personalities, preferred petting requirements, toy choices, irritation tolerance, vocalizations...

They tolerate one another, can be spotted snoozing in the general vicinity of each other — but no two ever get along all day long.

So when the three finally agree on something (past the collective attitude that their tuna fish feast in gravy is always late), it gets my attention.

When I find them lined up shoulder to shoulder staring out the patio doors at *something*, I try to follow their gazes and track what they're tracking. By the time I get to the window, the *something* is long gone.

Or like when they've strategically placed themselves along the utility room hallway, all facing the same direction in crouched hunting positions. I try not to think about the *something* that they maimed and sent running into the walls to die.

The creepy bit comes in when they all *see* *something* that clearly isn't there. All six eyeballs glued to a perfectly white ceiling. No bug. No floating tuft of Stella Marie's long tail feathers. No random flicker of light from a suncatcher or reflection of a puddle. Nothing.

There's nothing there.

Yet all three *see* what I can't.

It's eerie. But we tease and declare the cats must've seen a ghost. Or they caught the changing of the guard as God swaps out one of our guardian angels—because the good Lord knows we've worn out quite a few celestial beings over the last two years.

We also blame Little Miss Muse when some unseen force sends one or more felines down the hall in frantic tizzies.

But, a few nights ago, I swear I nearly made all three of our precious indoor adoptees permanent outside kitties.

All three were chilling out in bed with me—one of those rare moments, though all three were as far as they could get from one another, like same-pole magnets with their buffering force.

All three *heard* something. They raised their heads from their synchronized slumbers in unison. I dropped my book to my lap to watch this.

The hackles rose in unison – well, Amara and Malachi clearly engaged theirs, but Stella Marie's long hair doesn't allow for a clear show of startle.

Until she was so spooked by *something* that her hair parted along her spine and she slowly raised, crouched.

I put aside my story, swung my feet off the bed, and if I had hackles, they'd have been raised.

Goosebumps is what I got. Right along the back of my neck and down my arms.

The cats disembarked the bed. Plop, plop, plop.

They stalked out of the bedroom, single file, into the hallway.

I followed them. (The Hubs was of no use, sound asleep and sweetly oblivious to all things that *don't* go bump in the night...)

Three tails poufed. Or puffed. Poofed. What's the word? Bushed out. Bushy freaked tails and prickling fur coats. Synchronized fear-gaits. All four of us stopped in the hall, listening with pricked ears because they still *hear* *something* and I, well, I didn't hear it, but I was part of the search party.

I shone my phone's flashlight down the hall.

Nothing. I didn't hear anything.

The cats took a few cautious steps forward, I followed them.

As if I were brave.

As if I were following a trio of guardian Rottweilers about to take out an intruder and not three little rescue kitties all poufed, puffed, and poofed. Hackeld even. (For you zoology/vocabulary geeks out there, the precise word is piloerection. As in: *Their piloerections caused their hair follicles to stand on end because of an adrenaline-fueled flight or fight response.* But some folks may take offense to that word, piloerection, so we shall say bushed.)

The cats and I secured the kitchen. Then we moved to the living room and utility room. Likewise, those spaces were free of all scary *somethings*. But the trio insisted, as evidenced by their gaits, liquid black pupils, and piloerective— I mean *bushed* responses, that *something* was still amiss.

For the next fifteen minutes, I agreed with them, falling prey to the invisible, silent *somethings* that don't make a noise in the dark. *Something* that remains unnamed and only sensed by the most intelligent of all life on earth — the ever-perceptive cat.

Until I'd checked all the locks and behind all the doors, I agreed with them. I even got brave enough to peek out a window or two for that *something* that may be circling the perimeter of the house.

I threw them out their favorite Backyard BBQ Temptation treats and watched them try to decide whether to pursue *it* or have a snack. The snack won out, and we went on with our night — me back to my book and the trio – still in agreement something was amiss – smoothing down their bristled fur with stress-relieving baths.

The *something* went about with his/her/its night as well, and all piloerecting – I mean poofing – subsided.

So... Happy creepy October, y'all. May your *somethings* be nothing and may your follicles remain un-piloere—

I mean un-bushed.

Looking Back: The Adult-ish male child and I try to spend some time each week diving into a movie franchise of some sort or another. Last October we went through the Conjuring and Insidious movies. During broad daylight, though, because my puffed, poofed and hackled response is quite strong after dark.

A standard scary movie trope is the freaked-out character looking under the bed or in the closet for the *something*. I posed the question: Would it be better to find the *something* and know or to not find it and wonder?

The question isn't as simple as it first sounds.

Especially when piloerection is involved.

Little Miss Muse says the scariest thing she's ever experienced is when her author cleans out a perfectly fine cabinet instead of sitting down to write. I don't think she's wrong...

145

GET 'EM BEFORE THEY'RE GONE

An age-old marketing tactic in the advertising world is the ticking clock. You've all heard that urgent infomercial telling you the deal won't last on that impressive supply of miracle cleaning products you'll never use.

You've heard it in local car sales spots when the dealership would love to put you in a new vehicle in honor of Presidents Day or Tax Season. From the rate of speech to how many times the screenshot changes in just thirty seconds, these commercials scream "Hurry, Hurry, Hurry!" — even if they don't come right out and say "Hurry."

Something as simple as your weekly grocery store flier does this. The sale's only good for a week. Hurry, hurry. Jump in your new car, freshly cleaned with your not-as-good-as-what-you-used-to-use products, and drive down to the market to save $0.35 on mustard. (You'll spend $35 in gas to get there, but hey, a deal's a deal.)

And look out when those marketers pair their ticking clock tactic with scarcity. The idea that supplies are limited. (Well, in this age, with the shipping containers floating in a forever holding pattern in some ocean, that may be the case, but go with me on this...)

Not only will the deal price end soon, but you may not even be fast enough to score that eco-friendly bottle of glass cleaner, your new-to-you car, or that jar of mustard. There's a shortage, don't ya know?

Hurry, hurry! Get 'em before they're gone!

And then there's the nagging tactic, based on the science that potential customers will become buyers after having seven or more reminders to hurry, hurry, get 'em before they're gone.

Well, seems my brain has tried to run that trifecta marketing campaign on me of late. Clearly, I was not my own target audience.

There was this naggy little voice in the back of my head that said (at least seven times, probably more than that), "You should write that awesome blog post about amusement parks before the idea floats away. Hurry. Hurry. Time is wasting. Energy is limited and we don't know when we'll get another shipment."

That naggy brain also employed the skills of Little Miss Muse to do her song and dance all over the place as I struggled through day-to-day issues. "Use these ideas or lose them! Hurry, hurry!" was whispered, hummed, sung, and shouted from her lavender lips as she beat me over the head with her little wand.

I'm still picking glitter out of my hair.

So, to appease the thyroid-fogged, overloaded-with-life-junk brain and to hush up Little Miss, I at least made a list of blog ideas to return to later. I even chose purple paper to further please her. I'd promised to return to the list when things were calmer and clearer and use these ideas until they were all gone.

So today. Today is relatively calm. My head is much clearer than this time last week or last month or last season.

And I pulled out my purple list.

I count seven blog post ideas on my little sheet. Two I used under time pressure and wrote with a muddled mind. Well, good for me. That doesn't get next week's blog written. What's next?

"Something Different." That's it. That's what I wrote. What's different? I've a vague recollection that it would've been a cool piece, but the idea eludes me now. Like a bird flown from a cage. I didn't hurry, hurry. And now it's gone.

"Red Hat" is another one on the list. Did I see a red hat? Want a red hat? Are we talking Red Hat Society? It's like trying to recall the coolest dream ever, but vapors replace the concrete images that once sprawled behind my eyelids.

"Needed Things." Perhaps this was supposed to be my grocery list? Again, like a disappearing dove in the hand of a skilled magician, Poof! The premise is gone.

"Amusement Park." Yeah. I've got nothing. I know I've no desire to go to an amusement park. I know we've been on a rollercoaster of a ride this entire year, making 2020 look like a walk in an amusement park. But that's it.

"Real Life Stories" with a quote from Neil Gaiman. I thought I knew where I was headed with this one. I actually started to write it today three different times. Trashed all three attempts.

I sit back in my chair and moan.

I lost out on the limited time offers. The quantities ran out on me before I could restock my mental cupboards.

Little Miss is tsk, tsk, tsking at me from the corner. "You should've hurried when I said. You should've sat your—"

I stop her there before she can insult my rear or further wound my ego.

I toss my purple sheet into the trash.

Little Miss edges closer to my workspace, messing with her new purple eye shadow and making a powdery mess all over her pudgy fingers. "I'm just sayin'..."

She's such a nag.

I know.

Hurry.

Hurry.

Hurry.

Get 'em before they're gone.

Or at the very least, take better notes...

Looking Back: This happens more frequently than I'd like to admit. Lately, it's been scene notes that have expired before I could write the chapter. Get a cool idea, jot a few sentences. Then... nothing. Like this time 422 days ago, we're still on a roller coaster—ran by clowns and unicycling poodles—and I find foggy brain is a default setting.

Little Miss Muse hangs on the back of my office chair as I write this, reminding me that she's all out of that particular eye shadow—oh, and her wand could use some wax.

I'll start her supply list on the back of the purple paper I wrote the next writing "reminders" on. I'll not need it, anyway.

146

HAND WASHING AND KINDNESS GLANDS

A sign hangs in my bathroom above the towel rack.
It says Don't Be A Turd Today.

It's quite possibly the best thing I've ever bought from the décor aisle.

It's also quite possible that this bit of wood and paint has kept me from hitting "send" too soon. Or Googling lawyers for various and sundry reasons.

Or from community service.

After this awful last couple of years of people being downright horrible to each other, a "be kind" wave has swept social media posts, t-shirts, and restaurant marquees as a reminder to, well, be a decent human.

(I think it's generally depressing that we must be reminded to be kind, but I digress since, clearly, I need reminding...)

And we all should be decent humans. Unless you're a muse or a cat, it's only right. Muses and cats have their own set of demeanor rules, and no amount of "Don't Be A Turd" signs would ever course-correct their impending interactions.

I can be naturally kind (you know, when you're being sweet without having to put your mental energy on high throttle to be sweet). But, in instances when I've had no alone time to recharge, in instances when those around me are all being, well, turds, or in instances when life chaos has sucked me dry, I must dig deep into the will power to keep my cynical, pessimistic, smart-mouthed attitude in check.

Those "Be Kind" reminders are sweet. But I'm a hardhead most of the time, and I need a little more than a gentle nudge to course-correct. I need boulders and neon and to be told as many times as I wash my hands in a day not to be a turd.

Just don't be a turd.

And then I can exit the bathroom into the "real world," take a breath, and try again to steer clear of turd-classified behavior.

I have friends who ooze mercy, grace, and kindness. They would never need a "Don't Be A Turd" sign in their bathrooms. I enjoy their company. Over the years, I've tried to learn how they do it. How do they remain so... nice... even when those around them are clearly selfish, clueless creatures. I've concluded they were born with an organ that I wasn't. You know, like some people have an extra kidney or a third nipple?

They have an overactive kindness gland somewhere in their being, whereas I must manufacture and replenish my kindness stash daily.

I have other friends who would never need a sign like mine. Because their signs read "Be the Best Turd You Can Be." I also enjoy their company because I can relate to their pessimistic, cynical view of the world, and I envy (just a little bit) that they've lost that "I wonder what people think of me" filter. They say it like it is and let the cards fall wherever.

I land somewhere in the middle of these groups most days, firmly in the second during times of crisis (we've been in a crisis of one sort or another for over a year) or times when I haven't filled my cup with "me time" to write with reckless abandon.

And, most days, as I'm washing my hands and reading my sign, I can reset. Wrangle up a few more drops of kindness, or at least tolerance, and go about the day. Put a lid on the cynicism, pessimism, and expect-the-worst mentality.

Other days, I'm tempted to Xerox that bad boy and plaster the anti-turd message on every wall of the house.

Carpet the floors with it too. Because my wildly swinging mood and snarky opinions matter very little in the grand scheme of eternal significance.

I've had multiple interruptions while writing this.

Little Miss Muse nagging me about word counts. Cats smelling bad. He-who-shall-remain-nameless-because-he-means-well. Cats with ping-pong balls. He-AGAIN-with-one-of-those-kindness-glands-I-lack.

I can feel that spot where my kindness gland should've grown. The void is red-hot along the edges and hollow to the core.

I think it's time to go wash my hands.

Again.

Looking Back: I still have the sign. I still need the sign. The He-who-shall-remain-nameless is my dear Hubs. I think he has two kindness glands.
Little Miss Muse enjoys being a turd on occasion. She claims it gets my attention back to the works in progress—if for no other reason to get her to shut up.
For Christmas she may be getting a "You're Simply the Best Turd" sign—in purple glittery puffy paint, of course.

147

SO... I'M A JERK

Despite what the blog a few weeks ago may have portrayed, I really do try hard not to be a jerk. Or a turd. That's why I have that sign hanging in my bathroom to begin with.

Apparently, though, jerkiness happens.

"Fetch," this month's free fiction, has caused some folks a bit of anguish. Anguish they wished to "let me know about" in no uncertain terms.

I've gotten phone calls.

I've gotten an email.

Facebook message.

A person in person telling me that I'm, well, a jerk.

Jerkiness is relative, though, because I didn't understand what got folks so riled up.

"Fetch" got them riled up. Burrs under their saddles, even.

I didn't intend to be jerky when I wrote it. I saw the ending of the story in my mind before the beginning formed – one of those rare instances where I even wrote the last page or two before I wrote the beginning. I thought, "Ooh, that'd be interesting." So I wrote it—

Hang on.

Little Miss Muse is stomping on my desk, claiming credit for this tale. I have to settle this.

"*We* wrote it. *We* did." She's being a jerk.

"No. *We* did not. *You* were hanging out in Golden Nugget's shark tank swimming pool and giving the lifeguards grief when *I* wrote this in the hours before the anthology workshop. Remember?"

The flicker of realization running across her face tells me she remembers. She raises her fat fist in protest and opens her mouth to shout—

"No, ma'am. I'll give you credit when you deserve the credit. *I* wrote this one. *You* were swimming." Sometimes you have to be a jerk to your muse.

She tilts her chubby head to the side and glares at me. She's a little lopsided with her purple eyeliner today. I know this is not settled, though. She'll pour out floods of purple fury later. She's stomping away.

Muses. They want to take credit for everything...

I'm back.

Anyway, "Fetch" yanked, pulled, and otherwise jerked the tears right out of peoples' faces.

Some folks had all the feels.

Some folks had the sobs.

Some folks had choice words – aimed at me.

On second thought, perhaps I should call Little Miss back and give her the credit after all. She can field the flying fury. I should probably set her up with her own email account...

At any rate, "Fetch" has been gaining traction, lots of shares, and lots of reads. It'll be up here on the blog site for another couple of weeks until it's replaced with something Christmas-ish.

Read it for free while you can.*

If you miss it, you can read it in All the Feels Volume 3. This collection also has other really jerky stories in it, I'm told. A good little collection if your ductwork is backed up or you're emotionally constipated.

But that's just my jerky opinion. You'll have to read the book and come up with your own verdict.

*I RUN my blogs through Grammarly to help me catch blatant typos. Even Grammarly thinks I'm a jerk. It wants me to change this rather direct, possibly forceful sentence to one of the following:

Could you read it for free while you can? Or *Please read it for free while you can.*

You can imagine what I told Grammarly to do with its polite suggestions.

Looking Back: I've also received similar reactions to some of the more twisted mysteries. Apparently I'm a jerk more than I even realized. Little Miss Muse pouts in the corner. The last time we were in Vegas, she was banned from the shark tank swimming pool—for life. "Do you know how long muses live?" A grape-scented tear wriggles out from her eyelid. I feel sorry for her, just a little. I promise her a trip to an exotic-for-her location, but she has to promise to behave.

To not be a jerk.

Especially around sharks.

She tilts her head, her curls bobbing into her eyes. Her wings flutter and the tears stop. "Like France?"

Heaven help us. We're likely to start an international incident...

148

BLOWING UP BISCUITS

Someone asked me if I was cooking for Thanksgiving this year.

No. No, thank you. And here's why:

I've never been shy about owning my culinary shortcomings. I dislike cooking, prepping, planning, cleaning, stirring — basically all the -inging of trying to feed others or myself.

I'm the first to look for convenient shortcuts and the first to sign up for pitch-ins (as infrequently as this introvert goes to pitch-ins) so I can get the slot to procure napkins or potato chips. Please, please, don't make me cook for acquaintances and strangers.

I've burnt things, undercooked things, undercooked while burning things, misread labels, dug directions out of the garbage for the 12th time because I can't hold a three-step process in my head, and forgotten I was cooking altogether and set fire in the oven.

I may or may not have accidentally killed a raccoon from throwing one of my sloppy disasters out the back door.

But the other day, folks, I hit a new height in kitcheny mishaps.

My presence wasn't even required in the kitchen.

There was no appliance on—oven, toaster, stovetop, or otherwise. The microwave lay quiet, silently hoping I was done for the day and wouldn't explode something inside.

The Hubs and I were in the living room when we heard two loud pops.

Since we were watching Hawaii 5-0 (or some other cop show with frequent gunfire), it took me a second to realize the sound wasn't coming from the television.

Next culprit: Cats. One of three. Or a duo. Or they'd teamed up against the formidable Little Miss Muse, and that 'pop-pop' was her throwing Molotov cocktails concocted from purple glitter bottles to escape their feline fury.

But a quick headcount revealed all three kitties equally startled by the popping.

So I investigate. Kitchen. Hall. Office.

Can't find anything. Figured Little Miss had been clomping about in her lavender stilettos and banged into a wall. Or, more likely, a backfiring car had zoomed through the neighborhood.

I open the fridge for a water.

And there. On the bottom shelf.

Two out of three biscuit cans had given up, doughy puffs oozing from their seams. One can literally blew its top off. I don't know how long those cans had been in the fridge—I didn't check the expiration date. I figured I'd stored them wrong, or perhaps I insulted them as I took them from their quiet grocery store cooler and placed them in my cart. Maybe they sensed their fate in B.A. Paul's kitchen—half of them doomed for black, crunchy crusts, the other half scalded but raw in the middle.

They cried "Uncle, Uncle" before I could get my hands on them.

There was one can left. Standing silently by its fallen comrades. I tossed him in the garbage, too, lest he blow his bottom off and bust open the gallon of orange juice in biscuity protest.

Fast forward.

To three a.m.

To that sweet, sweet spot in the night when you know you're asleep, comfortable. Stress dream-free, even.

POP!

Then three cats.

One after the other.

On my head.

On my stomach.

At my feet.

In tribal agreement that something was amiss.

And Little Miss. On the headboard. Tsk, tsk, tsking me for even thinking she could be at fault for any of this. "It's just not my style."

"Yeah, right." I throw off the cats and the covers and the five of us stagger down the hall following the beam of my phone's flashlight until I reach the kitchen and

step

in

something.

I cringe as I reach for the light switch, positive that the slightly moist, certainly squishy thing beneath my foot is Stella Marie's latest hairball.

As the kitchen floods with light, I'm relieved, then confused, then confused some more as I discover a perfectly round, raw biscuit under my toes.

My eyes adjust to the bright. I see more biscuits.

On the floor next to the garbage can.

On the floor in the middle of the kitchen.

On the countertop fifteen feet away.

The cats appeared confused and still slightly poofed from their startle. But I still wondered if they had something to do with this. Maybe pilfered the trash for the first time since their adoptions. But there were no teeth or toe marks in these biscuits. They just blew utterly, wholly, out of that one lone can that had survived the refrigerator.

I gather the dough, toss it back into the garbage, toss the cats a few treats in apology that I'd disturbed their slumber. Thanked them for alerting me to the impending danger of flying dough balls.

"What about me?" Little Miss stood in the hallway, blocking my return to my nice, warm bed.

"What about you?" I tried to nudge by, but she'd have none of it. I was in no mood for more drama at three in the morning.

"You blamed me for the whole mess."

I sighed and went to the office where I keep a hidden stash of grape bubble gum for such occasions as this when Little Miss pitches a fit.

She took the offering, shoved three pieces into her mouth, and nodded in acceptance of my apology.

It was my fault, after all.

Blowing up those biscuits.

I didn't store them right.

I was too rough when I unloaded the groceries.

I threw a can in the garbage where the dough rose and rose until it erupted all over the kitchen.

All my fault.

I settled back into bed. Just as that sweet slumber began to wash over me — POP, CLACK, POP, CLACK, POP.

Miss Muse. Grape bubbles. High heels on the hardwood.

"No."

"But I'm awake now."

"No, please." This is my fault, too. Little Miss's neediness at all hours of the night. I've ignored her for too long. "Please. Not now."

She put her lips nearly inside my ear canal, her hot grape breath washing over my cheeks. "I've got a story idea—"

So, for this and many other instances like it, I shall not be cooking for Thanksgiving this year. My kitchen needs a break. Our tastebuds need to regenerate from the last meal I attempted. The cats can't handle it. I'm exhausted from the care and keeping of Little Miss Muse.

And I'm out of grape bubble gum.

Happy Thanksgiving to you all — no matter how you celebrate or what you may blow up in the process!

Looking Back: Christmas Dinner 2023 is exactly four days away as I write this. I'm sure Blog #192 will have something to say about it. I already have

sweaty-pit anxiety over it. I'm hosting. For flesh-and-blood and for dear friends. I'm sure there'll be blood and maybe no friends after I'm done trying to crock-pot a turkey and bake a ham.
Biscuits are NOT on the menu.
Little Miss Muse believes I'd be better off writing while someone else does the cooking.
She's certainly not wrong.

149

THIS IS NEW

"This is new."

We utter this phrase frequently in our home, usually due to the change in a cat's behavior. Or a loved one's aging process. Or a sound the house makes.

Sometimes "This is new" is just a simple observation. Like when Amara chooses my lap over the lap of the Hubs. It doesn't last too long before she's back drooling on him, but hey. It was new. For a moment.

Once in a while, "This is new" translates to "How cool!" Like when one of my titles starts selling to a handful of strangers across the world for no known reason. Or when I tasted my first white chocolate Reese's Cup–pure bliss!

Or "This is new," with every vowel sound drawn out in cautious utterance, could mean "This is gonna cost us money." Like when the refrigerator starts making popping noises or the clothes dryer sounds like it's giving birth to a moose.

Lately, with our stress loads and wonky health issues, "This is new" means something is amiss in our very cells. We're off-kilter, our bodies doing new things that are mostly unwelcome.

Hubs is recovering well from major surgery. So "This is new" happens multiple times a day. We don't know where his "new new" will land. So it's all new.

I came across some childhood photos the other day. My grandmother loved – and I mean loved – sticking me smack in the middle of the daffodils in her yard and snapping as many photos as she could way back when. Me smelling the daffodils. Me picking daffodils. On and on.

But, in adulthood, daffodil pollen can send me to bed for a week. I'm allergic. This is new.

I burnt myself in the kitchen a couple of years ago (imagine that – me mishapping in the kitchen—this is *not* new). I doctored the blister and covered it with a bandage. The reaction I had to the bandage was worse than the burn. This is new. An adhesive allergy.

Bifocals. This is new.

Peanut butter makes me gag. This is new. And incredibly unfortunate as I've just discovered white chocolate Reese's Cups. (My heart is broken just a bit...)

Allergic reaction to the flu shot last year. This is new.

I've had so many "this is new" moments (like hot flashes and night terrors and things I won't mention here) that I sought the counsel of a specialized doc. New Doc Guy, we'll call him.

I have a Back Guy, who tells me I'm unhinged every time I see him.

I have an Eye Guy, who tells me I'm a few clicks off normal twice a year. (To be clear, this is what he *says* twice a year; I'm a few clicks off normal year-round.)

I have a Primary Care Woman, who I love, but her head tilt when I explain my issues tells me I've sprouted zebra stripes.

Now, it seems, even my un-right wires are doing new things.

So, at the insistence of a bestie, who recommended New Doc Guy, and who also looks at me as if I've sprung zebra stripes, I made an appointment.

I tell my story. All the new things.

The nurse nods and types and nods, and then... pauses. "What now?"

I start again. With all the new things.

"You're a mess, aren't you?"

"Yes. That's why I'm here. So you folks can take all these new things and make them go away." In other words, erase my zebra stripes, please.

New Doc Guy comes in. He reads the notes. Asks the same question as the nurse.

I start again. With all the new things.

"Wait now, what?"

He pulls out a hot pink legal pad and starts writing frantically. I become distracted by the legal pad, since I have a notebook fetish and all (this fetish is not a new thing, but a distracting condition at the very least).

I focus back on him, but I keep one envious eye on that hot pink legal pad. *I wonder where he got that...*

New Doc Guy is saying, "—problems. You're a complicated mess."

"Why, thank you. That's the general consensus."

He explains my labs. Tells me yes, my thyroid is liken to a wicked stepmother, but it's probably not the only culprit. Turns out, instead of a solo operator, my thyroid gland is a member of a gang. Street thugs even, wreaking general havoc all over my system:

From "too much" of one hormone and "nonexistent" of another. This is news to me.

From general inflammation. This is new. (Or it's not new, just new to my awareness.)

From dietary sensitivities — Dairy, eggs, and wheat don't like me anymore. This is new. And incredibly unfortunate. (There goes Reese's Cups for real — at least for now.)

But New Doc Guy thinks he can help. This is good news.

He hands me new meds to quell the drive-by chaos the gang of endocrine glands do on a nightly basis.

A dietary supplement list longer than my arm to calm my inflammation.

I'm still thinking about white Reese's Cups and that hot pink legal pad when he says, "Oh, by the way. Let's take your blood pressure again."

What did he expect, after telling me all this? That my numbers would be normal?

So.

I'm also the lucky winner of a blood pressure medication combo package, lest I pop a cork before the other issues settle down. This is new.

Before I left his office, New Doc Guy also handed me a packet five inches thick of what I should and should not eat. Guess where Reese's Cups landed?

So, I'm off to do food prep.

Meaning cleaning and chopping veggies and fruits. And not unwrapping white chocolate Reese's. Or regular chocolate Reese's. Or even scrambling an egg.

This is new.

All new.

And with my wonky culinary skills, we may end up with a new kitchen before it's all over with.

But, perhaps with time, a few of my zebra stripes will disappear or at least fade. And in the meantime, I'll drown my sorrows by shopping for one of those hot-pink legal pads...

And maybe a new pen to match.

Looking Back: Folks, if your fridge is popping, just go buy a new one. Right now. There's a supply shortage, and you'll end up living out of a cooler for two weeks if you don't get a jump on it. Ask me how I know...
I'm likely to find out that the moose-dryer-gone-donkey-in-labor will end with us doing the new thing of drip-drying clothing all over the house. We should go buy a new one. Right now. There's a supply shortage.
Some of the above health ailments have abated, for now, while newer ones rear their ugly heads. We're all a hot mess in the B.A. Paul household. I blame it on the CIRCUS.
Little Miss Muse enjoys watching the CIRCUS. "Story fodder, for real!"

I'm in no mood to write about what I'm living through. I told her to grab that hot pink notepad and take her own notes... we might use them in another decade or two.

150

HAPPY ON PURPOSE

In our town, there's a "Walking Man." He's a tall, slender, older gentleman who, well, walks. Everywhere.

For years, we've seen him all over the city, walking briskly, meandering, or strolling, never seeming to take the same route. Or maybe he does have a route, and we're the ones with no pattern to our travels. Main roads, side streets, residential areas. Everywhere.

Hot, cold, rain, snow, wind, humidity. The man walks.

And he waves. He waves at Every. Single. Car.

Every. One.

Oncoming, from behind, at intersections. Doesn't matter. Each motorist is gifted this man's greeting.

If the car is coming from behind him, he raises one long arm in the air, and that's that.

If the car is coming toward him, he does the same, but with a little more "oomph."

If the driver makes eye contact with him and waves back (and believe me, I always try to make eye contact with this man and wave back), he'll throw both arms to the sky and shake those babies in glorious salutations.

And his grin... it's contagious.

It's the kind of smile that makes you think he left his home base to journey that particular road at that particular time to find you out driving and make your day a little brighter. Like he and his impossibly long arms did this on purpose.

The Hubs and I were out early a few days ago and saw him. It was cold and damp. He was wearing layers and a bright orange safety vest. We were coming up from behind. I rolled the window down, slowed and waved at him out the window. In the rearview mirror, we were rewarded with a double-arm wave, shining eyes, and the most impossibly happy smile.

Then we smiled.

And then I realized those muscles— my smile muscles—haven't seen much activity of late. I'm talking about those muscles that operate of their own accord with no conscious effort. The "genuine" smile muscles. Oh, I've done a lot of fake smiling and polite smiling. Those muscles are different. But the "genuine" ones seem to operate a little deeper and without the need for fake or polite influence.

Little kids exercise their genuine smile muscles every day unencumbered and without hesitation. They don't need a reminder to be happy. Happy just happens. Ever hear a baby belly laugh at a pet? It's one of the sweetest sounds on the planet. Ever watch a couple of three-year-olds crack up at a joke that no one but the two of them understand? Ever witness a group of kids get the "giggles," and no one can stop laughing long enough to hear some grumpy adult boss them into the next task?

The Hubs and I have had a list of troubles as long our arms this year. Our friends and family have, as well—many of them facing things that would crush even the most robust of souls. The world feels heavy. Happy took a back seat to survival. Typically, November prompts Facebook folks to list one thing per day for the month to be thankful for. In years past, my feed was filled with these posts.

Only one person that I know of did this for the whole month. I didn't see anyone else even attempt it.

The world is heavy. Homes are heavy. The holidays are heavy for some. Happy won't just happen. We'll need reminding.

But Walking Man reminds me I can wave. I can smile. I can shake off those heavy loads for a few seconds. A few minutes. Some hours. An afternoon. And be happy on purpose.

Do something I love.

With someone I love.

Or be happy alone with a fuzzy blanket and a cat in a peaceful house.

Or be happy on purpose with Little Miss Muse dancing on the desk, ideas flying from her glittered wand, the smell of grape bubblegum filling the space around my laptop...

And I can do it the next day, and the next.

Hot, cold, rain, snow, wind, humidity... Okay. Maybe not in the humidity. Humidity takes my "genuine" grump muscles through a thorough workout.

But all the other temps and precipitations, I can, by gosh, by golly.

On purpose.

With intention.

Be happy.

The encounter with the Walking Man reminds me I don't have to simply survive or cope or get through.

The encounter with the Walking Man reminds me how good it feels to let those genuine happy muscles stretch.

The encounter with the Walking Man reminds me I know how to roll down the window. Slow down. Stick my arm outside. And wave. Small, simple actions, compounding on one another to bring about a happy response for more than just myself.

Happiness and smiles, indeed, are completely contagious.

So with the new year creeping up on us, with all of its heaviness or happiness and everything it'll bring in between those extremes, remember to find those happy-on-purpose moments. Roll your window down. Slow your pace.

Shake off the arm's length worth of woes, wave to the heavens...

And smile.

Looking Back: Wow, I needed that reminder. We find ourselves in an even

more difficult position than what we were experiencing 373 days ago.
Happy doesn't happen. We have to exercise the muscle or we'll get stiff. And
turd-like.
Little Miss Muse, still slightly miffed about the shark tank, agrees.
And we're off.
Together.
To get some fiction words down on paper—whether they make sense or not
—simply because it makes us happy.

151

JUST IN TIME FOR CHRISTMAS

I t's been a year.

It's been a long 24 months, actually.

In the last couple of weeks, I had to move the blog's home on the turn of a dime, and with my lack of tech-ish skills, that was a huge stressor. I've still not settled in or "unpacked" everything for bapaul.com's new home, but it's getting there.

So those happy-on-purpose, giddy-little-jump-and-squeal moments are to be cherished to the utmost.

Unless...

Unless...

Your long-awaited author copies arrive in your mailbox, and that mailbox is across a busy road. A really busy road.

In that case, curb your enthusiasm until, well, you at least reach the curb.

And to avoid a fender-bending pile-up of gawking commuters, perhaps curb that jump-and-squeal dance move until you're behind closed doors—especially if you have the grace and coordination of this particular curvy girl.

I'm sure more than one passerby thought about calling for help when they saw me pull out my Ellery Queen package. I'm glad they didn't, though. I wouldn't know how to explain the sheer joy of author copies to our community's finest EMTs.

But author copies are the best.

Author copies remind me I *actually did something* in 2021 — other than just survive.

So, without further ado, here's my bit of shameless self-promotion:

Ellery Queen, Baby!

Second sale to this wonderful publication, and no less exciting than the first one.

My story, "Stone Still," is in the January/February 2022 issue.

Short and sweet. Giddy-little-happy-on-purpose blog.

May your Christmas be merry and bright, and may all your dance moves bring smiles and joy to you and yours—and may they not summon the EMTs!

Looking Back: I cherish those "proof of doing something" reminders. Life bogs down and dreams get put on hold, but those little moments are so important.

I had one just yesterday. An email letting me know that a submission had been accepted and will be published. By the time Life All Over Again *hits the shelves, I'll hopefully have announced this officially!*

I was glad this was an email, and not a snail mail thing. My giddy-little-jump-and-squeal nearly threw my knee out of joint. I'd have been down in the road for sure...

Little Miss Muse holds out a chubby hand. "It has no gum in it. For the work I did on that piece."

I'm tired of arguing with her for credit on who does what for each story I *ahem* we write. I break into another secret stash and fill her palm with grapey goodness.

All is well. And no EMTs were involved in the process.

152

RIGHT IN THE EYE

My poor Eye Guy. I feel so sorry for him when I show up and need an exam requiring dilation. It takes all my might not to kick him as he puts those demon drops in my orbs. I also felt sorry for my mother, who I'd asked to help me with some drops while we were on a shopping trip. My eyes were red and grainy from too much dry air and too much screen time, and she was happy to help. Until she nearly had to chase me around the hotel room and across two beds to get them in.

I can't handle it. I cannot — I mean *cannot* — put drops in my own eyes without *running from myself*.

Contacts are not in my future. If eye surgery of any sort is in the cards, they'll have to knock me all the way out and chain me to the table.

In the last few weeks, it seems my eyes have been taking more than their fair share of hits. "But don't you wear glasses?" you ask. Why, yes. Yes, I do. Either they were on top of my head, or not on my face, or the mini-blinding projectiles managed to evade the frames and hit their target. Here we go:

I'm not a fan of hairspray. I don't like the way it smells or how it makes my hair feel. But when you've been blessed with baby-fine strands and very few follicles, sometimes hairspray is a must, especially in the dry winter months.

You know. Where you walk across the carpet and the electrons vibrate from your socks up to your scalp, raising every hair on your head to the heavens.

Or when those electrons plaster that hair against your cheeks or your forehead and you're forever trying to wipe it out of the way... I use just a little to keep this annoyance down to a dull aggravation when I must be around people. I don't use aerosols—I think they smell worse than the pump kind. Hair gel works for about half the day, but by the time drama and trauma and chaos take hold and I've run my hands through my hair for the twentieth time, it's back to fly-away static.

Usually, one bottle will last me a year. My 2019 spray finally ran out a few weeks ago. Likely lasted that long because, well, 2020 sucked away most opportunities for "don't scare the public" hair.

Enter 2021 supply chain issues, and I was forced to buy an aerosol or travel three counties over to hunt for my not-too-smelly brand elsewhere. I'm not *that* dedicated to anti-static-ing anything.

Well, I dropped the aerosol can on the first go and didn't know I'd buggered the nozzle.

The next day, I aim carefully, so as not to plaster the wall behind me, trying to hit a particularly fly-away spot, and bam!

Right in the eye.

That's ONE.

The other day, the Hubs put away the dishes for me. We have a few pieces that I usually keep down on the counter for easy reach. He "puzzled" one into the cabinet—a glass loaf dish that I never bake a loaf in (see Blowing Up Biscuits), but it is good for leftovers we may have that were cooked by someone else...

I open the cabinet.

Bam! Loaf pan to the eye.

That's TWO.

Stella Marie, my beautiful long-haired kitty, loves pens and pencils. Especially the ones on my desk where she'll "inspect" and "supervise" their use. I sit down to the desk this morning, and she manages to step on one that's half-off of the corner of the desk. The pen somersaults, airborne, and...

That's THREE.

Kitty litter box clean-out time. While unwadding a Walmart bag to contain the scoops, I usually do that little "flick" maneuver to get the bag to open all the way.

Evidently, the last time I bought elbow macaroni, several pieces escaped from the box, ending up in the bottom of this particular Walmart sack.

My "flick" sent elbows ticking against the wall and across the floor. All but one. That one piece of pasta mimicked the pen's somersault trajectory and, bam!

Right in the eye.

That's FOUR.

It was a different eye. So both eyes traumatized, barely able to see to pick up the pen or the pasta...

I bought grapefruit today for the first time in a long time.

I shall wait until tomorrow.

And wear goggles.

And learn how to duck...

May your hair, husbands, and cats not bring you blindness in the new year. May none of your challenges be so great that you must run from yourselves or your mothers.

And if 2022 starts off with even the slightest twinkle that could echo the drama and trauma of 2020 or 2021, punch it right in the eye!

Looking Back: I must've missed my punch. I never took boxing lessons or karate. Maybe that would've helped. 2022 remained unscathed as we, its meager inhabitants, struggled to reign in our CIRCUS rings.
2023 will start off with our CIRCUS in full force—and a Couch Lady on speed dial.
Little Miss Muse says she'd have been a therapist if the muse thing hadn't have worked out.
I'm glad for everyone's sake that the Muse thing worked out.

153

MEET CASS

This little fella belongs to my Adult-ish Male Child. The poor thing was loose on the streets, begging, ill, and covered in all manner of critter-y crawlers, sure to be road fodder or a snack for some wild dog (the cat, not the Adult-ish Male Child.)

My son called for him, and he came running. Since our three kitties are spoiled beyond belief, they "graciously" donated some beginning supplies to the rescue baby, and vet appointments were secured. (I am positive at this point, however, Amara has done a year-end inventory on her spring collection and has found it lacking... Perhaps that's why she's been stomping up and down the hall for two weeks, giving us the death glares.)

We discussed names. I threw out some suggestions—all girl names because, you know, the Adult-ish Male Child googled how to sex a cat. He was fairly certain, like 90% certain, this was a girl.

"You sure? 'Cause every cat the Paul household has procured and named has turned out to be the opposite of what we thought. Then we have to go through the whole name-picking chaos all over again."

"Well, I'm 80% sure."

By the time we get to the first vet appointment, he was 75% sure it was a girl. He'd picked out a boy cat name, too, but was now 70% sure he'd keep that one in his back pocket for the next cat. This one, he was 60% sure was a girl.

The baby was pitiful. Snotty and oozey and itchy. Poor thing... (The kitty again, not the Adult-ish Male Child.) It hung close to my son as we waited in the exam room. I think it wanted to purr, but it was just too sick to do much but cuddle.

The vet tech comes in.

"Oh... look at the poor thing. Let's see what we've got here." She flips the kitten upside down, lifts the tail... "Congratulations! It's a boy!"

Well.

So.

Adult-ish Male Child shrugs, puts the girl kitty name in his back pocket for the next cat, and declares this guy to be Castiel. Named after a character from Supernatural.

(Side note: Adult-ish Male Child also named Amara after a character on Supernatural. Apparently, because I've not watched the series yet, Amara was "The Darkness." That explains a lot — especially those death glares. So I cringed a bit when another Supernatural character name is chosen.)

On with the exam...

Mites. Fleas. Worms. Check, check and check.

Upper respiratory infection, eye infection, malnourishment. Check, check, and check.

Wormer, ear drops, eye drops, antibiotics... Yup. Yup. Cha-ching.

I warned my son that since the kitten was so sick he'd not really "met" the real Castiel yet. It'd be a while before he could see the cat's true personality.

Fast-forward a few weeks, and Cass "showed up." He started playing, gaining weight, and generally being a total terror on four paws. Eats, poops, plays and plays, and rarely sleeps. And during this time, I was especially glad neither Cass nor the Adult-ish Male child lives with us.

Cass would come for visits, stopping at our house for a litter box break before heading to the vet. He's like the worst two-year-old ever.

Touching everything. Never stopping. Caring not that someone wants to talk to him or pet him or even get a good look at his face.

He. Never. Stops.

My three cats are miffed when he visits. They watch him from a distance, hiss a little. Spit a little. Glare at me like, "This rotten cousin keeps touching our things. We don't even play with our feathery-flamingo-on-a-string—it's strictly for decoration."

Amara—The Darkness—realized he is the recipient of her missing springs and hates him with a raw, raging passion.

The photos above are for one of his follow-up visits for vaccines. The first pic shows happy-go-lucky Cass. Curious, playful.

Then the vet comes in and says he's old enough and healthy enough. "It's time to discuss neutering."

The second pic shows Cass when he gets the news that his life will be forever, uh, altered.

And the third. Poor baby. He realizes he's just a wee little kitten and powerless to stop the impending doom of the vet's scalpel.

I remember the second day of 2021 when our collective countenances were aligned to the first photo.

Happy, curious, peeking around the corner at what's to come.

I remember January 6 of 2021, too. Yeah... Snip, snip. And the hits kept coming for folks across the globe—all year long.

For our family, the world chaos was coupled with more snip-snip events, a few check-check-and-check events, and a half dozen or so, yup-yup cha-ching moments.

Time to crawl into my bitty kitty carrier and pout, 'cause there's nothing I can do about any of it. Powerless.

As I write this, it's the second day of 2022. I'm aligned once again with that first photo's emotion. "Let's see where this new start goes..." I've set some new schedules for writing and the day job juggle.

Little Miss Muse is psyched out of her lavender-loving mind. The story ideas are pouring out of her faster than my fingers can type them down on the to-do list.

(Little Miss Muse also likes it when Cass comes for a visit. Their energy levels are a match made in heaven. Never stopping. Mess-making. Constant motion. Never sleeping. Cass and Little Miss are soul mates. At least until Cass's life is forever, uh, altered.)

I'M FEELING BETTER since New Doc Guy has adjusted some things. I've set some personal health milestones for 2022, and with the help of New Doc Guy (and a few attitude adjustments from the Back Guy), I'm looking forward to more progress.

I've promised Adult-ish Male Child that I will complete Supernatural this year. That's a lot of ghostbusting, but alas. He's been on my case for years, and I can't seem to get out of Season 1. He promises things get better.

We discussed how to do more of those "Happy on Purpose" moments in 2022.

Here's to 2022 and all the progress and forward momentum it can bring. Praying/hoping/wishing any and all snip-snip events remain at bay, for alas. We are just wee little humans with little control over anyone else's scalpels.

Looking Back: A wicked sinus infection floored me for two months, during which time I did, indeed, watch Supernatural.
You can find a pic of Cass in the appendix. He fits right in as one of the most psychotic members of our CIRCUS. His Snip-snip did NOT calm him down.
Little Miss Muse believes Cass is misunderstood.
This coming from a Muse with the attention span of a tuxedo kitten on catnip...

154

BOOK SALE LESSONS

It came out of the blue—at least for me.

The return of our library's book sale.

What bliss!

In years past, I'd spend hours (sometimes spread across multiple trips) scouring this sale. Adding to my To Be Read (TBR) Piles. Adding to my grandmother's TBR Piles. Looking for gems to flip on eBay (those were few and far between... too many sharks in that pond beating me to the punch). Looking for unusual and out-of-the-box homeschool must-haves.

On several occasions, the ladies at the checkout would say, "That's the one. Get ready." And they'd clear a space for me to bring my finds so I wouldn't herniate four discs lugging around my treasures.

Before the sale, the wonderful Friends of the Library volunteers would lug and tug and pull gobs of boxes—and I do mean gobs—of donated books, set them up on tables in the two entryway hallways of the library, and watch people crawl/dig/sort/claw through the madness. It's quite cramped and one of the only few activities I'll subject myself to where there are way too many humans per square foot. Comicons are another where I'll tolerate a crowd.

Other kinds of crowds often contain awful bits of humanity, and this introvert would rather not, pandemic or not, thank you very much.

And, unfortunately, that tiny space and the crowd that crams it full is why 2020 didn't happen—at least I don't think it did. At least it didn't happen in my head because I would've skipped it in the spring of 2020, and in the fall of 2020, the cases in our area were tanking hospital resources and our own family was hard hit by that wretched bug.

If they brought it back in the spring of 2021, I wasn't aware. That was another dark, dark time and I either missed the announcement or the sale was still off.

But this year, I was driving to the grocery store on a rare day when I was going in person to buy bread and toilet paper, and an even rarer day when I hadn't managed to make the 8:00 time slot where most of the town is still in bed or just waking. (See, crowds in the grocery store, no thanks.) But despite my lateness, the sky was clear and blue and beautiful, and I passed a sign at the park.

The park!

That the library book sale was in one of the 4H buildings. Large, open space. High ceilings and gobs and gobs of elbow room.

I may have screeched the brakes a bit on the SUV (don't tell the Hubs) and tossed a few bits of gravel pulling down the lane to the sale. Little Miss Muse accompanied me on this trip to ensure I replenished her grape soda and lavender nail polish (muses care very little about supply chain issues—they want what they want, when they want it). She went flying hard into the passenger windshield – I'm still dabbing up glitter from the impact.

"A little warning next time."

"Wear your seatbelt."

"It's not even garage sale season yet." She brushed her tutu and straightened her bent right wing.

I ignored her whining, parked, and went in. The building is slightly more than a metal pole barn—cement floor, high metal roof, plumbing and electric, but cool despite the industrial sized heaters hanging from the ceiling.

The tables were spread everywhere. Books and boxes everywhere —some of the tables were sagging and complaining. Only a few browsers were shopping. A few ladies were working the checkout and condensing and sorting the piles.

It took me a minute to figure out who was shopping and who was working—because, let's face it, if you're a Friend of the Library, you're likely a lover of books and cannot help yourself from creating your own TBR stacks.

Little Miss Muse fluttered and flitted from one end of the building and then back to me. "Where do we start? Hurry up because they've got no concessions here." She grabbed her poofy stomach as if she'd not eaten in days and would starve in the next five minutes.

"We start at the beginning and work our way through the tables."

"All the tables?"

"Yes. All the tables."

She rolled her eyes, muttering something like, "You don't even have a book in these piles. You won't sit down long enough to finish —" I flicked her rear and she stopped. My periodically lengthy procrastination due to trauma, drama, and illness was not up for discussion. Not here.

I did a cursory sweep, getting the lay of the land, noting where to spend more time. Picking up a few books here and there and slipping them into my tote. Slipped one under my arm like a lucky charm... (no judgment now, this is my thing. You have your thing.)

Then I shopped in earnest. Three hours? I think. I lost track of time. I didn't feel the seconds. I didn't check my phone. I just zoned out of the world and into the sale. (Similar sensations come over me in Half Price Books, which is why I don't shop Half Price Books when I'm with other people as it would be downright rude...)

I think Little Miss had three strokes and a coronary, just sure that the grocery would be all out of bubble gum and nail polish by the time I got done at such a late hour. I crammed that tote full of TBRs. Even started a "bonus" pile up at the checkout. Found favorite authors. New-to-me authors. Series runs.

I have a few cool anecdotes that came out of our time spent at the sale. I'll save one of those for next week.

In the meantime, here are some important *Lessons from the Book Sale* that I jotted down, just to keep me fresh and on my toes for that next glorious event:

1. Always keep a large reusable shopping bag in the car for unexpected book sales or that random garage sale that may also have books.
2. Tattered copies are to be considered. Tattered means someone—or more than one someone—cared enough to read the book through. Or. Or. They had a cat with a vicious vendetta against all things shelved. Either way. Spine damage doesn't bother me when I'm just looking for a good tale.
3. Books don't go bad. A good story 50 years ago is still a good story now. Maybe better...
4. You find your tribe at a book sale. Fellow booklovers searching for their TBRs and other fun surprises. Fellow booklovers helping you search for your TBRs. Everyone searching for everyone else's TBRs. Folks joining in the melee of yelling out authors and titles and subject matter to be on the lookout for.
5. You find lost friends at a book sale. A former neighbor works the sale. I also got to catch up with the mother of my childhood best friend.
6. Tell your Muse to buckle up, buttercup. And be prepared for sudden stops.
7. Enjoy the moments when you can. You never know when the next shut-down, life roll, or business model implosion will take away or delay one of your favorite things.

Most of all? Groceries can wait. Who needs groceries? (Little Miss would like to add here that all humans need groceries, and all muses need their fixes and to ignore that part about groceries.)

Looking Back: I've read all the TBR pile from that trip. Onward!
Little Miss Muse says if I wrote as much as I read—
I interrupt her here. "Stories feed you, my dear. More so than grape soda
and bubblegum."
She hangs her head and flicks off a novel from the bookshelf. Cats go
scurrying from the room.
"This one next, then."
It's a Mark Dawson novel. For the fans of Jack Reacher.
It should be thrilling... And Little Miss will learn how to be a better sniper.

155

GETTING THINGS STARTED

Want to do a little time travel with me today?

When this blog hits, it'll be the 24th day of 2022. I'm not sure how many days you've experienced of 2022 because you could be reading this on the 25th, 29th, or somewhere in July past the halfway point.

But the content goes live on Day 24.

As I write this, however, it's January 4. Four whole days in this new year, and I'm getting ramped up with several writing goals and challenges. One of those being to stay on top of blog posts now that Web Guy — due to no fault of his own — has sent me off to do my own thing (Kinda on my own. 'Cause even though bapaul.com has a new home, doesn't make me tech-savvy about the whole switch-over process. Web Guy is still on speed dial).

My concern with the switch was that I no longer had that "external" blog post deadline that Web Guy served as for so many years. He did, after all, faithfully post 149 blog posts for me over the years on the old site. 149!!!

#150 landed on the new site, and with it came the realization that I well and truly am the master of my own domain. No pun intended. I don't even understand domains... And Little Miss Muse is of no help, melting into a purple pile of gloomy goo anytime I need to work on calendars, scheduling, or edits.

Muses hate all things structure and time-sensitive.

So to protect my future writing time and clear my head, I've been churning out blog posts and timing them to go live on the right dates. The words count toward my daily word count goal. Today, I'll have finished one complete short and be well on my way to finishing the second. Not too bad given the standstill I was in over the last quarter of 2021 with health and family.

And, despite trying to figure out where to start (like trying to get a new roll of toilet paper going after the factory superglued the ends down), it feeeeels sooooo good to be writing for concentrated periods of time!

Writing is my dopamine release mechanism. I guess it's what joggers/runners feel once they hit the zone, driving them to spend more time on the track. I wouldn't know about the running thing. If I'm running, you'd better run too 'cause something has transpired that requires immediate action.

I'm a better human when I write every day. (At least until a real cat gets into the real toilet paper or chews up my outline, or knocks over the space heater...)

So, for the writing goals and challenges, so far, so good.

I imagine those of you reading this right now (24 days in) are also doing pretty well with your resolutions or goals. Even if they've slipped a little, I'm sure that back on Day 4 you were crushing them!

(I may have to amend this come Day 24 when this goes live. Perhaps I've given it all up and moved to Madagascar to sell water on the side of the road while Little Miss romps through the jungle with the meerkats. Who knows. Anything can happen.)

I'm still untangling the novel work in progress. I'll write new words on it, go back and fuss with the storyline. I think somewhere in the muddied-up 2020 and 2021, Little Miss and I tried to write two books, one on top of the other. It's a tangled mess. Here and there, a chapter belongs in book 3, not book 2. I don't recommend this method of creating.

It's maddening. Like a contractor building two separate houses on the same foundation, one wall belonging to house A, the ceiling belongs to B, and the floor slopes. Oh, stuff's happening. It's taking shape. But you'd have better luck having your cat undo that super-glued roll of toilet paper into something, uh, useable than living in that house.

So, in a nutshell and to avoid boring you to tears with more rambling or math, here are my 2022 writing goals:

- 1500 words per day
- One short story per week
- FINISH THE DUMB BOOK 2!...
- AND ITS SEQUEL!
- Continue a free short story on the first Monday of each month, and blog posts on all other Mondays.
- Avoid moving to Madagascar to sell water bottles with meerkats and Miss Muse.

On Day 4 of 2022, I believe that this is a very doable list; I even buffered in "life happens" weeks to lighten the pressure if life does indeed happen.

There may, however, be some side effects to this plan. Some of which those closest to me may notice:

For those local folks, if you see me out walking in a daze or unable to verbally communicate, it's because it takes me a good half hour to shake off "story brain" and put on "I'm in public brain." It's a side effect of opening up that creative gate and letting Little Miss Muse have a lively little romp through the nerve pathways. Please don't call the men with straight jackets. My daze will pass. Unless I'm wrapped up in a roll's worth of toilet paper like a Halloween mummy. Then maybe call the Hubs or the Adult-ish Male Child. Something has glitched out...

If you see me smiling for no good reason or appearing to have a conversation with some invisible force, I'm still firmly in "story brain" and if you interrupt me too abruptly, Little Miss Muse (that invisible force) will get grumpy. You may catch a glimmer of her lavender rage haze, and I'll make no logical sense for a few seconds as she withdraws her magic wand from my mind. Be patient with me. My human-to-human English will come back online, and we can have a chat as Little Miss goes off to pout and polish her wand.

If you see me teary-eyed, hand me a tissue or a wad of toilet paper (unused, preferably), and give me a hot minute to collect myself. Sometimes I've dug deep into that "feely" part that rarely shows up in an INTJ persona and poured it out on the page. Or I killed a favorite character. Or I want to kill a favorite character and just can't pull the trigger. Or, more than likely, I'm rage crying because I'm not tech-savvy and I'm fighting a battle with my website or InDesign or can't get that stupid cover to size up the right way. Ugggg. InDesign. Tech. Grrrrr.

And that reminds me, no matter if you see tears or hysterical laughter coming from me, and no matter how far we are into 2022, if you see me running...

Run.

Looking Back: Oh, how optimistic I was on Day 4 of 2022. If I'd only known...
'I even buffered in "life happens"' Haha. Not enough buffer on the planet.
There was no organized CIRCUS for me at this point. Shortly thereafter though, the clowns moved in with lots and lots of luggage.
I'm tempted to reel a little at that goal list that I missed. But, I won't linger there. I can't. Sometimes you can work the dream, and sometimes the dream must wait.
I did, however, "fire" InDesign in favor of a much more not-a-tech-friendly version. Since that move, I managed to churn out quite a few short story collections, so the year wasn't a total bust after all...
Little Miss Muse hates waiting. She's ready to get on with these works-in-

progress (WIPs) that are weighing her author down because she's got soooo many more ideas to churn out.

She's not wrong. 2023: The Year of Whipping the WIPs.

There. I declared it. When this goes to publication sometime in late spring, we'll see how many of those bad boys we've conquered...

156

SWEET VALENTINES

Ages ago, before the world went berserk, I went to Vegas.
I'm ducking now. It's a reflex.

When I hear that sentence — I went to Vegas — come out of my mouth, I cringe and duck. Any sentence regarding myself in Vegas, actually:

I'm going to Vegas.

I stayed in Vegas for a week.

I had an insane time in Vegas.

I met the coolest people in Vegas.

I'm going back to Vegas this year. Maybe twice.

Because I was taught — either directly or indirectly, I've no idea — that Vegas was a "bad place." And people who go to that city go there to do things they don't want anyone to know about. And when you do things you don't want people to know about, you're likely up to no good.

Likely, this Las Vegas fallacy was planted by my overly-opinionated grandmother — intentionally or not, I've no idea — during my primitive brain-forming years. This lady also impressed upon me that any word for flatulence other than "toot" was foul language and that it was amoral and possibly illegal to write checks or mow the grass on Sundays.

Bless her heart and God rest her soul. I digress...

At any rate. I went to Vegas in February 2020 to an insanely cool Anthology Workshop put on by WMG Publishing. A panel of professional editors was there to buy short fiction for their upcoming projects. One of those projects was Sweet Valentines.

We wrote the stories the November/December prior to the trip, and when we arrived in class, the panel would discuss each story, and the lead editor had the final say in whether the manuscript "fit" his or her project.

The submission for Sweet Valentines was the most challenging for me to write. I paced and fitted. Little Miss Muse paced and fitted with me. She'd give me a spark, and I'd snuff it out.

It was quite agonizing. (Agonizing in a fun way, much how football fans agonize over their favorite team losing. I don't understand why they keep watching if it causes that much pain. Likewise, some folks don't understand why I keep at this writing thing. We do it because we want to. Because it's fun agony...)

The parameters of the story were simple: The editor for Sweet Valentines Anthology wanted the following.

Short.

Sweet.

Romance.

Valentine-Day theme.

Simple, right?

Until I try to write romance on purpose. Boy meets girl, then... What?

Little Miss tried to keep killing off the characters. Nope. That's not sweet.

Little Miss wanted to place it in a dark, dreary forest with a ghost. Nope. That's not Valentines. "But it could be sweet." She wasn't getting the rules of the assignment. Generally speaking, muses hate rules.

So, I did the best I could. I left the romance parts "off the page" and wrote a sweet, very short Valentine's Day tale. You didn't see anyone meet.

You don't see anyone kiss.

No one goes goo-goo-ga-ga, weak in the knees. There's very little romance. But a whole lot of it, just not on the page. It's hard to explain.

And, apparently, when the editor was reading the submissions (over 50 of them, I believe) to decide what to include in her project, she got mad when she read mine.

She also said she threw her Kindle across the room and swore at me.

Swore at me! (Not in person, and not mean. Just a few choice words of utter frustration from the sounds of it...)

Because she loved the story, but I didn't follow the rules. It didn't fit a true romance structure.

But it fit everything else.

So she had it on the "maybe" pile. Then the "no" pile. Then back to the "maybe." By the time she got to Vegas, it was a no. Or a maybe. Firmly undecided, I do believe, and still very much aggravated that I didn't "write a romance."

Until the panel chimed in. The other editors believed it fit the nature of the project quite well.

So, the short story "I Remember Paperclips" made it into the anthology.

Next week, it will be featured here on the blog for the month of February as free fiction.

In the meantime (and thereafter), you can get it from WMG here until I tuck it away in a second upcoming volume of Spunk and Spice.

And then you decide: Is it a romance? Not a romance?

To remedy this "I can't write romance (or romantic elements) to save my ever lovin' life" issue, I'll be taking a class. Likely live in Vegas.

Where, in my case, what happens in Vegas comes home with me and gets a blog post...

(And all you dirty-minded people just took that last line to the extreme, didn't you? I'll send Little Miss over to your house. Y'all can deal with her for a hot minute. She's about to wear me out...)

Looking Back: That was a fun, fun week. Something amazing to look back
on right as the world came to a standstill in March of that year.
The second Volume of Spunk and Spice is, indeed, out—largely due to the
fact that I fired InDesign and went with easier-to-navigate software.
Little Miss Muse starts in again about the shark tank swimming pool.
Purple goo is beginning to puddle at the corners of her eyes.
I'm gonna have to pull off Memory Lane for a while to console her. Maybe
look at plane tickets to France. Or at least schedule my passport
appointment.

157

BUT IS THE PIZZA HERE YET?

I know, I know. It's Valentine's Day. I should write something sweet or sappy or romantic-ish.

Romance isn't my strong suit, but I've been told "I Remember Paperclips" isn't half bad. That's all I've got to say about that.

And actually, today is last night for me (remember that cool time-travel thing we can do when we write and read), and I'm watching the Super Bowl. And writing this blog. I've been living dangerously lately with the deadline thing—in day job responsibilities and writing life.

I don't like football.

I like football as much as I like obligatory holidays.

I watch because the Hubs and the Adult-ish Male Child are watching. The Hubs's team isn't on the field for this one. We're next-state neighbors to the Bengals, so that's "our team" for the night. And they've got the whole underdog thing going on, which I can get on board with. Until I'm bored with it.

My son doesn't watch football much at all. So he's already started with the questions. "What just happened?" "Why are they running like that?" "What color of uniform are we rooting for again?"

But the most important question: "Is the pizza here yet?"

No, it isn't. The pizza is late. Restaurants in this area are grossly understaffed. We might get our order before the World Series.

I also tune in for the occasional commercial. So far, we've got the McDonald's "Uhhhhhhh" and the announcement of an installation in one of my favorite franchises: Jurassic Park. People, the raptors are coming back with original cast members in June.

I can't wait for June...

I digress. Presently, I can't wait for the end of this game. I didn't sleep last night and... wait. Dolly Parton just needed to get something off her chest—her words, not mine.

Good grief. There's too much going on in this room. Four cats (we grand-kitty-sat for Castiel Monroe while Adultish-Male Child tromped around in the Sonora Desert). Little Miss is throwing a fit because not one uniform has any hint of purple in it... and why can't the cool guy with the purple hair be on "our team?"

Yet another pizza ETA request.

I don't know when the pizza's coming, guys. Any time now...

A loud groan from the menfolk tells me our team of the night is behind. And they're blaming themselves. The Hubs and the son. They tell me that whatever team they root for tends to lose, statistically speaking. So, my sincerest apologies to the Cowboys, Reds, and Hoosiers. It's the Paul family's fault that you've lost any game y'all have ever played in the last 45 years or so. Sorry for your luck.

When I watch any sporting event, about halfway through I start genuinely praying that the game doesn't go into overtime—I'm over it before the first half/quarter/timeout/commercial break. It doesn't help that game clock time transitions into dog-year time when you're just not a fan...

Oh. My. Gosh. Guys! Arnold has a mini pegasus named Peggy. I don't even know what the commercial was advertising for. Mini winged horse. Next best thing to a unicorn.

And how many of you totally fell for the floating psychedelic QR Code commercial? I did when it turned purple and Little Miss shocked me into action. But I was too slow. So yet another commercial that I have no idea what they were advertising—

Goats! Avenger Goats. Star Wars Goats. Up Goats. Goats everywhere...

Cue the cat fight. Amara Mino is not a fan of Castiel Monroe and sent him flying into the wall. Stella Marie excused herself to wait in the bedroom until the pizza comes and Malachi Maxwell sits in the corner shaking his head. Malachi, after all, has told Castiel all week not to be in the same room as Amara Mino...

Little Miss finds this much more amusing than grown men chasing each other. Though she does feel bad about the purple-haired man's injury.

And the pizza's here... Hot, steamy, and delivered by a young man with an impressive man-bun and sweet disposition, even if he was terrified of our slightly steep but snow-covered drive.

Half time. My favorite questions come from the interviewers chasing down the coaches (who clearly have nothing better to do at half time): "What do you do to win the game?" or something along those lines. And the reply: We need to make more plays.

Well.

There you have it.

How to win a Super Bowl.

Make plays.

Head slap...

And the halftime show is gonna cost me major $$$$. Little Miss spotted two pairs of boots and a tracksuit that she'd like to have custom ordered in her chubby-little-imp size. With holes in the back of the tracksuit for her wings...

The second half in a nutshell: The hours of rest my middle insomnia stole over the last seven days has caught up with me. I can't even pretend to be human, let alone upright...

Good night boys and goodnight kitties...

From this paragraph forward, I'm writing Monday morning.

So good morning...

Google tells me the Bengals lost. (See my blanket apology above to all the teams my guys ever root for.)

I bet the post-game and post-post-game interviews went something like this:

Tell us how you did it: We made the plays.

Tell us why you lost: We didn't make the plays. And the Pauls rooted for us.

And that's a Super Bowl Wrap.

You all have a lovely day. Do something you adore with someone you can tolerate. Or do something you can tolerate with someone you adore.

Either way... go out there and make plays.

Looking Back: I recently watched the overtime bit of the World Cup with a friend in France. No, I wasn't in France, and she wasn't here, but we messaged. Apparently, America gets their network feeds much faster than France gets theirs, so if you ever watch the overtime bit of a World Cup with someone in Europe, don't go "Uh-oh" in your message too quickly... it tends to ruin the effect.

Little Miss Muse couldn't find anyone wearing purple in the France v Argentina game, so she has nothing more to say about that game.

I just hoped both teams had fun...

158

IN AND OUT OF THE POOL

W hen I was a kid, one of my favorite things in the world was to go with a friend to her aunt's home. This aunt had a pool. A real pool, mind you. Not one purchased from Kmart's front curb (Or 3D—how many of you remember the store 3D???). Not one with turtles or overweight fish decals painted on the sides that my dad would throw in the back of his pickup.

And not one that had to be blown up.

And not one that had to be filled before the sides would stay up.

A real pool. With a filter and a ladder and floating bleach tablets —the whole nine yards.

It even came with rules.

The number one rule was don't pee in the pool.

The other rule that was shouted by the aunt and the cousins and the uncle was: No in and out. Get in and stay in—or—Get out and stay out. (Unless you really had to pee...)

When I was little, I thought this rule was for our comfort. Because once you get out, getting back in was rough. Temperature changes and all. And once you were in, getting out was rough for the same reason, especially on overcast or breezy days.

Nope.

I realized during our *nice try* attempt at a pool hybrid for our kids that the temperature of the water had NOTHING to do with this rule.

Our model had a pump and a ladder, but the sides were held up by water and you had to blow up the rim with a hand pump. So a pool, but not a pool, even though I bought the floating bleach tablet thingies.

I played chemist Every. Single. Day. And dumped hundreds of dollars of quality chemicals into the pool every morning and shocked the pool after every storm only to have algae and scum gunk. Never again...

But... the rule?

Get in and stay in.

Or if you get out, don't get back in.

It was because of the dirt. The grass. The hundred other what-evers that jumped up from the yard and stuck to the bottoms of feet or lodged between wet little toes and drug into the pool. And hid under that blow-up rim and created more gunk and slime and algae, requiring more cleaning and skimming and vacuuming and, well, you get the picture.

In and out of the pool.

Bad idea.

Same with writing projects, I'm finding.

The water's fine when you're all the way "in." From the hold-the-breath contests to see what character A decides to do with that dilemma I just threw at him. Handstand contests between A and B side stories. A tad of Marco-Polo-ing (especially when I held my breath too long and forgot where I put a character—that's always fun).

Like riding atop a magical unicorn floaty that bobs and sways with the water as the ideas pour out uninhibited and some magical being (likely not a muse, as muses are such fickle beasts) refills your Canada Dry Zero Sugar Ginger Ale that finally found its way out of the supply chain logjam and brings you strawberries and white Reese's cups to keep your brain fed while you create...

It's also fine when you're all the way "out." As in done. Completely. Dried off, manuscript sent off to the proofreader or the editor or on to a submission of some sort. Done. All your muscles relaxed and warm and washed in a calming peace. And if you close your eyes and concentrate, you still feel as if you're floating on your unicorn...

But man, oh, man. Getting in and out? Over and over? Starting and stopping?

I explained to a friend that some of the stories I've written so far this year feel like they have square wheels and I'm pushing them uphill in mud. She replied at least I'm making interesting tracks in the mud.

She's an optimist.

I think I'm just tracking mud...

And grass.

And a hundred other whatevers that jumped up from the yard and stuck to the bottoms of my feet or lodged between my not-so-little toes and drug into the manuscript.

And then I have to play major chemist (aka editor) and dump and subtract and cut and skim gobs of content to rid it of those junky, scum-producing issues. Yuck, right?

A thousand interruptions of life and a brain that swears it has ADHD (but likely it's Little Miss Muse or one of three felines causing a ruckus). A sinus infection that's hitched a ride multiple times since the second week of January (playing its own game of in-and-out-of-the-nostrils, I suppose, dragging in more issues with each pass it takes at me). You name it. Events, illness, or generalized stress sending me searching for the ladder to get out of the pool before anything is done.

But today is Monday.

A new, fresh start to the week.

Another chance to pump fresh air into my unicorn floaty, refill my Little Miss Muse's not-diet grape soda and bring HER her favorite purple bubble gum (because, let's face it, we live in the real world and I'm here to serve HER) and get back in the pool.

Hopefully to stay in the water for more than a day...

Looking Back: I'm doing this in-and-out thing with Triage, a novel that was sparked by a short story I wrote for that Vegas romance workshop. No, it's not a romance, but it does have a guy and a gal trying to figure out life and feelings amid corporate espionage. And death. The death part makes Little Miss Muse happy.

The book was coming along nicely until Thanksgiving. Then more CIRCUS. Then more holidays in the CIRCUS. It's one of those WIPs to whip in 2023.

Little Miss Muse is at the white board with her purple marker. She takes a deep inhale off the tip and then begins spilling storylines for Triage onto the wall as she grins like a fool.

She's high, though, now. So none of the lines make sense, but we'll take a photo of it later and maybe stick it in the back of Triage to show what it's like to work with a Muse who likes the smell of dry erase markers.

159

BANANA BUTTS

It's been a nutty few weeks. Retractable sinus infections, day job drama, family chaos, and winter weather that can't decide if it's winter or spring or fall...

Also a furnace that may or may not have been trying to kill us. (The furnace was fine, but my ongoing sinus issues have created a problem with my sniffer, prompting emergency checks of our major appliances—long week, folks. Lots of "Are you sure you can't smell that?" going on.)

Add to this the War. (Enough about that. Moving on with this silly, distracting post.)

Moving on to our black banana butt issues.

I kid you not.

Black as night and nasty as you can imagine (The bananas' tail ends, not our personal tail ends... Gotta watch those dangling modifiers and unclear descriptors. They'll get you dirty-minded folks all stirred up.)

At first, I thought I'd bought a bad batch. It happens.

But they were fresh—the green kind of fresh because I knew we wouldn't need them for a couple of days. I always hang the banana bunches on a rod in my kitchen. They look nice there. All visible, within reach, and inviting.

And then.

Black butts.

They weren't turning black from the stem down. They weren't ripening with brown splotches uniformly. Black as ink from the bottom tips, the rot creeping upward.

With ooze and everything.

I threw them out and scoured the area.

And bought more bananas. A little riper, a little more yellow, because it was a day or so later and we would be eating them soon.

I hung them on the rod again.

Aaannd... you guessed it. Black banana butts.

How is it I can't buy a good bunch of bananas anymore?

I used to base my decision on which bunch of yellowy goodness had the most impressive movie advertising sticker. Call me crazy—many have, and many will—but I found shopping for this elongated fruit much more fun when Dole or Chiquita decided to adorn them with fun Disney or Avenger characters.

Don't slam it—these series runs were even listed on eBay for a time. I'm not sure if they still are.

You can read my original Bananas Stickers! post if you so desire.

But this was nuts! Two batches.

Then we figured it out.

One of the felines—we didn't know which one at the time—had been gnawing on the ends of the bananas. We discovered tiny puncture marks along the peel where the black grew and spread. Tiny tooth marks.

Someone has a new hobby. (Turns out it's Malachi Maxwell with the fruit fetish. We caught him mauling a Granny Smith Apple the other day.)

So. No more bananas hanging beautifully on the kitchen rod.

Now we must store our bunches in the cabinet.

Do you know what happens when you store bananas in the cabinet? No one remembers there are bananas in the cabinet. Out of sight, out of mind.

And we end up with brown banana butts. Actually, the whole peel turns brown. If Grandma were around, she'd tell me to make pudding or banana bread with the aged fruit. Or to cut the black oozing ends off the bunch and eat them anyway.

Ummm... no. One can't unsee a black banana butt such as those Malachi created.

And I don't cook. I wouldn't have the ingredients on hand for pudding or bread, nor would I go shopping for those items on purpose.

I don't cook.

That's why the cabinet isn't opened that much.

And why we have such a banana issue.

I'm looking into a citrus spray for our countertops to avert the cats from surfing their way into trouble. Hopefully before they learn how to use the toaster.

But, knowing my gang, they'll enjoy the citrus, learn how to open the fridge, and partake of the Hub's orange juice and clementine selections.

Here's hoping your week runs smoothly, no matter what oddball challenges you face.

And that your bananas are perfectly enjoyable right down to their butts.

Looking Back: We still store the bananas in the cabinet, but we're better at remembering they're in there—most of the time, anyway. Banana Stickers!
is Blog #75 in Life Along the Way...
Little Miss Muse hides her head as we reread this post.
I prod her about the issue.
Apparently, she encouraged Malachi to try the bananas in the first place.
Of course she did...

160

DEAR WHOEVER

D ear Mr. Magic Wand Guy...
  Wait. Maybe that's not right. Perhaps it's Magic Wand Gal or Imp or Muse. One can never know.

Dear Magic Wand Company...

Well. Maybe that's not what they're calling themselves these days. Did ACME buy them out? Did their American-based business get shipped overseas? Is someone drop-shipping for them on Amazon? One can never know.

Dear...

Dear...

Dear Whoever,

I'm writing regarding an order placed approximately four decades ago. I wrote this request in colored pencil (green, I think) by my own big-girl self. This, I'm sure, was witnessed by at least one of my parents, possibly both of them. The request was also passed off to one Santa Claus and perhaps the Easter Bunny and Tooth Fairy—whichever of your colleagues was on duty back then.

The item was on page 54 of your Fall catalog. I remember that quite clearly (don't ask me why, some things just get stuck in the memory files).

And the item number was MWTW-400. Standard black body. Standard white tip.

You know.

The *Magic Wand That Works*. I was a rather courteous child, so I know I did not add the upgrade of White Rabbit-500 (we already had rabbits that would do just fine, Thumper and Coco). Nor did I request the Black Hat-783 model (only boy magicians wore black hats in my days. I was going to wear a silken scarf with bright yellow tulips that belonged to my grandma—start a new trend).

I also knew better than to ask for something as hard to handle as Unicorn Eggs (we lived in the wrong planting zone for those, the entire wrong continent, actually) or Pot-O-Gold complete with three bonus wishes from your in-house Leprechaun.

It seems that you carried a Big Stick Box-Of-The-Month Club subscription that I may be interested in. Though I would've had no use as a young girl for such big sticks, I do vaguely remember the description saying something like, if on rare occasion your Magic Wand That Works fails to do as advertised, a Big Stick swung with just the right force and with just the right aim could also solve a vast array of conundrums where other methods fail.

Shy child that I was, I also avoided the more ostentatious MWTW-9000 in shimmering lilac with rose gold tip, though my Little Miss Muse now believes that would've been the way to go.

Perhaps an ostentatious order such as that would have been, what? Lost in the mail? Stolen by porch pirates? Fallen victim to magical money laundering schemes? Suffered supply chain issues?

Does your company, Dear Ma'am (or dear Whoever) carry insurance for lost packages?

See. I spoke with my mother just the other day about this item. She remembers placing the order, even though she had no idea what I could possibly want with a Magic Wand That Works. I also believed neither of my parents truly understood the magic of unicorns or the possibility of fairies, but I digress. I hold no such grudges against the supernatural or unknown.

So, I hope this wasn't a cultural misunderstanding between realms of logic and whims of fancy.

And now... now?

Now, you see, dear Sir or Ma'am (or Miss or Muse or Imp or Elf or Whoever), the world has gone bat butt crazy, and a MWTW-400 would come in quite useful.

I wouldn't even be selfish. I'd share it with anyone who might need a Magic Wand That Works, provided they do good with it. Whatever their version of good is.

As a matter of fact, I do believe that I would like you to fill my original request for the MWTW-400 and add to that the MWTW-9000 in shimmering lilac with rose gold tip.

I also believe, Dear Sir, or Dear Whoever, that because my order has been delayed by so many moons, your company should upgrade me without extra charges.

And toss in free shipping.

And a tracking number. Insurance for the full amount.

And I'm saving this request on my hard drive, to the Cloud, and printing it in triplicate should litigation ensue.

P.S. Just go ahead and sign me up for the Big Stick Box-Of-The-Month Club. I know I'll owe extra for that one, but a few of those within arm's reach isn't a bad idea... I'm tired of speaking softly, anyway.

What the heck. Throw in a Unicorn Egg. Species #321, please, with the lavender mane and see-through horn. I know someone in France who can plant it for me.

Looking Back: If that order had ever come, the CIRCUS wouldn't have set up shop in my living room.
Little Miss Muse is still looking into the lost order. She believes she knows someone in accounting.

161

TIME TO ESCAPE

S ometimes you just gotta get away.

Away from the routine.

Away from the ruckus.

Away from the never-ending news reel of life...

But what to do when you can't hop a plane and leave your habitat? What to do when you can't even hop in the car and drive around the block for a mental respite (or a mental breakdown, whatever may be your priority...)

Take a story break.

The world of indie publishing (self-publishing) has opened up quite the travel agency, if you ask me. Short stories and novellas existed in traditional forms, but now, with the touch of a finger and an e-reader you can escape—if only for a moment. Authors in control of their own stories means they don't have to write only what big publishing houses are willing to print.

They can write anything.

In any length.

In any genre.

And send it into the world for us to find and enjoy.

And some of the "Big Name" writers are catching the wave, too. Free at last, free at last...

So, Little Miss Muse and I have curated a mini travel guide. All you need to know is what you're in the mood for and how long you've got.

Wait. That last bit... that sounds like a prognosis instead of a time management issue—*how long you've got.*

How about: All you need to know is what you're in the mood for and how much time you have to spend.

There. That's better.

(Full disclosure: I need this information in a place I can find it quickly. I always learned more in school doing research than anything else. But it seems I'm forever looking up these word counts, and nothing sticks. Perhaps "curating" them for the blog will allow me to retain the information and save yet another internet rabbit hole chase. I fell down three such holes doing this blog and bumped into Alice and the Queen of Hearts on my way back out.)

So the first issue: How fast do you read?

Not techy or work-related words. Fun words... Words that make you feel something other than the urge to quit your day job or go ahead and hire the fridge repairman because the manual that came with your new computerized appliance is written in Greek and Ancient Alien 2.1.

Personally, I don't read every single word in a book I'm trying to enjoy. I start reading slowly, getting the feel for the main character and the setting. Who's who and where's where kind of thing. Then, if the author has grabbed my curiosity, we're off. I skip words, skim paragraphs. I can get through a standard-length novel written by a master in about three to four hours (Grisham, Koontz, James) if I'm not ill or brain-twaddled from the day job.

However, give me an anthology of short stories, and it will take me much longer because the characters, plot, genre, and setting can change with every "chapter." My reading speed tanks on short stories.

The "feel" of the book affects my speed, as well. I tend to speed through thrillers faster than Jack Reacher shops at a thrift store for his next outfit. But with a book like "Where the Crawdads Sing," I found myself slowing down to enjoy the setting and the mood.

Give me a straight-up romance, and I'm asleep by chapter five. So. Many. Nights to get through one of those.

Generally speaking, according to the "experts," adults read between 200-250 words per minute. Your mileage may vary depending on if you're a voracious reader or if you like to meander through the tulips chapter by chapter.

If you're morbidly curious, Google "reading speed test." Lots of calculators out there.

I was morbidly curious, so I tried this one: www.freereadingtest.com

My speed was 391 with 100% comprehension. But it wasn't romance... it was science. If they had offered me a romance snippet, I'd have been at 10 words per minute with squinting and pauses for forehead-slapping. (See, internet rabbit holes will get you cool information, but not so great for forwarding progress on the work-in-progress.) I also read A LOT for my day job, so I don't have the luxury of reading slowly.

Little Miss Muse racked up 1519 words per minute with 50% comprehension. And then she clickety-clacked off to do other things. Numbers bore her quickly with all their logicy-logic.

So... here's the rundown on story lengths, whether you need to escape to the bathroom because your in-laws showed up or you're ready to hunker down for a couple of afternoons.

Novel: Lengths tend to vary based on the genre. Extensive world-building needs more pages, whereas sweet romance set in a modern-day coffee shop, not so much. *Gone With the Wind* clocks in at over 400,000, *Dune* at 188K, *Lord of the Rings* (all of them together) about 580K, and Harry Potter patters along through his series at over a million meager words (who says kids can't dig in and hang on for a "big book" experience?). The average novel length is 50-70K.

Novella: 10,000 to 40,000 words.

Novellette: (Yes, it's a thing): 8,000 to 17,000 words.

Short Story: Over 1000 words (about the average size of one of my blogs, give or take Little Miss Muse's interruptions and what the cats may be destroying in the next room, cutting things short). An average short story of mine is about 5k, but they can go up to 10,000.

Flash Fiction: Likes eggs in a frying pan—don't leave the stove, it's not gonna take that long to finish. Like seconds to minutes. Like the in-laws don't even have time to pound on the bathroom door to ask if you need medical attention. In 500 words (and quite often less than that), you give your brain cells a mighty minute or two to focus on something else.

And now Little Miss Muse is tap, tap, tapping her lavender stilettos with the cheetah print. It's time to refill her grape soda on the rocks and get back to the fiction word count...

... before someone starts pounding on the door and asking if I need medical attention.

FYI: This blog is 1032 words before this sentence...

And I guarantee you it took me much longer to write it than it did for you to read it.

Looking Back: I'd forgotten where I put this information... I needed it just the other day. Completely and totally forgot that I'd even wrangled it up. How odd it is to read back over some of these posts. Some of them stuck. For others, Little Miss Muse and I are nose-to-the-screen wondering where my (our) train of thought was heading...

I also have that sensation with some of the short stories I've written. I can't remember how the plot goes. I'd be the first one to flunk a multiple-choice test on my own creation, for sure.

Little Miss Muse says she believes it's time for me to escape. Not into a book mind you, but to a mountain cottage with lavender shutters at the base of some purple mountain majesty to catch some of her ideas and put them into writing.

I think she's right.

162

EVEN MY SHEEP ARE MALFUNCTIONING

A good night's sleep hasn't been had in these here parts by this here writer since sometime in 2021 —and that may even be stretching it.

The one-hour nap cycle (one hour fitful rest, one hour staring at the ceiling) I have gotten rewards me with the "no one will listen to me" dream. Or a "I can't find my_____" dream. Or "I'm late for a very important date, Mr. Rabbit" dream.

Then there was the week of nightmares, where I knew I was in a nightmare and couldn't move. Prayed for one — or all three — of the cats to jump up and down on my head at three a.m. and rescue me from impending doom. (Amara actually came through for me one evening. She got extra tidbits of happiness from the treat jar for her heroics.)

My over-the-counter sleep aids get me started, but nothing has proven to get me through the hours of two a.m. to six a.m. with any real success. A pillow-beating, blanket-fighting, why-do-I-have-all-these-arms-and-legs-good-grief-I-have-more-appendages-than-a-colony-of-octopi kind of restlessness.

Oh, oh. And I completely adore the Princess and the Pea remix. Meaning any slight wrinkle in the sheets or the pajamas or the air itself causes me to get up, readjust, and or roll about like overcooked rotisserie chicken.

At least the chicken is getting some sleep.

My sheep are malfunctioning.

So... I've been reading at night.

Last night, Mr. Dean Koontz came up with a wonderful idea.

And let me stop you right there.

Why, yes, in fact, I do enjoy Mr. Koontz at nighttime. Because I can count on one hand — one little digit actually — the number of times my dreams had anything at all to do with my choice of reading materials, especially the fantastically fantastical ones. If anything, my reading-related dreams are fitful rearrangements of real-life day-job juggle of legal, medical, and plumbing (yes, pipes and toilets) marketing firms. Dreams where writers don't listen to me, I can't find my laptop charger, and I'm behind deadline, Mr. Rabbit.

Anyway, here's the bit that made me laugh out loud. Then I had one of those moments where you let your book rest across your chest, and you stare off into nothing and consider the possibilities...

"Oh, Jocko rarely sleeps. Sometimes he sticks a fork in a wall plug and knocks himself out for an hour. I don't know why it doesn't kill him, but it doesn't, and I've learned to live with it."
– Erika 5, "The Dead Town", Dean Koontz 2011

Anyway, when Little Miss Muse and I came across this delightful little paragraph, she nudged me hard to the temple, very close to my black eye (yes, a real black eye—story for another day). "You should try that."

"It would kill me."

"It doesn't kill Jocko."

"Jocko is a fictional character."

"I read that paragraph ten times. It doesn't even kill him once."

"He's not human. Jocko is a literal lab accident." I rub my sore eye and pray for a coma.

"At least you'd be getting some sleep. You've been looking like a lab accident."

"It could put me in the hospital."

"That could be fun... they have *real* sedation. And purple Jello."

Only a Muse would think admission to a hospital would be fun.

So, before this blog devolves into a soppy puddle of more whining than I care to write about and more complaining than you care to read about, I'll bid you a good day.

And a good night.

Now. I hear Little Miss rummaging in the silverware drawer. Curious little imp will try anything once. I need to stop her.

But I do wonder which of my wall plugs carries the highest voltage...

Looking Back: Jocko remains on my list of top five favorite fictional characters. I have not yet tried the fork-in-the-wall-socket method of sleep aid.
Little Miss Muse said it works quite well. Knocked her out for a whole ten minutes. Longest she's slept at a time in forever...
I realize this is about the time the outlet under the office window went dead. Now we know the rest of the story.

163

WATER YOUR UNICORNS

A dear friend gifted me a plant.

Me.

A plant.

But it was in a very sweet "Let's Just Be Unicorns" planter, so I forgave her. (You know who you are, Miss L., and you know I love you...)

You see, I take care of plants about as well as I cook.

As in, I don't take care of plants.

I get the urge once a year for about a week to dig in the dirt. I may overspend on annuals like petunias or dahlias or impatiens.

I may even mulch and plot and plan out color-coordinating flower beds, refresh flower pots, and get everything looking cheery and happy right after the Indiana winter finally gives up. And I swear THIS will be the year that is different from all the other years previous. THIS will be the year that I become a gardener.

Then.

Just like that, I don't care anymore. Like a switch is flipped in my brain. I had fun. I did the picking out things and the planting things, and now on to the next task.

Which has nothing to do with flowers. Or watering. Or keeping anything alive other than the cats and us humans.

If anything is still blooming by Independence Day, it's because dear Hubs has watered and weeded and generally brought them from the brink of death after encountering my two black thumbs and lackadaisical attitude.

It got so bad in the last few years, that we literally purchased metallic sunflower sculptures, sprayed them with rust-proof sealant and planted *those*. They're on year two and still blooming. So. There.

So when Miss L. gifted me the planter, I was filled with questions:

What is this plant?

How do I take care of it?

Will you still love me if I kill it?

Will you still love me if one of my cats kills it?

She thought I was kidding. I was not. "You just give it a little water once in a while." This answer made my black-and-white logic brain hurt and spurred even more questions.

How much water, exactly?

How often is once in a while?

"You know, about once a week, and about a medicine bottle full of water."

Like a bulk horse-pill vitamin bottle or a tightly controlled-substance-sized bottle?

Well, after that was all sorted, I found a place for my unicorn in the sunroom, in a glass curio where the cats can't eat it and where I'll surely remember to water it.

Because it's a unicorn, after all. And how cool is that?

Nope.

I have not remembered on my own to water my unicorn. Not even once.

I've set a reminder on my phone, complete with a little unicorn emoji. WATER YOUR UNICORN. In all caps. Because otherwise, it's like the dinger on the oven—I don't pay attention to it, either.

However, I'm proud to say that several weeks in, and I've not killed it. At least I don't think it's dead. It could be that Miss L. is trying to boost my confidence and planted a fake plant in real dirt, and I've been watering plastic this whole time. I'll have to ask her next time I see her.

I was on my way to water my unicorn (a day late even though the reminder had screamed at me in all caps) and noticed I'd left a burner on the stove set to low. I was cooking the air above the burner. That was the second time in a week I'd left a burner on.

Then I remembered I forgot to switch the laundry around.

And then, and then, and then.

And then I sat down and made more reminders to ignore and more lists to lose. Because my mental capacity is shot. It seems I can do a good job at the day job, or I can manage general living. Lately, I cannot seem to figure out how to do both.

And the day job is about to suck the life out of me...

So. As a public service announcement (and a lopsided personal to-do list) here are a few things you may find falling through the cracks of a fragile, worn-out mind:

1. There are wet clothes in your washing machine. They're done. They're molding.
2. Lint trap in the dryer.
3. You're about to run out of toilet paper. Or deodorant. Or both.
4. That oil change decal reminder slid off your windshield a month ago. You're overdue for a lube.
5. The furnace filter is clogged with whatever floats around in your home. Here, it's cat dander and Little Miss Muse's glitter powder.
6. There's a banana turning black somewhere. In a cabinet. In a lunch box. Under the car seat.
7. You didn't send the attachment with that last email.
8. Your phone has been on silent for three days.
9. The library book is overdue, and Redbox wants their DVD back now.

10. Don't even smell that milk. And in one more day, your grape juice will be wine.
11. You will not remember why you walked into that room. Going back and forth won't help. Give it up.
12. There's a window open somewhere. It's raining.
13. The television remote may be in the refrigerator next to the wine… Uh, I mean grape juice.
14. You still didn't get that attachment onto the blasted email…
15. Your glasses are on your head.
16. Check the batteries in the smoke detectors.
17. You do not have Band-Aids. Or Neosporin. Just put them on the grocery list.
18. That doctor's appointment is closer than you think. Put the ice cream away. Eat a salad.
19. Never mind number 17. Put salad on the grocery list with the Neosporin and Band-Aids and toilet paper and deodorant and cancel the doctor's appointment.
20. Refill your blood pressure medication. Oh, wait. You need a doc appointment for that.
21. Do you have all your little children with you? Or for us empty-nesters: Are you missing a cat?
22. That bill is due now. And you don't have any stamps. Or envelopes.
23. Easter is next week. Or, if you're reading this after April 2022, the next holiday is coming faster than you'd like.
24. That email with the attachment went to the wrong recipient.
25. Seriously, the blood pressure medication is a must. Rebook the doc appt.
26. Are you cooking? Right now, like, are you cooking? It's about to boil over, burn, scorch, burst into fiery flames. Your oven dinger has gone off twelve times and you've ignored it—

Oh, wait. That's me. Right now. Dingers and alarms and worried cats. Oh my! Muses spinning out of control!

Gotta go...

Enjoy your week.

And for goodness sakes, go water your unicorns!

Looking Back: Well, Miss L. had to come to my house and diagnose my unicorn.

It was half dead.

I repotted the succulent in the wrong kind of soil, and even despite me forgetting to water it, it was drowning.

I have one sprig left of my unicorn succulent.

For now...

Little Miss Muse says I'd have more time to write if everything were artificial. Artificial plants. Artificial cats. Artificial Husb--

Stop. I do believe that would be a blow-up doll, Little Miss. No thank you.

164

GHOSTS WITH A SIDE OF CHEESE

One of the coolest things ever is to know someone who writes books. And writes books that you like. To see them lined up on the shelf and know that you *know* them.

The Ghost Detective Series by R.W. Wallace is pretty darn cool. Love the ghosts. Love the French backdrop. Love the mystery surrounding the cemetery's inhabitants.

Mostly, though, I love knowing that the escape these books provide is brought to me by someone I call a friend.

So, when she puts out a new Ghost Detective novel, I buy it.

Sometimes, I like ebooks to read on my iPad, synched with my phone. When I need an escape, I can read it anywhere, anytime.

However, when the Hubs wants to sample the paranormal pages written by someone he knows by proxy, one must purchase the paperbacks. No problem. I also intend to have her sign them one day, so, yeah. Paperbacks.

I enjoyed the first three books and passed them on to him.

As soon as he finished one, he'd start nagging me to nag her to get the next one out as soon as possible.

Just a public service announcement: Nagging your favorite author doesn't make them produce words faster. If the author is relatively new, nagging causes stress-induced rage fits (at least that's what it does to me and Little Miss Muse). If the author is well known... well. They won't listen to you anyway.

So, when the fourth installment in the Ghost Detective Series came out, I ordered the paperback as soon as I could.

The Hubs got to it first. "I need it to read on my lunch break." He flipped through the pages and glanced at the end.

Now, I have my own ritual I do when I pick up a new paperback. I examine the cover—all points of it. I check out the copyright page for the year (weird, I know). I read the dedication and the previously published works page. All a getting-to-know-you dance before the fun begins and the story wraps me in sweet escape.

But this flip-the-pages-to-the-end practice of his makes my toes curl. One should only flip through the pages of a novel to enjoy the aroma of the crisp, fine pages. Not to glance at the words and get a hint as to what may happen... ugg. But, to each his own.

"That's fine," I say. "Gives me time to finish the one I just started." I've enjoyed discussing the books with him. I enjoy knowing he's got something cool to do on his lunch breaks other than listening to some dumb sports scores.

Then he did it. "Since you're not getting any of your own writing done, I mean."

Cue the internal stress-induced rage fit and fake smile He's my biggest fan. He's my biggest support. But man, oh man. That "why haven't you gotten anything done" line, no matter how sweetly or innocently delivered, strikes a nerve.

Through clenched teeth, I replied, "It's fine. I'll finish reading the one I've already started."

Fast forward weeks later, and I'd finished reading the one I'd started and several others to boot. A nonfiction guide, as well. But I digress.

He returns the paperback to me. "It's a little rough. Tell her we need the next book."

I won't tell her any of that. At least not directly... *wink*

And I was confused. The Ghost Detective stories are not "rough."

Her writing is not "rough." The woman is multilingual and writes in better English than any English teacher I ever had (Sorry, Mrs. Yeager).

I thought maybe she killed off a mainstay character or things took a dark turn. But that didn't seem right. I shrugged it off and carried on.

I retired for the night. Book. Pajamas. Water bottle. Cat. Fuzzy blanket. Little Miss in a corner with a brand new box of glitter to occupy her while I sleep. I settled into bed. I start my getting-to-know-you dance.

And came to the Previously Published/Also By page.

I found writing. In ink.

In the Hub's handwriting. Tiny, tiny little numbers that made no sense to me. But they sure look like they'd make sense in his workplace setting.

Fling the cat off the bed.

Untangle from the fuzzy blanket.

Knock over the glitter bottle. Dodge an empty grape soda bottle from an angry Muse.

Pad down the hall in my pajamas to where the Hubs is dozing in the recliner.

And let the confrontation begin.

"Did you do this?" I show him the page.

He shrinks into the recliner. "Yeah. I must've not had any paper. I was in my truck reading during my lunch break."

"You have SKIN! Write it on your wrist or arm or big toe next time."

He apologized and then said, "It's gonna get worse." I shrugged that comment off.

Back to the bedroom. Apologize to Little Miss. Apologize to the cat. Readjust the blankets. Skip the rest of the pre-reading dance.

Ready for chapter one and my escape with a trusted author in a cool series: Here we go:

A tiny, tiny piece of a Cheeto or Dorito or cheese cracker falls onto my chest. Maybe all three. (Spoiler alert: I did find all three...)

"Are you KIDDING ME??!!"

A cat cries out in terror.

Another mishap from Little Miss Muse and a few choice words of her own. Not in English. Not in French. I didn't ask for a translation.

But no reply from the living room.

Second chapter? Cheese powder smudge highlighting an entire word.

In Chapter Three, he had peanut butter and must've gotten interrupted because the page is dog-eared.

And Chapter Fifteen? I don't even know—sending to the crime lab for forensic analysis.

When the Hubs finally made his way down the hall to the bedroom, I was livid. Covered in crumbs. The bed looks like I've had a gorge fest. Many, many cheese-puff highlights throughout the pages. I've never experienced such a frustrating "escape." Going along, wondering where the next turn will take the main characters. What new cemetery they may visit. Where the next twist may be.

And the next twist turns out to be a Cheese Curl!

"Really?"

He shrugs. "I *told you* it was going to be rough."

Well, *then* it made sense.

I've read books from the library that have been through *hundreds* of people without this much STUFF crammed into the pages!

But hey, at least he's enjoying his escape. Everyone deserves a few moments of peace with some perfectly paranormal dinner guests. Or lunch buddies, as the case may be.

I gave him another paperback that I'm not so attached to (I don't personally know the author, and I read it FIRST!) to keep him occupied until she gets the next novel out. (That was not a nag for her to get the next novel out. Not a nag at all...)

So while you all go check out R.W. Wallace's page, I'm off to source e-readers for the Hubs — complete with a bulk supply of screen wipes.

Then, I've got about ten more chapters to go. If my deductive skills are on point, tonight's offerings will consist of one more murder, three new clues, a new ghost, ham grease, Twinkie fluff, and a hint of Cheeto dust.

Looking Back: The Hubs has declared he read more in 2022 than he has in his whole adult life. Kudos to him! R.W. Wallace has new titles out—you can find her website listed in the appendix.
I've since started collections of other author's books, and, yes, I read them first. I can't bear to see the orange-yellow carnage on the page if Hubs enjoyed them before me...
Little Miss has a crush on a Sultan, another author's muse. She swears she has a stack of those books hidden somewhere in the house—maybe that's what's in the freezer...

165

LAMENTING THE LIZARDS

E very year when the weather breaks, the little, little...
Hang on a second.

Let me Google it. I know it's not a gecko or a salamander...
Wait just a second.

Skink. They're called skinks. Five-lined skinks to be precise (and boy, am I glad that's an 'i' and not an 'a' in that lizard's name, or y'all'd be emailing me post-haste) come out all around our property to sun themselves and soak up the heat along our brick house and window ledges. (And the photo does, indeed, show a five-lined skink. I thought I'd have to compromise and use an insurance lizard for this week's blog.)

Well, in Indiana, sometimes the weather breaks, and sometimes it reboots three times and then you get frozen five-lined skinks, but that's another matter.

We have a three-season room addition on our home, built before we moved in. One of the huge selling points. It's on a slab and not very well insulated. The original exterior brick makes up one wall, and the other three are mostly windows. We might turn on a little heat out there if we're hosting Christmas or some such goofy nonsense where I actually have to cook and *at the same time* pay attention to what I'm cooking. That way, if I do accidentally give someone food poisoning, at least they were able to enjoy the best room in the house while they partook of the poisonous feast.

I'll occasionally let the cats out there in the winter. The sun shines the brightest in the mornings in that space, and they catch sight of the sunbeams. You know, those rays of warmth that dogs and cats alike seek out as if the beams are their species' long-lost mothership calling them back to their home planet.

Anyway, when the weather really does break, humans and felines all enjoy that room quite a bit and I leave the doors open to the main living room and enjoy the breeze.

The other day, I was doing my get-the-room-ready cleanup of bugs and general dust layers from it being mostly closed for a while. It was a typical Indiana spring day with a rogue snow shower blanketing the freshly sprung dandelions with a decent inch of snow. But it was melting, and my spirits were rising, so clean the room.

I moved one of the cat's little napping huts (don't make fun... I'd have a napping hut or three if I could get away with it) and there it was.

And there went my mood, melting faster than the spring snow.

A petrified lizard tail.

I squawked. All three cats had re-gathered in the room with me after the vacuum stopped its evil sucking. "Guys, it's too early for lizards. Waaay too early."

Poor guy (or gal) probably came in about the same time the dandelions popped out and got his season of sunning off to a bad start. Hopefully he lived to tell the others not to slip into the cracks around the back of the Paul house. Stay in the front. Out of sight. Out of mind.

Last season, I can't tell you how many tails I swept up. Stella Marie even brought me one no bigger than the tip of my little finger — still wiggling. I never know if the lizards have been consumed or if the "eject and run!" method of survival worked in their favor.

I feel sorry for the things, I really do. I enjoy watching them sun themselves; many have the shimmering blue tails—well, the ones at our address have stubs, but you get my drift. They scale the bricks with their little suction-cup toes. Sometimes I sit out front and if I'm still enough, some even emerge from the cracks in the sidewalks and run over my feet. I always warn them, though they don't listen.

"Stay in the front. Spread the word."

My cats are well-fed. They lack for nothing (napping huts, right?) They only hunt for the sport of it. Criminals, all three of them.

A few seasons ago, one of them managed to bring in the other half of the lizard (or the other 80-85% of him, I suppose) — still wiggling. He left a slender, bloody trail from the doorway (his tail had been eaten or dropped in the sunroom) where he skittered all the way to the cats' feeding station and hid under their water dish mat.

Clearly not the brightest bulb in the box, but hey. He was traumatized.

Who knows what I'd do if some creature caused me to eject a body part.

Come to think of it, I've been in no fewer than seven situations in the last ten days where that defense mechanism could've come in handy. Drop an appendage faster than a five-lined skink and run.

Drop several appendages. Who needs them anyway? I'd have to learn dictation as I'd have no hands to type out new fiction, but... to get out of anxiety-producing social situations? Or mind-numbingly dull events? I'd consider it a viable option...

Then skitter off to the safety of fuzzy unicorn blankets, unfinished manuscripts, and murderous cats.

Poor little lizards...

Looking Back: That particular napping hut had to be tossed. The cats now
have a napping Christmas Tree bed which they take turns in.
It's the end of January as I re-read this. In just a couple of months, the cats
and I will be at this activity once again:
Warn the skinks. Scare the skinks. Sweep up parts of the skinks.
But it'll be spring and that'll be a good thing.

Little Miss Muse would like to try her hand at making mud pies and could I please order some pretty purple flowers to put on top of her dirt crust.
"Like a grave plot right in our back yard, you see." She seems proud of this analogy.
I think we need to discuss this plan...

166

PREMEDITATED PATIENCE

The things on my list of things I'm running low on are the only things I'm *not* running low on.

Does that make sense? I may have just confused myself—not hard at all, these days.

Items I'm in short supply of at the moment:

- Months in the year
- Days in the week
- Minutes in an hour
- Decision-making power (I have hit a wall. Right, left, middle? I don't know. Where are the Reese's cups?)
- Filters (the kinds for your mouth and your facial expressions that protect those around you from what you really think)
- Eyebrow girdles (much like a filter, but it's the mental strap you place around your forehead to keep your eyebrows from lifting all the way to your hairline when you don't believe what you're being told)

- Neck braces (to prevent Bobble Head Syndrome, again, stopping odd tilting of one's head and general bobbing when you don't believe what you're being told)
- Sleep (middle insomnia is still raging its head)
- Energy (may have something to do with that sleep thing)
- Rows (I have gobs of ducks; I'm down to not enough rows to put the little quackers in)
- Notebooks (Little Miss begs to differ, having just tripped over a pile of them in the corner of the office. I beg her to check her "low" stock of lavender glitter. She's quiet now. Touché.)
- Patience (the variety needed on the spur of the moment to deal with impromptu drama)
- Reese's cups (of the white and milk chocolate varieties)
- Grape bubblegum (I succumbed to the Muse's favorite always-low treat. I think grape bubblegum is nasty, but it keeps her happy. One must always keep the Muse happy.)
- Magic Wands That Work!

BUT PERHAPS THE thing I'm in desperate need of the most is Premeditated Patience. That variety of longsuffering one must muster up when attending an event/outing/appointment and one would "rather not," or "can't even," but alas, one must persevere. Muster up a smile or at least a concerned face. Nod appropriately so as not to break one's neck brace. Only extend the eyebrows as far as the girdle will allow and no further.

Premeditated patience requires the following:

- Lay out the outfit the night before to ease the burden of decision-making the day of.
- Pre-fluff the fuzzy unicorn blanket before leaving the house to ensure it's ready to receive a weary soul into its warmth upon return.

- Discuss with the felines that one of them must be *The Cat of the Day* and join the weary soul in the fuzzy unicorn blanket upon the master's return.
- Position the Reese Cup, fresh notebook, and a fine-tipped pen near the Post-Event Location (be that the sofa, the recliner, or the bed).
- Discuss with Little Miss Muse the necessity of quiet and calm. No new story ideas will be accepted for a period of four hours after any event requiring premeditated patience. Muses are not to wear their clip-clopping violet stilettos during this time, nor are they to pop grape-scented bubbles in their master's face. (Little Miss is furious, now. She says I'm not her master. I say she's my creation. She says I'm her charge. We'll have to come up with a more acceptable term for our relationship—which will also require premeditated patience).*

---

*THIS IS AS FAR as I got in writing this blog before a family emergency whisked me away for nearly a week. I was already running low on certain mental capacities, then boom!

In and out of the emergency room. In and out of hospital rooms. In and out of the car so many times to take care of business, I can't even count. (I lost the car twice on Wednesday. Never parking in the same spot and lack of sleep/energy... I hope I gave a good show to anyone who saw me meandering with my remote raised above my head, pushing the lock button, hoping to catch the honk of my weary SUV in the lot.)

My thoughts drifted back several times to how patience regenerates. Mine regenerates oh, so slowly, and if I've spent patience with a patient or a doctor or medical facility, I've no patience for anything else. A "hit the wall" kind of mental block. Thankfully, the end-all crisis of last Monday/Tuesday has softened down to a dull, concerned roar for the moment. But wow.

My head is spinning, and now I really do need that neck brace.

Here's hoping your week doesn't deplete your stock of filters or eyebrow girdles...

Looking Back: As in so many of these blogs, when I first started re-reading, I had a hard time remembering even writing the piece. Until I got to the interruption.

It's been 258 days since that medical event for my loved one and was fraught with frustration. And would you know it, the rest of the CIRCUS never quieted down during this event.

Little Miss got real quiet real fast during the start of that ordeal. Scary when the Muse goes mute...

167

WINNABLE DECK

Ages ago (and I do mean multiple decades' worth of years), I used to sit at my grandma's kitchen table and watch my mother play solitaire. I was fascinated with the shuffling of the cards and the way she dealt out an ever-growing pyramid of piles, nice and neat.

I was equally confused as I was fascinated. What card goes under what? Are Jacks or Queens more important? What goes on that magical Ace pile hovering above the main play area? Does it matter if it's a club or a spade? Finally, she taught me how to play this lonely soul's game of kill-time-with-52-pieces-of-cardstock.

I became quite proficient at dealing out the playing field. I also became quite proficient at fudging the rules when the necessity arose —I was, after all, only cheating myself and didn't even have a sibling to brag to about my false victories. Alternating red and black cards couldn't be messed with, of course, but that didn't stop me from sneaking an unturned card from the bottom of one of the piles or "accidentally" placing a Club on the Spade pile.

(It was forever before I could call those shapes by their proper names. I remember calling Clubs "clovers" and Spades "the pointy ones." Then, in high school, I learned euchre, where Clubs are Clubs unless they become a Spade because the only-once-in-a-while powerful Jacks said they could do that—and then only sometimes. Otherwise, the Aces ruled. Hearts and Diamonds joined the melee and would switch their teams up anytime they pleased, or so it would seem to a beginning euchre player...)

I'd put the cards away for months—even years—at a time while life got busy. Then, once in a while, I'd shuffle and deal out another round or five and kill some time.

Fast-forward many more years, well into the digital age, and now one doesn't even have to shuffle. Or worry that a cat or dog or Muse might mess up seven carefully stacked piles. All one needs to do is open an app and push a button or click a mouse. (I find playing digital cards to be much like reading ebooks. It's certainly convenient and sometimes enjoyable, but there's nothing like the feel of real paper in your hands.)

With the many, many hours of waiting and uncertainty with medical crises over the last six months, and given my limited attention span and brain power, I found a solitaire app and began to play a hand here or there in a random hallway or waiting room. Something to do other than fuss or fidget. Something to focus on rather than the news that may be coming with the next professional through the door. Something that only took a few minutes instead of, say, trying to write a short story or blog post in between nurse visits.

The first thing I noticed is that the app won't let me cheat.

The second thing I noticed is that computers aren't fair. Like some evil feline mastermind coded the program.

The third thing? The option for a "winnable deck." (Well, maybe that's how you cheat.)

I could choose, if I wanted, to have the app deal me out just the right cards in just the right way so that there was a surefire way to win the game. What evil mind game was this? If it deals me a winnable deck, that doesn't guarantee I won't flub it up and lose anyway. Then what would happen to my already fragile psyche?

Evil cats. That's who programmed this app.

I was dumbfounded. A surefire win. Where's the fun in that? And

Little Miss, who'd reluctantly accompanied me to all these medical events, said, "Where's the fun in the cheating you'd be doing if you could?"

Touché.

Then she added as she pulled out a long string of grape bubble gum and twirled it around her fat little finger, "You'd do yourself and me quite nicely if you'd give us some winnable decks."

"What?" I took the gum from her lest it ended up under a seat or on the bottom of a urologist's loafer.

"Set us up for a win, why don't you?"

You know, I hate it when the Muse is right about life affairs outside of the writing desk. Especially when the Muse is a little imp in a purple tutu who should be working on the next story plot instead of telling me how to live life. I start to argue, but she interrupts.

"It's either that or you put away the writing for as long as you put away that first deck of solitaire cards. Wait till the air clears and the planets align."

Ouch. She's right.

She's full of snark and sarcasm, having done two perfect pirouettes on that punch line about the planets.

We attempt to set up winnable decks: Lay out clothes the night before work or school, preplan meals, put the bills on autopay...

If all goes as it should, the moves add up to a successful day. (Or, in the Paul household, the cats knock the clean black slacks onto the floor to use as a bed for six hours, the refrigerator goes out five hours after purchasing a load of groceries, and the autopay bill was taken out four times by some tech glitch—likely programmed by Kitty the Terrible, but hey. We tried.)

Little Miss Muse is lovingly referring to my haphazard approach to the writing life since the beginning of the year. Goals have gone by the wayside. Streaks have fizzled to streams then to trickles then to nothing but annoying little guilty drips. Piles of notebooks and new pens sit untouched. Calendars hung with the greatest of excitement at the end of December remain mostly blank, a reminder that Life stacked the deck in its own favor for the first five months of 2022.

As my shoulders slump with this realization, she crawls into my lap. Something she rarely does. She reaches for my cheeks with her chonky hands.

"It's okay. Life happens. Life sucks. Life is a game. Life is a circle. AND IT MOOOOVES US ALLLLL!" The cats flee the room as she breaks out her best Elton John.

I attempt to shove her off my lap to no avail. "Will you please—"

"Shhh... We got this. Let's redeal. And if that deal doesn't work, we'll reshuffle." She shrugs. "Or start drawing from the bottom of the pile..."

I laugh and place my hands over hers, my tears (from reality and from her off-key singing) wet our fingers. And mix with the purple taffy goo she'd left behind on my face...

Several events have landed on my calendar that I'm looking forward to. Ones that can reset, recharge, and redeal the mess that was the first half of 2022.

With Goo-Gone in my Amazon cart along with a fresh stash of grape-flavored-everything, we'll start a new winnable deck. At least the first few cards, anyway.

I'll toss in an apology card for the unfortunate urologist and call it a good start to a new deal.

Looking Back: Funny how I thought, 135 days into 2022 that this would be as bad as it would get.

Oh, honey. There wouldn't be enough trick card decks to stack '22 in our favor even if I'd hired the top ten magicians in the world.

Some years are like that.

I had to learn (and am still learning) to look for salvageable moments and be grateful my three cats don't know computer code...

Little Miss wants to learn code. I pointed out a few posts ago she wanted to try mudpies.

"Why not both?" she whines.

I can think of a thousand reasons why. National security being top of the list...

168

CURSED CURSOR

It's blinking at me.

I think it's keeping time by the second. I've sat here long enough staring at it and four of its cousins, so I should know. A steady tick, tick, ticking away of moment after moment. Taunting.

Laughing.

Daring me to write.

Something. Anything.

It knows I have deadlines.

Day job deadlines. Dream job deadlines. Household and family deadlines. All with their respective cursors.

Blink, blink, blink.

It knows I can't stand the haphazard tapping of Little Miss's high heels, the slurping of the cats as they bathe themselves on the bookshelf above my desk, or the random throttle revving of Mr. Redneck Guy and his dilapidated motorcycle down the road. Even the birds tweeting outside my office window are getting on my nerves.

Not to mention the donkey calls of the, well, donkey from the farm two properties down. (Why? Why a donkey? I can hear him braying over the air conditioning.)

So it just keeps blinking.

Steady, silent.

I fear it may become sentient, read Poe's "The Tell-Tale Heart" and start thumping right out of the monitor, driving me the rest of the way insane. (I worded that very carefully. It's a short drive, and a few may argue I'm already insane. I can own that.)

The cursed cursor. One is waiting for me to DO SOMETHING on each of four other documents. Waiting for me to finish up, get started, continue on, or perhaps have a unique idea, then save/close/send the dumb document and move on already.

And lest anyone confuse the tiny vertical blinking line in a Word Document with the three small dots or the twirling circles, let me elaborate. The three small dots means YOU'RE doing something and I'm waiting on you. The twirly thingamajigs indicate SOFTWARE is doing something and I'm waiting on it.

The evil vertical blinker, on the other hand, is waiting on ME to do something. Anything. Usually of a productive nature. Usually requiring the stringing together of coherent words one after another to form likewise coherent sentences, then paragraphs, then scenes or blog sections or conclusions to letters to insurance companies, doctors or clients or, or, or...*

*AND RIGHT HERE, I temporarily lost the ability to be coherent. Because four other blinking cursors in four other documents are waiting on me. They've synchronized their blinks, creating a nearly audible thumping away of the time as midnight approaches, and I'm still stuck back on something that should've been done Tuesday.

A quick glance at the calendar tells me this is the last full week of May. A pang of panic has started in my toes and creeps up my spine.

Another document opens. A fifth cursor adds itself to the silent melee.

So, before the five start taking cues from my ducks-not-in-a-row and the unicorns un-watered, and before they start multiplying like bitty blinking bunnies, I bid you adieu.

May your vertical cursors not blink at you for more than a few seconds, may those folks behind your three little dots send their responses quickly, and may your twirling thingamajigs spit your content out with lightning speed.

Looking Back: I try really hard not to get myself into those "every aspect of life needs me right now" moments. Those times where a half dozen people and the screen itself crosses their arms and taps their toes bidding me to hurry up and solve their problems.

When the CIRCUS is hopping, though, sometimes things fall by the wayside and pile up. Cursors, three little dots, and twirling thingamajigs all converging and conspiring against the clock on the wall and the days in the calendar.

Little Miss Muse says she's glad she doesn't have to deal with such things. She just lives life from one grape bubble to the next and by the thread of her nearly-thread-bare tutu.

169

SOMETIMES SNAILS

I've been told I'm one of the hardest people on the planet to buy things for.

Family and friends typically stress over those gift-giving occasions like birthdays, anniversaries, and Christmas.

I don't—they do.

Perhaps I'm hard to buy for because I don't really care about the stuff money can buy. I'd rather have peace and calm and an afternoon with a cat with a fuzzy unicorn blanket (of which I have plenty—both cats and fuzzy unicorn blankets). Another reason is that if I see something I want, I typically get it for myself, thereby robbing others of the joy of gift wrapping that bobble, blanket, pen, or whatnot themselves.

When I show interest in an object, say unicorns, I tend to receive lots of unicorn gifts. I have a small unicorn collection now. (Not by any stretch as large as the one that I had as a child. That one likely pushed 500 pieces...)

I also have a fountain pen collection, and I enjoy the occasional "treasure hunt" to locate vintage tropical bird figurines. They go nicely in our sunroom.

I also like owls. I'd like to go to one of those owl nurseries and play with orphaned owlettes that have learned how to ride mini skateboards. What fun! Or I'd like to spend an afternoon at a rescue that rehabilitates injured owls. That would be enlightening.

My family knows I like owls. The Hubs bought several nice ones for me for a birthday or anniversary here and there. Right now, they're in a drawer, though. The unicorns are in a box.

Because Castiel Monroe, my grandkitty, is insane, and when the Adult-ish Male Child drops by with this cat (who loves car rides more than I love unicorns), Cass takes out his insanity all over my house.

So for the protection of owls, horned horses, and Cass, I've put them away until the supply chain loosens up and the curio cabinet I want becomes available. (The vintage toucans and parrots are safely behind such a barrier. At least I think they are...)

Not long ago, the Hubs and Adult-ish Male Child accompanied me to pick out flowers (I have no idea why I'm trying real, live flowers again. But alas... it was something to do.) I like purple. Little Miss likes purple. But sometimes, just sometimes, I'd like a different hue.

But the Hubs and Adult-ish Male Child (especially him, though I can't figure why), would point me toward purple pansies, purple petunias, purple, purple, purple.

Sometimes red might be nice.

But we already started with purple, so here we go. Four purple petunia plants to match the pretty purple pansies I got for Mother's Day. (Dear Hubs, they really are pretty, and I really do like them. This post isn't about purple pansies...)

Then the Hubs sees an end-cap display of various critter planters. "Hey, look! There's an owl!" (He loves pointing out all the owls when we're out). "Do you like those?"

"They're okay."

"Do you want one?"

"No."

"Why?"

"I like the snails better." I wasn't trying to be difficult or obstinate, but I suppose I came across that way.

To which the Hubs says he can't see any snails. Because he was focused on the owls.

"I don't want any of those planters, actually."

"But they're owls."

And snails. Don't be snobbish with the snails. Besides, I didn't want any new planters because that would've meant having to pick out more flowers. Purple, probably.

And then the Adult-ish Male Child says he would've picked owls out for me, too.

But hey, guys? Sometimes snails would be nice. Sometimes red works, too.

Sometimes changing things up makes life interesting. Get out of the rut.

(Little Miss Muse begs to differ. She has her standard stash of Muse fuel and fidget items, and she declares she will not deviate from grape bubble gum, purple soda, firecrackers and lavender stilettos. Purple glitter is also the only glitter that works... She cries from the top of the bookshelf that she's not in a rut; these things are vital to her creative process.)

I didn't realize *I was* in a total rut with my go-to read-for-enjoyment choices until I signed up for a class in July. The required reading is entirely outside my preferred genres. Titles I would never have considered giving a second thought. Because they weren't owls or unicorns.

They were snails. Red snails, even.

Per the class's instructions, I won't discuss particulars here, but folks, there's a wide, wide world of cool stories out there.

This summer, try reading something outside your "norm." You may always prefer owls and unicorns, but sometimes snails can pack an impressive punch.

Looking Back: That class taught me a lot and was grand fun. The required reading reminded me Grisham, Koontz, and Child aren't the only ones in the game. As rough as '22 was, I thoroughly enjoyed branching out my reading...

...as long as I read the paperback before the Hubs could get to it with his cheesy fingers, that is.

Little Miss Muse moves closer to the freezer and spreads her chubby arms out wide. Blocking it.
Now I'm almost convinced that she and the Sultan are up to something.
Possibly a collaboration.
Or she's reading smut.
We'll have to have a talk about this...

LICKING LIGHTBULBS

Malachi Maxwell is, by far, the most mentally challenged animal we've ever owned. He makes up for it by having a heart that's, by far, the purest.

I blame his lack of brain function on the rough start he had as a kitten—abandoned, abused, malnourished, and nearly died three times before we finally brought him into the house:

1. Hammock net mishap
2. Fell out of tree
3. Fell out of tree again

While his two sisters thrived and succeeded at anything they put their little paws to, poor Malachi would lay to the side and just watch. By the time he would muster up enough gumption to try the activity the girls were involved with, he'd forget what to do, become clumsy, get his toes stuck in the carpet/tree bark/my clothes, and go back to watching.

We adopted him. He was so needy, I'd tuck him into an old purse, sling it around my neck and keep him close while I worked lest he try any of the following:

1. Fall off the table
2. Fall off the desk
3. Fall off the bookcase
4. Fall off the cat tree
5. Fall off...

Somehow, this poor boy didn't get the memo that cats are to land on their feet. He never relaxed into the fall—he'd full-on panic and "keep" falling, hitting every object/protrusion/item he could on the way down. Like watching a Looney Tune goof in slow motion.

As he grew, he tried to damage himself further:

1. Head stuck in reusable shopping bag handles
2. Head stuck in Walmart sacks
3. Whole body stuck in the box springs
4. Concussion on oven door that I slammed shut a mere microsecond before he tried to leap into the 400-degree oven
5. Toes from all feet stuck in carpet, in epic Twister board fashion

He also has things that he "can't even."

He "can't even" with strange men.

He "can't even" with dingers, buzzers, or alarms (in real life or on the television).

He "can't even" when I'm not in sight.

During these times, the poor guy runs away, or—my favorite—sits down, throws his eyes toward the ceiling, and rolls his head back and forth. When I say he "can't even," he really can't.

But his newest way to damage himself and curl my toes has to do with lightbulbs. One of his favorite spots is above my desk atop the bookcase. He rests there while I work or write. And, as you can see from the photo, there's a nice, bright lamp. It gives off gentle heat, and for the longest time, he'd just lay close to it.

Until recently.

When he started licking the lightbulb.

I can't even.

When my kids were young, I'd utter sentences like:

1. Don't hammer yo-yo halves to the shed floor.
2. Why are you crying? There's nothing to cry about.
3. Don't drive the lawnmower up the side of the house.
4. Don't bite her.
5. I don't care if he's staring at you.
6. Who stinks?
7. Barbie Dolls aren't toilet wands.
8. I don't mess up your favorite things, why must you mess up mine?
9. Why did you microwave my pad of blue Post-It Notes?
10. Don't fall asleep while I'm at the grocery store or he'll microwave my blue Post-It Notes.
11. It hurts because you've cut off your entire thumb tip.

(Okay, some of those weren't directed at my children; some of those were pleas to the Hubs...)

Now, I find myself uttering similar phrases to our kitties:

1. Don't bite her.
2. Why are you gagging? There's nothing to gag about.
3. What are you staring at?
4. Who's biting the banana butts?
5. Who stinks?
6. Don't put your head in Walmart sacks.
7. Don't lay on the stove.
8. Why are you crying?
9. Put your toes back in.
10. I don't puke on your favorite things, why must you puke on mine?

And my latest plea?

1. Please, oh, please, Malachi Maxwell. Don't lick lightbulbs.

And it's not just the one near the top of the bookcase that he's after.

He's after the lamp on the end table.

He's after my reading light near my bed.

Basically, if it glows, he wants to lick it.

I'll scold him. Move him away from the temptation. Turn off the bulbs. He wants to lick them so badly that when I stop him from doing so, he "can't even" and rolls his head and eyes at me.

I don't know why he wants to lick lightbulbs. Maybe he's trying to catch a clue or a hint, or an idea...

Hey, wait a minute.

Perhaps that's the answer to the current writer's block.

Perhaps a nice taste of illumination would grease my imagination gears enough that Little Miss Muse can start working her magic...

"If you start licking lightbulbs, I'll have you committed. It'll be the first time a Muse has gone to court to win guardianship over their author, but, if you lick lightbulbs, I bet the judge would grant it to me." Little Miss, reading over my shoulder as I type this, is disappointed in me. "Would you like a roommate or are we springing for a private padded room?"

Before I can snark back at her, she pulls out her firecracker and bejeweled Zippo lighter and adds, "I've got all the ideas you'll ever need, lady."

I glance up at the bookcase where Malachi has assumed the position, head over the glow of the lamp, mouth opening...

Oh, the drama.

I can't even.

Looking Back: We still have lightbulb issues. We also have tissue box issues. And dish towel issues. And his blanky must be just so before he can relax.

Poor Malachi Maxwell.
Little Miss, given the year we had in '22, believes it may be time to rethink whether I should attempt a mouthful of glowing glass to get us going again.
No, Little Miss. I think we'll be okay.

171

FAVORITE NEW WORD

Warning: For those with low tolerances for bathroom humor, just skip this one.

Autocorrect has been a real pill the last few days. Either that or I need glasses.

I know I'm brain-fried from life events, daily chaos, and the sweltering days of... Spring? (as I write this the official start of summer is still six days away and already 93 degrees with a 108 heat index). Add to that the occasional hot flash, and, yeah. Beth is brain fried (so a short but maybe not-so-sweet post this week).

But, still. I mean. When I'm trying to type *suppose*, and I'm only off by a single letter, there's no way any intelligent AI should suppose I'm trying to say *sensual*.

So I reached up to make sure I'm wearing my glasses. Yes. I was, and I know I didn't get that many letters off.

Sensual someone gets the wrong idea?

I mean, suppose someone gets the wrong idea?

My favorite all-time autocorrect occurred this week. The sentence was ~~sensual~~ supposed to read "We shall see."

Autocorrect decided to teach me a new word and corrected it to "We shapp see."

Shapp?

What even is a shapp? Why is this nonsense word even in the AI's dictionary?

Turns out Milton Shapp was a Pennsylvania governor back in the '40s. Upon digging a little further, Merriam-Webster doesn't list *shapp* as a word.

But the Urban Dictionary does…

Shapp is a verb. "To lose any/all control of bowels, especially to defecate on floor."

Another meaning: "To do something bad and then hang around a few hours, not helping clean up."

No matter what you think of the Urban Dictionary, it has saved me from making a fool of myself a couple of times. I simply cannot keep up with the slang and changing meanings of words and phrases.

Apparently, Merriam-Webster can't either. And it seems like anyone younger than me by more than five years speaks English, but not *really* English.

Also, given some of the Urban Dictionary's front-page, featured definitions, I've clearly lived a sheltered life. (Note to self: Have a culturally astute editor read anything written for YA audiences and younger… jeez.)

At any rate, shapp was a well-timed autocorrect given our recent life events. Either definition would fit. I'll let you use your imagination to protect the medical and emotional privacy of those involved.

The Hubs, the Adult-ish Male Child, and I threw around fun banter, changing the part of speech and adding suffixes and prefixes to the word at length. We needed the laugh.

We laughed so hard that I feared one of us might give a demonstration of our new vocabulary word.

Either or both definitions.

I'll let you use your imagination.

Another autocorrect turned "About ten o'clock" into *ataraxia*.

Well then.

This one Merriam-Webster has under control.

Ataraxia: A state of freedom from emotional disturbance and anxiety.

So, ataraxia is an antonym of shapp.

It's also an antonym for hot flashes and 108-degree heat indices.

I wish to attain this ataraxia condition. It seems a might more favorable to the other conditions I and the ones closest to me are currently dealing with.

Ataraxia. A favorite new word!

And though *summer* is *not* one of my favorite words (or events), I do wish you an ataraxia-ish start to the season — with no shapping about (either definition!).

Looking Back: I actually left a note to myself about the editor... Someone who knows more than I do about slang and current buzzwords. Help me keep my foot out of my mouth... or at least out of my manuscripts.
Little Miss Muse thinks dictionaries are overrated and language should be felt more than coded into little black marks on a page.
This must be why two/to/2/too show up willy nilly when she's on a roll and I only serve as her transcriptionist. The first time I typed 2 for too, I thought it was because of lack of sleep.
Nope. Just Little Miss shapping about in English.

172

I'M ON IT

We're nearly halfway through 2022. Yesterday was the first day of summer. Supposedly the longest day of the year. And, boy was it loooongggg. Complete with seven hours of IV hydration in the ER for the Hubs, another two hours on the road, and an hour waiting on the pharmacy—in triple-digit heat indices. At one point, little black warning spots flashed around the periphery of my vision, telling me a bad thing was about to happen.

Then I lost my keys. Keys I'd had in my hand as I loaded a few easy-on-the-newly-hydrated-one's things into the car. I felt the keyring slide off my finger. Figured they were in the passenger floorboard. Nope.

Figured they landed in one of the sacks. Nope.

Perhaps they slid directly into the popsicle box. After flinging popsicles all over the car... Nope.

After fifteen minutes of searching the same spots over and over and multiple black flashes (Can black spots even flash? Why yes, yes they can), I opened the back door, got eye level with the floor, and saw the key ring lodged in the perfect "can't see it from any angle but this very one with my butt sticking out" position.

I was on it the whole time.

Little Miss Muse points out that if I was really *On It*, I'd have not lost the keys right under my fanny to begin with.

Then, this morning, eight large buzzards in our backyard took turns showing off their massive wing spans—not in flight, but in a standing-guard position—and staring at our house. It sent chills down my spine. Little Miss thinks they're smelling the rotting manuscripts growing moldy black hair in the To Be Done files on my computer.

A quick look at my writing numbers at this halfway-through-the-year mark sent my shoulders slumping past my hips and chills down my spine. Scarier than the eight buzzards, those numbers.

What happened? We're halfway through the year and *that's* my number?

Well, turns out *I'm On It* is the culprit for this lower-than-hoped-for word count.

A loved one with a fall and an out-of-rhythm heart? I'm on it.

Full-time day job with folks who can't follow directions? I'm on it.

A second lady with newly diagnosed debilitating seizures? I'm on it.

Five+ dollar a gallon gas and the near-futile search for cheaper transportation? I'm on it.

A third loved one with bilateral foot tumors? And a fall? I'm on it.

The Hubs and his life-altering gut flare? I'm on that, too. Until those little black specks ground me to the house for a couple of days.

I'm sitting in a camping chair in our front yard now. I think the buzzards out back have moved on to other roadkill, leaving my digital stink to me and Little Miss, but the front feels safer at any rate...

I'm letting the breeze blow away some of the stress. Birds chirping. Maple leaves dancing overhead.

I have two documents open. I type a few sentences here, then go to another document and add ideas to my "Re-start List." The good thing about word counts is that what's written won't go stale, and what's to-be-written will be waiting for me when my brain isn't foggy — and my loved ones aren't trying to qualify for Synchronized Imploding Health as if it's an elite Olympic sport.

Someday, I'll report this:

Finish the short stories I abandoned as I flew out to another emergency room? I'm on it.

Send those shorts to the proofreader? I'm on it.

Finish the YA trilogy? I'm on it.

Covers for the new trilogy? I'm on it.

Churning out content and having a blast doing it? I'm on that, too.

A tiny sweat bee likes the corner of my laptop — he's hung out with me from the start of this blog. His friend likes my knee, and another of his relatives enjoys flitting around my knuckles as I type. I feel one kissing my cheek. How sweet of them to keep me such lovely company.

Do sweat bees live in ground nests? If they do, I'm probably on it.

Looking Back: The halfway mark turned out to be the highlight of the year, but not the peak of the stress by a long shot. As for my restart list, I did finish those abandoned shorts. Even sent them to the proofreader. I have churned out new short story collections and kept up with the blog posts. The YA trilogy is set to be finished this year... unless life bursts open a nest of Murder Hornets and, well. We'll deal with that if it happens.

As for the other events: The hearts, brains, and feet are all stable and/or healing/healed. Day job remains full of folks who can't follow directions. Gas is under four bucks, and we found a fuel-efficient car for the Hubs. The Hubs, 209 days from the original post, is cautiously stable. Crohn's sucks.

Little Miss Muse is glad he's better. She doesn't mind his presence and he does nothing to thwart her antics. She likes his peaceful demeanor.

I'm so glad my Muse approves of my mate. I can't imagine what would happen if the two came to blows.

173

PRETTY ON THE TOP SIDE

Little Miss Muse and I (over)packed our bags, boarded a 7:10 a.m. direct flight to Vegas Saturday, and now she's finally overcome enough of the jet-lag lazies to feel like dropping a few lines of snark that she can take credit for.

Most of you know what's been going on behind the scenes at Paul Central (If you're behind, check out "I'm On It") — and most of it ain't been pretty.

Pretty ugly medical issues.

Pretty ugly stress levels.

Pretty ugly day-job deadlines.

Even the cats were giving me the stink-eye (though this could be because the suitcase was out and they weren't allowed to pack themselves into it).

I put a lot of pressure on the Vegas trip, not in the least of which is rest and relaxation — two concepts totally foreign to me as of late. Long overdue.

So, for the next couple of weeks, I'm not "ON" any of my normal stuff.

Because things were getting pretty ugly. And it was time for a breather.

My view from the plane before takeoff was overcast. Nothing special. Some would even say an ugly, dull sky.

But that all changed with our increase in altitude.

Oceans and oceans of gorgeous clouds. It was like a bird's-eye view of an entirely different world. I'd gaze out the window for several minutes at a time, then look away to chat with my seatmate (a very kind preschool teacher from a Vegas suburb) for a bit. When I'd return to my view, the "scenery" changed. Different formations. Whisps, and puffs, and chubby glacier-like beings floating in a sea of misty haze. This lasted until we crossed the Rockies, then the magic was behind us...

(Sorry for the grainy photo, folks, but the pilot wouldn't pull the plane over for me to get a better shot of those clouds.)

It's always like that. The clouds. They may be dull, even ominous, on the bottom, but they're pretty on the top side. I've flown above the clouds before, but this was hands-down the winner.

It's the whole "silver lining" thing. Another thing that's been short in supply, right along with rest and relaxation.

But time away gives perspective. A chance to stretch the imagination and enjoy new experiences and build new relationships...

To see the good in the last six months. Not just the ugly.

So far, my travel buddy and I have navigated more time zones than should exist (her far more than me; I don't even know how she's upright, quite frankly), mastered the art of calling an Uber, and braved the neighborhood Vegas Walmart. (If you're wondering, a Walmart is a Walmart is a Walmart).

On the horizon is a lot of fun, a lot of new memories to be made, and a writing class—

"At the Shark Pool?"

Little Miss Muse is getting antsy. She's got a brand-new swimsuit. Ready to wow the lifeguards at the Golden Nugget with her impressive backstroke (doubly impressive because she has wings).

I don't let her come to the conference room with me at these things because she just causes too much chaos, and all the other writers' muses are so well behaved. I'm afraid she'll rub off on them... So I let her swim. The Golden Nugget's sharks in their impressive swimming pool require an aquatic veterinarian after her time there. It gets ugly.

So she has a blast, and I get some learning done.

The skills taught in the writing workshop next week will be amazing. My first attempts at them could very well be... ugly. But with practice, they can make my writing stronger. And the whole thing has the possibility of helping me reset some pretty serious writing goals.

I'm not naïve enough to believe that all those issues I flew away from will be resolved when I land back in Indy. As a matter of fact, some of them will be roaring quite loudly.

But I've updated my Facebook background to remind me it'll be okay.

Because it's always pretty on the top side.

Looking Back: If it hadn't have been for that two weeks away midyear last year, I would've had a literal nervous breakdown. The memories made on that trip became my "happy place" as life roared all the louder upon landing in Indy.
And the writing class, which totally kicked my butt, totally was worth it.
Little Miss has mixed feelings about that trip due to the incident at the Shark Tank. It got ugly, folks.
I ask her if the Sultan was on this trip. And did that add to some of her misbehaving when we got home.
She declines to answer.

174

WE'RE ALL CHARACTERS

In the weeks before I left for Vegas, we had severe storms, with wind that couldn't decide which direction to blow and window-pane-rattling thunder.

Typically, the cats don't seem to pay attention to storms, but for some reason, these fronts were much different. All of them fussed and fought. Amara was particularly grumpy.

And poor Stella. The thunder would start ramping up, and her eyes would go wide and turn to giant black puddles—then she'd bolt from whatever surface she was on, which was a problem when the surface was my lap or a pillow near my head.

Her claws are so sharp you don't know anything's happened until the blood starts pouring.

One evening, she'd been sleeping at my feet. The thunder crashed; she got my leg and arm and nicked my earlobe when she made a U-turn on my head to flee the room.

Another time, Stella got me on the lip with a single toe as she leapt from the coffee table, misjudged how far to go to clear the back of the couch, and used my face to assist her escape. For a good while, my lip would crack and bleed when I talked or smiled.

The storms were on my mind regarding the flights—and whether I'd be stopped and asked why I look as though I'd been in a knife fight. Given the wrecked state of the aviation sector, I figured there'd be massive delays and cancellations. But, to my relief, everything went rather smoothly.

On the day of take-off, right off the bat, I didn't follow the instructions printed on the BACK of the baggage tag from the self-check kiosk, and I had to apologize to the woman at the counter who told me people make that mistake all day long. Well, maybe print the instructions on the FRONT, but I didn't say that. I was just glad to be rid of my checked bag and went off to do one of my favorite airport activities:

People watching.

Three of the more prominent characters:

Let It Go Girl

This little girl was about three years old, with dark hair that went EVERYWHERE. She wore a tattered Ella costume over Frozen pajamas—complete with a dingy cape which someone cleverly tied up in a big knot so it wouldn't drag the ground or get caught in the moving sidewalk. I get the feeling this girl and her costume are inseparable. That when it's time to launder it, she sits and guards the machines.

She sang loudly, "Let it GOOOOOO, let it goooo" out of tune and with no concern for rhythm (and just that line from the song—she never moved on to another stanza). Dad, holding tight to her hand, was pale and had that dead stare that sleep-deprived folks often wear. Mom sauntered alongside, likewise zombified. The girl sang from the gate, sang her way past me, and many minutes later, I could still make out her melody, such as it was, among a distant crowd.

Other folks smiled and commented how cute. Yes. Cute. But those poor parents wish they could bottle that child's energy and snort it as needed.

Lonely Big Boy and His Guard

A flat-affect stewardess tended to an unaccompanied minor, a boy of about ten years old. His face was bright but guarded when he came out of the chute, and the lady pulled him off to the side. Clearly, he was ready to be picked up by a family member or friend. He wore an ID lanyard around his neck, a baseball cap that was a bit too big, and he carried an overstuffed backpack. The stewardess stood stick-straight in her navy blue uniform about two feet from him and barely spoke to him at all. Accompanying the unaccompanied was not her favorite task.

Occasionally, he'd risk a quick glance up to her face, like "Lady, where's my person at?" but she didn't offer comfort or assurance or even just chat with the kid about his favorite sport or candy or anything. He was surrounded by an airport full of people but was all alone. His countenance fell by the minute. Those 15 long minutes likely felt ten times that for the boy. The stewardess got antsy, and her posture stiffened even more. He pulled out his phone, looking desperately from the screen to the crowd ahead of him. I could feel his anxiety from twenty feet away.

Turns out, anxiety is contagious from twenty feet away.

I started looking with him. Back over my shoulder. Is someone coming? Who is coming? Mom? Cousin? Grandma?

Did Grandma get lost?

Oh, heaven help us. Grandma got lost after the TSA folks pulled her aside and frisked her because she forgot to tell them about her hip replacement hardware, and it got her flustered. She could be stroking out in a bathroom somewhere, leaving this lonely boy with the never-smiling stewardess. Stella could walk all over that guard lady's face, and she'd never have to worry about her lips bleeding when she smiled. Because she never smiled.

Finally, finally, a blonde woman with the same delicate features as the boy emerged from the crowd. The relief flooded over him—and the stewardess actually relaxed enough to allow whatever crawled up her butt to see daylight.

Then the tears came. From the blonde lady and the boy who frantically pushed them away as fast as they fell across his flushed face. Poor kid. What a scary few minutes.

Had me going, too.

And I never found out what happened to Grandma...

Oh, wait. Grandma wasn't real. She was a character.

But aren't we all characters?

As I write this, it's Friday, and we're counting down to the writing workshop, which starts the day this goes live. We'll be focusing on characters a lot in that class, too, I assume.

I think character creation is much like people watching, but with your eyes closed and your fingers on the keyboard. And then you call in Little Miss Muse and let her do the rest...

We're about to call an Uber.

And I'm sure the driver will be a character.

Looking Back: If you want, you can flip forward to #194 where
FRONT/BACK instructions plague me. I'm sensing a pattern.
All of our Uber drivers were amazing. One gentleman was anticipating the
birth of his grandchild that day—and it happened to be my son's birthday.
One spoke French, and I was thrilled to be the third wheel for that
conversation and equally thrilled that I could understand a handful of
French words (granted they were so close to English, I may have been
cheating).
We had a guy that was so proud of his Tesla that I thought his chest would
burst. That is, after we figured out how to open the doors. The guy who
drove us—
"That's where I left it." Little Miss pipes up, eyes wide. She flits about in a
rambunctious ruckus.
"Left what?"
"My shoe. That one with the violet strap and the leopard print."
"Left it where?"
"The Tesla."
"Well, it's gone now."
"But it was my favorite shoe."
"We're not going back for it. I'll get you another."
"You can't get just one shoe—"

"A pair. I'll get you another pair." Gee. *Whatever happened to "feel" the language?*

"What will I do with the right one?"

"Anything you want."

She stares at me blanky for a split second. Annnd... she's off. Rummaging in the freezer.

We must have a talk about the freezer. My Muse is her own character.

175

THEN THE DUCKS

Little Miss Muse and I packed up our bags and headed back home Friday after two weeks away completely saturated in writing and relaxation.

The trip was much needed on many fronts, even though the workshop portion was insane and triggered information-overload symptoms. Sitting at the feet of the masters and soaking in the experiences and stories from all the other writers will do that—all in a good way.

But it was time to go.

Because. You know. Little Miss Muse was at her antics once again in the Golden Nugget's shark tank swimming pool.

By day three, two lifeguards had quit, and one shark filed a complaint with the aquarium authorities that a life of being well cared for and adequately fed was just not worth the hassle of seeing that little purple imp show up every couple of years. The great fish shed twenty-two teeth at first sight of her, and his dorsal fin will *never* be the same. (Who knew bottle rockets worked underwater?)

So on day four of the workshop, Little Miss had been permanently banned from the pool. I found her in the casino, wrapped in her purple polka-dotted towel. She was dropping coins into one of the slot machines. At first, I thought she was pouting. But on closer inspection, I noticed a pile of tokens at her feet, one lavender stiletto perched atop the shiny mound of coins, and a grin working its way across her chunky face as she won time and time again.

From across the casino, two burly guys were headed in her direction. I scooped her up in her towel, grabbed the high heel, and off we went to pack lest she be arrested.

She settled down once we got to the airport and agreed it was time to return to Indiana and get to work.

I've never *not* been excited about writing, but lately, more often than not, creating new words had to take a backseat to life and emergencies, and I missed it terribly. Immersion in the topic these past two weeks was heaven, and the writing was so much fun...

Then the ducks.

My mind started going to the to-do lists and the what-next tasks waiting for me once I landed. Ducks to put back in rows. Ducks to ship elsewhere. New ducklings to the journey that needed more attention than others.

Some ducks I knew about. Some were surprises.

Some are easy, one-off issues to check off the list and move on. Many are not.

So the goal for the next couple of weeks is this: Keep above the clamor of the noisy duck rows. If one waddles off to someone else's pond, so be it. If a duck decides to stage a protest, so be it. If a duck decides he doesn't want to be a Hoosier and wishes to move to the Virgin Islands, I'll buy him a ticket.

Little Miss Muse and I have decided to close our eyes and find our happy places in times of stress and chaos. Hers is the shark pool or at the slot machine, and mine is in a world that exists only in my imagination—at least until the words topple out of my fingertips onto a manuscript...

Because I'm back to the Hoosier cornfields, where the drama never ends and there's always another duck.

Looking Back: Five hours off the plane marked the start of a devastating family matter that served as a catalyst for the worst six months of my adult life... and that duck still quacks.

The reset goals I'd set in Vegas would be an arm's length out of reach. Then three. Then five.

Little Miss Muse and I had many heart-to-hearts (about her behavior in the shark tank and my spiral into anxiety). We've come to terms that I need a pro for my head, a Couch Person so to speak—and she needs to be patient as I learn to write in chaos.

Patient meaning no run-amok story ideas at three a.m. I need sleep.

Patient meaning no tormenting the cats when I have day job deadlines. I need money for bottle rockets and replacement tutus.

And, most importantly, patient meaning no Sultans or Stilettos in my freezer!

176

STICK A FORK IN IT

I hate cooking. Just thought I'd let you know this in case you hadn't caught on to this throughout 175 previous blog posts—a good percentage of which dwell on, or at least mention in passing, my loathe for kitchen-ish activities.

When I do have to produce something edible, I look for the fastest, easiest method possible.

Baking potatoes is no exception.

And when the heat index is triple digits, I try not to use the oven. So...

I wash the potato.

Wrap it in plastic wrap.

Stick a fork in it. (I kinda like this part. There's something strangely cathartic about repetitive stabbing.)

Then toss it in the microwave.

After this step, I usually walk out of the kitchen and completely forget that I'm cooking until something dings, chimes, buzzes, or bursts into flames.

Or, in the case of this particular baked potato... Screams.

I know, I know. It was simply steam escaping from beneath the skin and the wrap. But that spud had some lungs.

At first I thought it was a cat, but all three were accounted for.

Then I thought it was the neighbor's children playing outside.

By the time I figured out the high-pitched agony was coming from inside the microwave, Little Miss Muse had already loaded up her double-barreled bottle rocket gun and was about to light the fuse in a wholehearted attempt to protect her stomping grounds. (Literal stomping grounds. High heels on the hardwood floor all day that day as she paced and churned out ever-new ideas for us to write about— all while ignoring the work in progress (WIP) which needs some restructuring before we can move on. Muses hate structuring or anything with the prefix "re-." They believe their job is done with a carefree helping of word salad...)

I opened the microwave door and was greeted by a hot, humid cloud. I grabbed a kitchen towel and pulled the potato out to the counter.

And stuck the fork in it again.

Only half done.

To help it out, I stabbed it a few more times, then sent it back to its radiation inferno to finish cooking.

It continued to scream and whistle and whine. I've never met a root vegetable with so many complaints. Even the ones I truly did set on fire never complained as much as this potato.

It's like my WIP.

Fussing.

Whining.

Screaming.

A little restructuring is in order. Clear the slate a bit and pave the road for the characters to be able to do their thing and save their corner of the universe. Stab it with a red ink pen a few dozen times and see what leaks out...

If the red ink pen doesn't work, I might try a fork.

Come to think of it, I bet we all have some life circumstances that could use a red ink pen, a fork, some well-placed plastic wrap, and a hefty dose of microwave radiation...

Wow. I must be just a tick stressed.

It's probably hunger. Yeah. Let's go with that.

I'll refrain from outright declaring that I feel like stabbing something.

Oops.

Little Miss Muse is backing up into the corner, gathering poofed-tailed cats as she goes. She's aiming her double-barrel rocket launcher in my direction.

Time to go stab a potato with a fork.

Repeatedly.

Looking Back: I still feel like stabbing things with a fork. Repeatedly. Whoever my future Couch Person might be will either love to see me coming (fresh sand in the sandbox) or dread it (especially if Little Miss Muse joins me on the couch).

Little Miss Muse says there's no shame in seeking help. She declares this as she flicks her amethyst-bedazzled Zippo lighter a little too close to Stella Marie's tail feathers.

She says the Sultan had to seek a Couch Person when his author took a year-long sabbatical from writing. Muses can't handle writers on sabbatical without dire consequences. I know this from the stretches of time I don't write new words and Little Miss Muse's wings start to shed.

"He has one he could recommend. Wait just a minute and I'll get you a name."

Annndd she's back in the freezer.

I thought Sultans were a desert-dwelling people. If he's truly in there, I've no doubt he's been to a Mental Health Pro for Muses. Probably needs a follow-up visit.

177

THE PERFECT PLAN

I t's that time of year again... Back to School.

Perhaps it's been that time of year for a month or two, at least retail-wise. But with our family's three-ring circus complete with flying monkeys, I failed to notice.

It hit me hard when I took my aunt for her weekly grocery shopping. There. Right at the entrance of the store was a huge—I mean huge—display of Post-It Note products.

I think my mouth watered.

I know my knees went weak and wobbly.

But alas, my focus was on my aunt and her list, not my near-blinding office supply fetish.

But the display burned a hole in my brain until the next week when we returned to that same store.

"I gotta pick up some of these," I told her.

Then she remembered she needed a binder to control some of her paperwork.

My heart soared.

We wouldn't just stop at the Post-It Note display in the front of the store and then head straight to the bread and cookie aisle (Aunt adores her cookies). We would, indeed, make our way to the back where the full spread of back-to-school and office supplies were kept. We passed rows and rows of stuff I don't need.

Stuff I have too much of already.

New stuff I've never seen.

I picked up a pack of little Post-It flags (Yes, I did need more of those because I'm sure I owe my proofreader a refresh on her supply after the last batch of edits killed two tree branches-worth of sticky notes marking all my typos).

I also bought a rather hefty block of lined, super extra sticky Post-Its.

I have the perfect plan to plan out the perfect plot for my next novel (as the characters in my work-in-progress novel scream at me from the side of the road where they've been stuck all year).

I envision writing plot beats and scene snippets, one per Post-It, and slapping them all over my office walls. Perhaps immersing myself in a three-dimensional outline will get me going. Good plan, right? At the very least a good excuse to buy a rather hefty block of lined, super extra sticky Post-Its.

And then Aunt and I saw planners. Lots of planners.

Unfortunately, though, the selection included only "academic." Meaning they start in August and end next year sometime.

I prefer planners that start in January. A clean, fresh start to a clean, fresh year yet untainted by juggling clowns, ducks not in rows, and those dastardly flying monkeys.

In other words, my plan with a new planner is to totally forget about the year we're in (2020? 2021? 2022? Each one of those had its own dumpster-fire flavor of the year) and develop the perfect plan for the upcoming twelve months.

(Cue the smirks. Cue the chuckles. Cue the knee-slapping guffaws).

The perfect plan?

I could *possibly* find the perfect planner:

- Starts in January. (I'll forgive them if they added December of the current year. I can always rip out that gut-wrenching month if need be. Holiday drama, anyone?)
- It must be spiral-bound and lay flat.
- The cover must be waterproof-ish and wipe-clean-ish.
- The cover must be chew-proof-ish (because of the cats, not because I have lost my mind to the point that I am now eating office supplies... yet).
- The cover must be here-we-go-again-proof-ish. For when life tanks and the planner is crammed into a backpack to accompany me to doc offices, emergency rooms, and other office-type settings I'd rather not speak of here.
- Little Miss Muse prefers the cover to be some shade of purple. I try to appease her, but all the other points must come first. She threatens to spill grape soda on it and force it to be purple. Thus the previous point of waterproof-ish and wipe-clean-ish.
- The paper must be heavy enough for me to mark through my to-do lists with fiery flare.
- It must have sturdy plastic tabs marking the monthly spreads.
- New this year: The ink must be crisp enough to see through my I-can't-stand-these-blasted-bifocals.
- It must have enough space on each day to write down the medical comings and goings of six adults, a day job, the dream job, and, as it turns out this month, the plumber.
- I must love it enough to want to spend time with it every day for a whole year. After all, this planner becomes my right arm, my very brain, and, at times, my therapist.

So, the perfect *planner* is doable, even though I know the perfect *plan* doesn't exist. Too many monkeys, squirrels, ducks, and clowns.

And, oh, look. There's an ostrich in my duck row!

So, while I wait for the calendar people to forget about academics for the season and focus on a totally fresh, new year, I'll use my rather hefty block of lined, super extra sticky Post-Its to plot and plan other things.

Perhaps one of those lined notes will fill with other office supplies I can't live without.

You know.

To make the best of the upcoming year.

Sounds like the perfect plan.

Looking Back: On a positive Post-It Note, I have used that super-sticky lined pad to timeline out my novel in progress and set scene and beat reminders in front of my eyes. It helps me keep focused while Little Miss Muse dances around with twenty other story ideas while I just want to finish this one novel, pretty please and thank you very much.

Little Miss Muse thinks it's cute that I still try to plan things. Given how the CIRCUS leaves very little wriggle room for predictability.

I remind her the CIRCUS wouldn't be so lively so often if she'd stop setting fire to the clown wigs.

178

ACCEPTANCE

The phrase used to be "Not my circus, not my monkeys."

I held tight to that idea for the longest time, kicking pretty hard against what life threw at me.

In some instances, it's true: Most problems aren't mine. I have no dog in *that* fight. No skin in *that* game. The cliched phrases are endless to explain how one should stay in their lane and let certain people/activities/events/drama/emotions just go. Go. Go. Go.

But lately...

I most certainly have a circus.

Full of people/activities/events/drama/emotions.

And lots and lots of monkeys.

All mine.

A dear friend once told me I don't need to catch every ball thrown at me. This is true. And I've learned this skill to a degree. It brings more peace than trying to juggle life events that aren't mine.

But lately...

If I don't catch some of these balls (or get the barking, clapping seals trained well enough to do so) I get hit in the head. Or the gut. Or the heart... (heart punches are the worst).

I didn't ask to be the circus master. I've posted "Now Hiring" fliers for the position, complete with the promise of an epic sign-on bonus, matching 401(k), dental, vision, and a free poodle. Apparently, no one else wants the job, either, no matter how cute the cycling poodles may be.

Poodles still poop.

Elephants, yellow-haired clowns, and flying monkeys do, too.

So what to do?

No one wants tickets to my brand of circus. Even if I managed to sell a few seats, the legal ramifications of an audience member tarrying in my Big Top Tent would be massive.

A well-meaning friend sees me coming and asks what's wrong. I tell her about one—just one—ring of the circus and her eyes widen slightly, her eyebrows lift, and then she winces.

Another friend checks in. Sick of the Circus Ring One retelling, I tell him about Circus Ring Two. Turns out the eyes/brows/wince thing is universal.

A third friend asks. Ring One, Two, Three, or some other random number? I've lost track of the rings. Some circus master I am.

I decide to just smile, nod, and lie. "I'm fine." They know I'm lying, so I add, "You wouldn't believe me."

"Write a book about it."

The advice is sound. Usually writing makes me feel better, and, more often than not, real life gives great fuel to fiction plots.

But not this time.

Because, you see, fiction must make sense, no matter if you're reading/watching a true-life memoir or a romping unicorn space adventure complete with pew-pew laser pistols. The tale must have some form of logical foundation or it falls apart. After all, how many times have you read a book or watched a movie and walked away from the experience pointing out all the plot holes?

My circus life has waayyyy too many plot holes. None of which have gaped open large enough to swallow even one pooping, peddling poodle, so the plot holes are good for nothing but drama.

My circus life has waayyyy too many fallacies in logic. I wouldn't even know where to start writing a memoir. Because I couldn't market it as true life. It's too unbelievable.

My circus MAKES NO SENSE! This isn't how life is supposed to go. I stand in the middle ring complete with my top hat, tailcoat, and whip and shout to the performers, "That's not how it works! That's not how any of this works!" But my circus doesn't listen.

Uggg. So.

Acceptance is the next level.

Balls will be thrown (and maybe dropped). Poops will be dropped (and maybe thrown). And before the end of the event, more Rings will be added.

I know this now. It's just how it is.

My circus. My monkeys.

So, back to the What-To-Do-About-It question. I think a two-pronged approach to acceptance is my best bet at this stage.

Number One: Flex. Like tight-rope walker level of flexibility. (Though the rope-walker in my circus is dangling upside down with all her limbs wrapped around the wire. She's been there for five days. There's no net, and I'm not likely to purchase one since I can't seem to sell any tickets. So there she hangs.)

I'll write when I can.

Laugh when I can.

Take breaks and find quiet time when I can.

Scoop poop and fluff clown wigs when I can. Pluck worn-out flying monkey wings when I can—keep those bad boys in the air.

Number Two: Patience. It's a big, bad circus. But one thing about circuses that I must remember...

Eventually they pack up and leave town.

Looking Back: As you have likely surmised, my CIRCUS has not left town. 160 days from this blog's post date, it still goes strong. More on that later... Some days Little Miss Muse can't even and goes and sits in the freezer.

179

PURGE, PAINT, AND REGRESS

It's become clear that I have a set pattern when things are massively stressful or in times of great grief.

First, I purge.

I take all that emotional energy that many would spend sobbing or ranting and I throw myself into gutting a closet, the cabinets, or whatever cluttered-up corner I can get my mitts on.

Problem is, I've purged quite a bit over the last couple of years, and now I'm running out of things to throw away. Sometimes I throw out/donate/sell something that I have to turn around and buy again. These purges can become costly.

A few episodes ago, the Hubs told me I couldn't be anxious or purge-ish in the garage.

Meaning his stash of 50,000 nails (he builds things as much as I cook, so I don't understand why we have all these nails) and 5,000 golf balls (ok... he'll probably go through these before he retires) will remain secure.

I purged a couple of weeks ago. Moving piles of this and that to out-of-sight locales and the garbage when needed.

Next step? Paint.

Sometimes it's just a room.

Sometimes it's several rooms. The way the circus is going, I'll run out of rooms sometime next year and will have to find a Bob Ross tutorial and start painting my own "Happy Little Accidents."

I throw on a publishing podcast or an online writing class, turn off the world, and inhale the fumes.

This time, it was a small bedroom.

I started with the ceiling. I posted this update on my personal Facebook feed:

You don't know how much of a mouth breather you are until you paint a textured ceiling.

Afterward, in the fog of physical and mental exhaustion, I came up with a half-brained (fumes, right?) business idea:

Flavored paint.

I mean, I tasted that ceiling multiple times. The paint goes on very light pink then dries white. The flavor could be Candy Cane or Strawberry Vanilla Shake.

The walls are a minty green. I was sure I was going to run out before the room was done, and I did NOT want to buy another entire gallon just to finish four square feet. So I was rolling that stuff on pretty hard, spreading it as thin as I could, creating tiny splatter droplets that landed, well...

Turns out I was still mouth breathing (or gasping for air because I had to shut the door to keep the cats from licking the walls or using their tails to do touch-up work).

So I tasted the walls, too. Andes Mints? Avocado Delight?

(If anyone makes this a reality and someone locally decides to repaint in a Reese Cup Sunset or Tiramisu Beige, I'll help you paint.)

After wearing myself out purging and killing brain cells (and searing taste buds) painting, I regress.

When all the physical anxiety is gone, my mind wanders back to my childhood.

Ewoks and Wonder Woman.

Indiana Jones and Mr. Rogers.

Gizmo, ET, and Kermit the Frog.

I think my mind needs something soothing to land on, and these memories don't require extra thought, emotion or decisions. They just... were. Things Little Girl Beth loved.

I'll rewatch movies I've seen a hundred times. Search Pinterest or Etsy for unique takes on those retro characters. Anything to allow my mind to rest, I suppose. A therapist could explain this behavior more thoroughly, but I've yet to make that leap. I don't even have time to get to Back Guy, and he serves as a mighty fine therapist most of the time.

This Regression Round? Unicorns.

To the point where I spent way more time than I'd like to admit shopping online for unicorn bedding for my newly painted and freshly tasted mint green bedroom. I even texted the Hubs at work, asking if I could have a unicorn room.

"Yep."

Good answer, seeing as he won't let me touch his garage clutter.

I texted a friend and double-checked that since I'm a grown woman and all, would it be okay if I had a unicorn room.

She didn't see any problem with it. As a bonus, she even tossed out an epic short-story writing prompt that allowed Little Miss Muse to go off and play for a while. Which, in turn, pulled me out of the funky cycle and allowed me to start thinking about writing goals for the rest of the year. Ahhhh. To dream.

I have a good Hubs and good friends.

So, that was my week.

Circus. Purge. Paint. Regress.

And begin to dream again, just a little bit...

Looking Back: Ahh, back in the days when the CIRCUS was just the circus. I haven't decorated with unicorns, yet. I did add a bookcase to that room which gives me great joy as the shelves are double-stacked with my to-be-read tomes.

Little Miss has secured the name of the Sultan's therapist and is encouraging me to make the leap. So, at her behest, I am, indeed, on a waiting list.
But with a Couch Person of my own choosing, not that of the Sultan.

180

WEE WEE WEE...

...I want to leave home.
So with the stress of the current circus, even the Purge, Paint, and Regress failed to do its thing. Not because that process is necessarily flawed. No. It's more that This. Circus. Just. Keeps. Going.

My clowns are all bald now because the monkeys, freshly infected with rabies, snatched the crooked wigs right off their heads and, well.

Here we are.

Not a pretty circus. Even the poodles are protesting, their little unicycles' wheels spinning eerily. Not a rider in sight.

A while back, I talked about one of our catchphrases: This Is New. We've said that a few times this week.

Amara figured out how to "door surf." Two paws on the tip top of my office door, and two paws barely clinging to the top of the door trim on the wall. She was about to do the mid-air splits, and the Hubs had to grab her down. I don't know if she'd have landed on her feet, but I definitely didn't need another round of vet bills for a broken leg after a wicked virus of some sort worked its way through all three felines the week before.

She was evidently feeling better, though, and trying out some new acrobatic tricks for, well, the circus.

On a positive note, we did get the whiteboard paper hung in my office (which was what got Amara excited to begin with: packaging and new things and something shiny on the wall). I intend to use this board to outline and keep track of my would-rather-be-writing life.

On a realistic note, the whiteboard is still pristine. All because of the (and everybody reading can chime in here) CIRCUS!

"That was new," the Hubs and I almost said in unison after he put her on the floor and she went careening off the hallway walls, working out a bad case of zoomies.

One night this past week, after a particularly grueling few days of family crises, my body decided to try its own new trick.

Particularly my left foot.

Very particularly, my little piggy toe of my left foot.

Now, I've had muscle cramps, spasms, and Charlie horses in the past, especially during pregnancies. Eat another banana, take a potassium supplement, and those tended to ease.

But on this night? I was minding my own, tired business, chilling on the couch, when a cramp started in my left arch. No biggie. I wiggled it around and hoped it would calm down.

It didn't.

My left little piggy toe did a ninety-degree departure from the rest of the herd. All my pigs on that foot started to contort and curl without my willing them to. Looked like something out of a horror movie.

And. The. Pain.

Wee. Wee. Wee. As in squeals of agony, not joy.

This was new.

Ten minutes and a small hot flash later, I was still sore, but at least all the pigs were back in the "pen," and I could walk.

On a positive note, for ten minutes I forgot about my circus, and I saw this blog taking shape. The title.

The snark.

The ending.

And even Little Miss Muse taking the credit. (She's so bored, by the way. It's hard telling what will come out of my fingers the next time I have a writing session. I may need to devote a few hours to the most incredibly ridiculous short story ever to allow her room to play after all this drama and trauma I've made her sit in time out for.)

In the meantime, you can click on the links in the first few paragraphs to get an idea of life in the Paul household and why most writing endeavors have taken a back burner. And go read Four Seconds — it'll be up on the blog until the end of the month.

On another positive note, I have a couple of fun writing things planned. And I've refreshed Little Miss's supply of bottle rockets (my stress causes her stress, which needs a release of some sort).

We may even wiggle in a tiny three-day escape from (everyone, all together now...) the CIRCUS.

Perhaps the refresher will help me holler "Wee, Wee, Wee" all the way home...

...and be happy about it.

Looking Back: We indeed wiggled in a road trip to Chattanooga, just me and the Hubs and Little Miss. We enjoyed a day on Lookout Mountain and then found the Naughty Cat Café (such a cool rescue idea, check out their site).
We swung by Nashville on the way back north and had a nice visit with Aunt and Uncle where they took me to the coolest bookstore ever: Duck River Books, where they left me unattended. Poor Hubs turned into a pack mule getting my haul into the car.
"Four Seconds" (based in Chattanooga) is a short I wrote for the Vegas writing class that had to hit romance, historical fiction and espionage beats. Quite challenging, but the outcome wasn't too bad.
Anxiety does awful things to a human body. I've experienced that cramping a couple of times since... No fun.
Little Miss Muse says her constant ingestion of Grape Soda keeps the cramps away. To make her point, she pirouettes through the office, bumping into two cats and my gallery wall, nearly knocking Big Bird into next week. I think I'll stick with water and a banana.

181

TITLE GOES HERE

No, the title of this blog isn't a forgotten placeholder error. I've seen lots of that type of thing as an editor. Writers often use placeholders in certain spots to block out structures for articles or reports and then forget to go back and actually title the thing or come up with headings.

In this case, I didn't forget.

I just didn't know what to call today's hot mess or where to start, really; my mind has been muddied with life difficulties of late.

I'm also a tiny bit OCD about my pre-writing dance as I face the blank page and blinking cursor.

When I first start a blog post or story, I open a blank document and then save it right away to my desktop. That file needs the date, the blog number, and the title of the blog.

I'll stare at that title for quite a while. It brings focus—sometimes. It brings angst at other times when I'm not sure how I'll spin the tale. But it has to be there.

Something has to be there.

Sometimes I change the title a dozen times or more as I write. It drives me crazy not to have that top-of-page line to focus on. And, Oh.My.Goodness what a disaster if I don't have a short story title in the header of my manuscript before page three. "Title" seems like such a failure as it glares at me from the top right corner of the screen. It's something I know I'll have to address eventually, but having a working title can bring focus and clarity.

It also reminds Little Miss Muse that we're currently working on THIS PARTICULAR PIECE and not ANOTHER RANDOM IDEA.

It's a quirk.

Today, I came up with a half dozen blog ideas, five were really bad, before settling on this writerly ramble and then couldn't decide what name to save the file under.

I despised typing "Title Goes Here" in the Save As line, but it shook something loose.

I feel I'm in a state of constantly starting over with the writing goals and dreams. It's getting old. I'm ready to move on.

Then, once the CIRCUS settles or the latest physical ailment eases, I sit down at my writing desk and go, "Now, where was I?"

Oh. Right.

Title Goes Here.

Start at the beginning with the blank page, the blinking cursor, and an excited purple imp muse who's been way too long alone in the corner with her bottle rockets and lavender glitter bombs and grape-flavored bubble gum. She's ready to get to work.

But she needs a little focus.

Title Goes Here.

Then the next word, and the next. The next thought piles on top of the previous one. Word by word until full sentences fall from my fingertips and finally, finally, that glorious state of "flow" where it's me, Little Miss Muse, and, well, an actual story line...

Something will inevitably pull me away from the writing. Something always does. It's life in this CIRCUS of mine with all the crazy monkeys...

But I know by now I can always start again.

From the top.

Until the story is all told and...

The End Goes Here.

Looking Back: Even before the pandemic, this was my rhythm. Write like a nut for a stretch of time, churn out titles or coalesce them into a collection. Dab away paragraph by paragraph at a novel-in-progress.

After the pandemic, and not because of it, I don't believe—this got worse. My family members suffered great setbacks with their health, then, well. There's only so much juice left in the tank.

"Grape juice with a swig of grape soda followed by a Red Bull. That's what I'd prescribe." Little Miss never lacks energy—motivation, yes, energy, no.

"Gag me. And do you know what my heart would do with a Red Bull?"

"Not as concerned with your heart as I am with your fingers. Hook yourself up to an EKG and let's get going." Little Miss Muse can be a slave driver.

We have another self-imposed deadline. A done first draft of a novel in the next 30 days. Ha! And this on the heels of meeting my Couch Lady. Wonder how much juice will be left in the tank after she gets done re-working my inner thoughts?

Hopefully by the time Life All Over Again *goes live, Triage will be in proofreading...*

182

MONKING THE BRIDGE

Those who know me well know that I have a particular phobia/neurosis/aversion related to bridges.

I don't like them.

At all.

They swing.

Vibrate.

Jiggle.

Suspend themselves above water, forest, or concrete and promise to deliver one safely from where one is to where one wants or needs to be.

And I have trust issues.

So trusting that promise the bridge makes is a huge big deal.

Add to that the height of the things, and yeah. I'm a particular kind of hot mess on certain road trips. I watch the GPS screen to see snakes or vast blotches of water and stress over whether that blue directional line that I am following will indeed take me over certain death.

It doesn't matter if I'm driving or if someone else is behind the wheel. I'm a mess. Sweaty hands. Can't catch my breath.

Completely irrational.

Like Adrian Monk and germs, or his other 311 phobias. But all 312 of mine are wrapped up in bridges.

Monk also has OCD, wherein he must touch things. With just one finger... More on that in a minute.

The Hubs and I got away to Chattanooga last week. It was a nice little road trip. But the Ohio River and Tennessee River and who-knows-how-many high-up concrete interstate tangles lay between our corn field and our hotel at the base of Lookout Mountain.

I was, however, pleasantly surprised that this hotel was situated so that no Tennessee River crossing was required. The last time I visited Chattanooga, I had to cross the river multiple times a day. All that crossing did nothing to desensitize my bridge anxiety about *this* trip.

The first night in the city, we took a walk downtown. We meandered and read Civil War tidbits and intriguing Cherokee Indian lore and their fate along the Trail of Tears. Then we came to the mouth of a giant blue bridge hanging over the river. The Chief John Ross Bridge, I do believe.

And something in me said enough.

Enough of this nonsense and irrational fear.

Enough of being unable to control it (or anything else in the CIRCUS that is our life—I do believe this CIRCUS had a lot to do with what happened next).

Enough.

I started walking.

Right onto the bridge.

"What are we doing?" Hubs asked, more than a little trepidation in his voice. I can only imagine he believed that I'd either finally glitched all the way out or was suffering heat stroke—or both.

"What *are* we doing?" Little Miss Muse flitted around my head. I can only imagine she believed that I'd jump, forcing her to find another author to muse around with. And the author/muse relationship is so delicate, and I've spoiled her rotten. No other writer would willingly take her on. She'd have to hold another writer hostage with her bottle rockets...

"What am I *doing*?" I asked myself. I can't imagine willingly walking onto such a structure had I been in my right mind and heat-stroke free. (I think the heat index at the time was 98 or so—heat stroke was a possibility).

But I think I'd just had... enough.

I couldn't bring myself to walk near the water side, though. I put the Hubs there. I preferred to hang out with the speeding vehicles.

Made it out over the water, the cars rumbling the concrete beneath my feet. The walls closing in ever so slightly on the periphery of my vision.

Walked out to the beginning of the metal beast's gaping mouth.

And I Monked the bridge.

I touched that sucker. With one single index finger.

Just like Adrian Monk.

Then, with weak and shaky knees, I snapped a selfie with my guy to prove I'd done it, and we walked back, he and Little Miss worried the whole time I'd topple into the buzzing traffic or faint dead right there on the spot.

But I didn't die.

I felt like I had some sense of control. Or at least the illusion of it.

And the next day? I did the swinging bridge over a gorge at the top of Lookout Mountain in Rock City (after I was sure I'd be the only one on the structure).

I Monked that sucker, too.

And I didn't die.

Little Miss, however, may have suffered heat stroke and will commence filing workers' compensation claims tomorrow.

Monking those bridges did nothing to change the circumstances of the CIRCUS. But I did it.

It also didn't cure my phobia, as evidenced by my shirt-drenching anxiety when driving over the Ohio River through Louisville on the way home.

At any rate, tomorrow, I plan to Monk one of my manuscripts. Even if I only get so far as to point at it with one bossy index finger.

I also plan to Monk the writing schedule, a couple of cats (this is also called nose-booping, FYI, and two of the three cats enjoy it), and the ever-growing pile of shorts that need to find a market or be placed into a new collection.

One step at a time to regain some control...

Or at least the illusion of it.

Looking Back: That's all we have in the control department, right? Illusion? We like to think our schedules and calendars and wish lists are event- and emotion-proof. They're not.

And no writer on the planet has a schedule that's muse-proof, whether the muse is an imp or an iguana.

Little Miss Muse says it would be futile to try to Little-Miss-proof anything from her. She says this as she flicks her new Zippo lighter that she negotiated out of me to STAY IN THE CAR for my first Couch Lady session. The things one does to try to stay afloat...

183

IT'S BIG... AND ON WHEELS

As I write this, October has already chewed up and spit out eight of its days.

Eight.

Slow. Down. Please.

I love this time of year. Cool, crisp air. Zero humidity. The colors that explode in the treetops and then drop to the ground with glorious flare. But given the events of the CIRCUS over the last two weeks (all rings are aflame, the air burns with singed poodle hair, and this poor Master of Ceremonies has nearly had a straight-up mental breakdown—at the very least my first full-blown panic attack), I haven't been able to truly enjoy these early change-of-season days.

And now eight of them are gone.

And so is an hour of my life.

Last night, the Hubs and I declared that we would not give in and turn on the furnace despite the freeze and frost that would occur while we slept. We know as soon as that time comes, we become spoiled to the heat and there goes hard-earned money on temperature control. Hard-earned money that could be better put to use buying parts for the new-to-the-Hubs-midlife-crisis Jeep. Or a writing retreat. Or cat toys. Anything other than the gas bill.

I *hate* paying for temperatures.

(We also play this game in the spring, but the weather usually wins out quickly. I can always put another quilt on the bed. However, there's only so far one can go when one is hot and hot-flashing.)

Despite not turning on the main heating source, I am not against using a space heater to take the chill down a notch.

That is, if I could find the good heater.

One of our mini ones is about to give up trying. I think Malachi has spent too much time with his hind end near the fan and is clogging the heater's innards with his shedding.

The other space heater is shaped like a radiator. It's big. And on wheels. It gives off a subtle, calming heat. Amara loves it. Puts her toe-beans right up to the edge and goes all cat-in-a-coma. I don't have to worry about fur clogging anything, as there is no fan.

But I can't find it. Anywhere.

I have looked in closets. The shed. The garage. Behind furniture where I *know* I would never store a heater. Closets again. Shed again.

Racked my brain: Did someone borrow it? Did I donate it to one of the adult-ish children?

Do I vaguely remember this big one on wheels giving up this past spring and chucking it to the dump?

I can't remember.

But I should be able to. It's big. And on wheels, for crying out loud. How does one lose such a thing or forget the event that led to it no longer being on the property? I did find a newer, small mini one. With a fur-sucking fan. I don't remember buying that... Hmm. Maybe the radiator one did blow up.

One loses such a thing and/or erases such happenings from memory because of THE CIRCUS; I know this. But I digress.

I shall forgo the search and shop for a new one. Or make do with the two little ones. But today is gorgeous, and I need to be outside in it before the skies gray, the snow flies, and the trees droop with ice.

I need to further clear my head from the events of the last couple of weeks so I can focus on forward momentum. Calm my inner Circus Master. Let a few of those flaming CIRCUS rings just... be.

Some yellow-haired clown in a polka-dot jumper will surely come around with a foaming extinguisher and make a show of dousing the flames.

Mainly, I need to consider how to write and create and play with words and worlds and settings, all amid utter life chaos.

I met a great group of local writers last weekend at the Cambridge City Library author signing. It was an excellent experience that has Little Miss Muse and I hopeful.

It gave us a lot to mull over, from ideas to events to networking.

Participating basically wrote a permission slip for my little purple-winged imp and me to play and dream in the middle of the giant plot hole that is life. Turns out this particular plot hole is a big one. With wheels.

So I'm off to walk and ponder and enjoy the day before October slips away and Little Miss Muse discovers I've misplaced her purple suitcase full of bottle rockets.

The big one. With wheels.

Looking Back: The events surrounding this time nearly split me in half. Thus the need for the Couch Lady. Since the first of the year (a whopping 60 days so far as I write this), I have written every day, even if it's a measly 50 words. Every day. Words down.

That's a win.

So was finding the little band of writers in my neck of the woods. That author event spawned weekly writing sessions out of the house with the Living and Breathing folks that aren't in my CIRCUS. It's refreshing. Perhaps Couch Lady can give some tips and tricks on how to not let the passion die during times of great turmoil.

Little Miss, again with her favorite new Zippo, flits across the desk threatening to light day job to-dos and shopping lists on fire. "I've got a way to motivate you if Couch Lady doesn't come through."

I'm sure Little Miss has more than one way.

184

THE BRIGHT BALD BULLSEYE

I thought I'd end up going alone. A solo trip to our high school's auditorium to watch the drama department put on a rendition of *The Legend of Sleepy Hollow*.

But the Hubs surprised me when he said he'd accompany me. "You don't ask for much."

I suppose that's true. I don't ask for much. I'm not a shoe person or a purse person, or a get-me-the-next-best-and-brightest-doo-dad person. (Office supplies, though. But I don't *ask* for them. I procure and stockpile at will... But I suppose he loves me anyway.)

Nothing at all like Little Miss Muse, who stomps and squeals and demands all things glittery and purple in order to do her job. But I suppose I love her anyway...

Live theater has never really been my thing, either, but that may be our location and the need to drive for hours to find a production that might interest me. *Phantom of the Opera* for one of the Hub's birthdays was a neat one. I went to a few other little ones I can't remember – most of those in my high school days because some of my classmates were cast members. That's the extent of my experience.

But this was Sleepy Hollow. Sure to be fun and fit the fall season.

And since the high school is literally in our backyard, no travel needed.

We got our tickets and chose our seats. Hubs took the aisle, and I settled down next to him to scour the program. Then we reminisced, since both of us graduated eons ago from this same high school. The room felt smaller than I remembered. The stage wasn't as massive as I recall. The seats were definitely smaller, too (Yeah, yeah. I know why *that's* the case...).

Funny how time and age shrink places down to their proper sizes.

We teased about how we were in the splash zone if this was a show at the Zoo or Sea World. Or if we were in a magic show, one of us would be lugged onto the stage to be the punch line of the performer's joke.

Good thing it's only a high school play.

The lights went down, the curtain went up, and the performance began. The set design was fantastic, though I was concerned that the church house would topple at one point, as that was the entrance/exit for many of the background actors.

Ichabod Crane came on the scene, the wanderer in search of a class to teach. And his class turned out to be the audience at large. On a few occasions, he'd address us, never happy with our progress in our studies. Always threatening with a birch tree switch.

At one point, he was so unhappy with our academic performance that he left the stage, red dunce cap in hand, and proceeded down the aisle.

Our aisle.

And then I looked at my dear, dear Hubs. Who came because I don't ask for much.

And I knew.

There's no one else even slightly fit for the part. The other aisle-dwellers were ladies or men wearing baseball caps. Or little kids.

But my man?

He's got a bright, bald head just beckoning to be the walk-on (or, in this case, stay-seated) cast member of *The Legend of Sleepy Hollow*.

His scalp glowed in the stage light that followed Ichabod from the stage. The perfect bullseye.

And Ichabod hit the target.

On went the hat. All eyes on my man. I don't even know what Ichabod was going on about at this point, acutely aware of the long, pointy hat on my guy's noggin. Acutely aware of all eyes on him. And I was trying not to laugh out loud and drown out Mr. Crane.

Then, our strict schoolmaster yanked the cap off and retreated to the stage.

The Hubs took it like a champ. Even ended up enjoying the play more than I did, in spite of the involuntary participation.

It was a good night. Something different.

At one point, I felt guilty that I'd come. I should have taken those couple of hours to finish a submission to an anthology I'm aiming for. Or finish up the next short story collection. But, it'll get done next week.

That's my aim, anyway.

I'll just paint a bright bald bullseye on those projects and channel my inner Ichabod.

Looking Back: I found a pattern emerging in my life of late. One of guilt and full of "should".

I should be...

It would've been better if...

I could've...

I need to let the fun times be fun times. Learn to be present in the good moments and stop looking for terror around every corner (That's yet another side effect of the CIRCUS). Stop bathing in guilt for having an enjoyable moment or ten.

Little Miss Muse says guilt is a foreign sensation to her. "Most muses I know just move on." She owns all she does and lives to love life in the next second.

I can agree that I've never once seen her regretful for anything. Even that time she singed Stella Marie's tail feather with her new brand of bottle rockets.

185

BACK IN MY DAY

I never did find my trusty old heater—that big one on wheels.

So I bought a replacement. A radiator-style heater (no fan for cat fur to clog up) on wheels. But you know what? They don't make 'em like they used to.

I am quite disappointed with the new addition. It works. But not like the other one.

I miss my old one.

The more life chaos that jumps into our circus rings and further scatters our ducks-already-not-in-rows, the more my bones hurt and the wearier my soul becomes. Part of it is stress.

Part of it is middle-age-ish-ness. The heater on wheels dealt me a firm realization—in more ways than one.

Hot Mess Realization #1: If I double my current age, I'm more than likely a dead woman.

Half of my life. Gone. Poof! Like my old heater on wheels that went who-knows-where. That high school play we watched last week? They were all babies on stage. Babies, I tell you!

The thirty-something that just served me my blueberry muffin and Diet Coke is also a baby. Young 'un, even.

Forget middle-age-ish. I'm full-blown in the middle. Perhaps a bit past that, even.

Hot Mess Realization #2: I have old-ish bones. My grandmother used to back her hind end up to her wall-mounted gas heater years ago. She'd get so close her clothing would have tiny scorch marks tattling that she'd stood too long trying to warm her old bones.

I tried backing my caboose up to this new-fangled heater, hoping for a tiny bit of sting. A few good seconds of a thermal hug that would stay in my clothing long enough for me to get back to the couch and wrap up in my fuzzy unicorn blanket, trapping the comfort. Nope. This new-fangled device comes with way too many safety features and not an ounce of true fabric-singing, bone-warming output.

I could ride this radiator heater like a department store penny pony for hours and not even break a sweat.

Break a bone, maybe. But not a sweat.

Hot Mess Realization #3: I have become my ancestors.

When I tried to wheel the new heater to a smaller room, one of the casters folded in on itself. It's supposed to fold for easy storage, but not while in use. And the wheels are held on with plastic. I heard myself say—out loud: "They don't make stuff like they used to."

In that second, all of my grandparents, parents, and quite a few great-aunts and great-great uncles declaring their opinions of shoddy workmanship and the decline of civilization in general came out of my mouth.

How often did I hear one of them start off, "Back in my day..."? The struggles of getting to their one-room schoolhouse. The nothing-but-potatoes for dinner nights. The lone orange in a Christmas stocking. The landline telephone, complete with party line gossip. The days of going all the way outside to turn the antenna to pick up one network on a television the size of the Titanic. The frustration of untangling manual typewriter ribbons and hammers. Outhouses and the Sears Roebuck catalog pages.

After I think of the things they endured, my heater problems are indeed trivial. I could, after all, just turn on the furnace.

I began to wonder what I would tell future generations.

Back in my day:

- I stored my school assignments in a Trapper Keeper. (Certain styles of the original brand sell on eBay for over $100. Should've kept that kitten one...)
- I drank unfiltered well water.
- I rode in moving vehicles without a car seat — or seatbelt.
- "Streaming" is when the ribbon billowed out from the VHS tape when the VCR malfunctioned during a rewind.
- We had the same phone for 15 years.
- A massive wooden drawer system full of tiny cards with book titles was my Google.
- I had to be in the living room on time to watch Friends or miss the episode entirely.
- I had to switch chargers for my phone because Apple kept changing the port size.
- The network only went to 5G.

All small problems—if they could be considered problems at all. Not at all on the level of the lone orange in the Christmas stocking.

So... what to do with these Hot Mess Realizations?

Count my blessings. I have things much easier than those who came before me. However, I'm sure I'll occasionally play the age card and declare loudly how things were better back in my day.

I'll keep my chiropractor appointments. My Back Guy adjusts the joints and the attitude on occasion...

And, since I'm just-past-middle-age-ish...

Get the next book finished, Beth. Good grief! Time's a tickin' away.

And turn on the furnace so your fingers don't freeze to the keyboard.

Looking Back: The Hot Mess Realizations never stop, and have, of late, been coming at the rate of one a day. You saw me have one just one blog post back—about the guilt thing.

I've recently put stand-up comedy in my bag of tricks to cope with the CIRCUS. It has no plot, no dark and awful happenings, and occasionally I get a good, much-needed laugh.

My favorite comedy flavor by far is that Hot Mess Realization that the comedian shares from their own life that is relatable to much of the audience.

Aging. Relationships. Airports.

"I don't bother having realizations. And if I did, they'd not be all hot or messy. I'm immortal." Little Miss's breath reeks of grape soda as she reads over my shoulder. For good measure she burps and flits glitter over the keyboard.

She's not feeling one bit guilty about it, either.

186

THE SCARY THING IS...

I found my heater.

The big one. On wheels.

After I bought a replacement.

After I spent gobs of time and mental energy trying to locate the old one or determine who I gave it to.

It was in a blind corner in the Hub's man cave. I went in there several times to stand in the middle of the room and scratch my head. A garage-turned-interior-square-footage, we used to call it the Game Room since it held a pool/pingpong table. Now it's mostly empty floor space and a recliner so the Hubs can watch television surrounded by his Cowboys, Reds, and Hoosiers.

Yesterday I went in there to get my external hard drive from the fireproof safe so I could back up my laptop lest I lose all the words I've managed to accomplish in the last couple of weeks (Not many words, but hey, they were hard-fought words, and I'd like to keep them for as long as possible).

And there it was, between the safe and the treadmill, which we've not given much consideration to since last winter.

I stood there, hard drive in hand, and stared at the not-so-missing heater. How did I not walk all the way into the room when I looked before? Or maybe I did, and I just didn't see the thing because it had sat in its spot for sooo long that it became part of the room's structure as opposed to an individual item.

This blog goes live on Halloween 2022, and there's nothing scarier than realizing your Hot Mess Realizations are hitting hard. And that they were revealed to you in no uncertain terms by an inanimate object is equally disturbing.

Perhaps the SYFY network could market this concept. Radiator heaters turned invisible therapists. Radiator heaters vs. sharknados. But I digress...

I could blame the missed heater on my bifocals. At the time of the search, my prescription needed to be changed. Get my new glasses with stronger lenses, and BOOM! Heaters pop right back into the visual field from the abyss.

I could blame it on the never-ending outside stressors. Or my internal battle with thyroid-itis.

Or, we could call it what it is. Full disclosure: I'm officially certifiable.

The Hubs knows this. I don't know if he knew before we got married, but he's trapped now. He's signed a paper saying he'll stick around in health and certifiability.

Little Miss Muse already knew this. I think that's why she chose me to be her conduit. She needed a kindred spirit to wrangle her ideas.

And the scary thing is... I'm okay with it.

Color me crazy.

Dye me demented.

Magic-Marker me maniacal.

There it is. I'm nuts.

I think one must be slightly off their rocker to be a writer in the first place. Who else could milk three entire blog posts out of a space heater?

Happy Halloween, folks.

Stay safe.

It's nutty out there.

Looking Back: So the good thing is we have a heater on wheels for Amara and Malachi to stay toasty with as they watch squirrels and stray cats from the sliding glass door of Hub's man cave, and one for us to use in another room. Hopefully, I'll be more clear-headed next fall when I go looking for the heater(s) on wheels and not forget we own two.

Little Miss Muse says she still hopes I try to ride the one like a penny pony. "I'll YouTube it. Garner up some new fans. They'll buy all our books!"

Uh. If I stoop to that level of self-promotion, something truly awful has happened, and the clowns really are running my CIRCUS.

187

A WAVELENGTH SHORT

I've introduced Malachi Maxwell on the blog, and he's been a regular guest star with some of his antics. If you want a refresher or are new to this feline family member of mine, check out "Licking Lightbulbs." It gives a great recap.

And yes, he did take a spell of licking lightbulbs. We've no idea...

His newest trick was to remove a register cover in the living room floor. I went batty, running to and fro around the house looking for the two girl cats, fearing they'd discovered the duct open and were now partying somewhere between the floor and the crawlspace.

The girls, thankfully, were oblivious. (Heaven help us all if Amara discovers the vent covers are removable — she'll shove the other two into the ducts, replace the cover, and walk away like a boss.)

Lately, Malachi has discovered the tissue boxes.

All of them.

The kind of boxes where a single tissue sticks out of the top and dispenses one at a time.

He likes to remove the tissues from the box. One at a time. From all the boxes.

So we store our bananas in the cabinet, we've moved the lamps so he can't lick lightbulbs, and now, if you come to our house and wonder why all of the tissue boxes are upside down, you'll know why. We also have things sitting on the register vents until the poor, brain-damaged kitty forgets the vent covers are removable.

He can't help it. He had a rough start in life, and, despite our best efforts to get him on track, he's just...

Well.

Bless his heart. He just can't even with hardly anything.

When we moved the lamp away from the bookcase, poor Malachi was literally jaw-dropped and cried after me most of the day. He jumped to the top of the case, reared back on his hind legs, and put his front toes on the ceiling. He looked like a meerkat trying to worship the creator posing like that. He studied the ceiling, glanced at the floor lamp across the room, now out of reach, and went back to staring at the ceiling. Praying, maybe, that the higher power would prod me to replace his licking lamp.

The other day he was on top of the refrigerator, "measuring" whether or not he could reach the lights on the kitchen ceiling. He cannot. Reach those lights.

But, he seems to think his ideas are bright ones. He's a few wave-lengths short of a full spectrum.

Come to think of it, perhaps that's why he needs to lick the bulbs.

Poor guy. I, too, am plagued with the occasional "bright idea that isn't."

Many times, I overestimate the time and mental energy I'll have to get my to-do list done.

My recent bright idea was to join NaNoWriMo. For those unfamiliar, that stands for National Novel Writing Month. Basically, you set aside all sanity and write a novel in 30 days during the month of November.

At the time of this writing, I'm 14,000 words in to my 50,000 word goal. I'll keep you updated.

I'm currently in a love/hate relationship with this challenge. I love getting the words in. I hate the "hanging over my head" part of it—especially with Thanksgiving coming up and several doc appointments for several folks on the horizon.

I love the idea for the book (which is based on a short story I wrote for a class during the Vegas trip this past summer). I hate that my tertiary characters believe they need a spotlight scene every five chapters. They do not. Need a spotlight scene. They're tertiary.

I love that I'll have a finished novel at the end of this ordeal. I hate that I started a new one while there's a different novel in my work-in-progress folder that I abandoned and can't seem to return to.

I love that I finally feel I've broken through the significant writing block that has spanned many, many months. I hate never-ending day-job obligations that eat away a chunk of the day before I can sit down and have fun with words.

I must've been truly certifiable to try this challenge, this, of all years, given the CIRCUS. How dare I believe I can hold cast members and plot lines together when I can't keep track of the location of very large appliances in my house or remember that I'm currently frying sausage?

I must be a wavelength short.

I know I'm going to have burnt sausage.

Perhaps Malachi has some tips for me.

He can surely point me in the direction of the best-tasting lightbulbs.

Looking Back: NaNo did get me punched through the start of Triage, which was good. But the draft was so "dirty" I lost most of the words I'd accomplished because, well, the ideas were of the not-so-bright variety. Like less than a watt's worth.
So Triage, as I write this now, is set to have a fairly clean draft done by the end of March. Twenty-eight days from now.
Yay!
Little Miss Muse is in the corner rolling her eyes. I can read that look. "It's about time." She gets excited when I get excited. That's when the flow state starts.
That's when the fun begins!

188

SO, I WON'T BE COOKING TONIGHT...

I had a hard time with the title of this blog post. It could have easily been any of the following:

"I'm So, So Sorry"

"I'll Be More Careful If There's a Next Time"

"It's Just How Things Are"

"It Didn't Kill Either of Us, Did It?"

You'd think with four-plus decades on this planet, in which many of those years I was tall enough to reach the knobs on the stove, that I'd have learned even the slightest bit of culinary skill.

Nope.

And today, I'm telling on myself for something that happened this time last week.

Last Monday, I actually felt like cooking, likely due to being sick to death of eating the same rotation of simple meals or dining out too often in a town with few choices. I even printed off a recipe and made a special trip out to get a couple of things we didn't have in the fridge.

Cheesy chicken bake.

It didn't have too many steps. It wasn't complicated. It was something a little bit different, but not too different so as to send the Hub's already sensitive gut into total shock.

I even got a jump start on the recipe. Placed the chicken in a lightly greased 9X12 (a Pyrex deal that someone gifted us for our wedding. It's not seen much action, to be honest, which is why it's lasted so long). I dirtied up a second bowl to properly mix the cheesy/onion mixture. I dirtied up a real butter knife to spread the mixture on the chicken. I covered the 9X12 with Saran Wrap—the brand name stuff so I wouldn't lose my sanctification trying to get the appropriate-sized sheet from the roll—and placed the dish in the refrigerator.

On the morning of Monday, November 14th, that's the last good thing that happened to that chicken.

(And since dear Hubs reads my blog on Mondays, usually while he's on his lunch break, here is where I apologize. For everything. And where he'll decide before he comes home what he wants for supper, and he'll cook it himself or he'll take us both—or just himself —out to eat. Because I sooo won't be cooking tonight after he reads this blog.)

When evening came, and it was time to actually bake the chicken, well...

Let's just say I'd written quite a few words that day on the novel-in-progress.

And let's just say I'd done quite a bit of day job work, which also requires brain cells.

And let's understand that the later it gets in the day after all that brain work, the less my brain works.

I preheated the oven.

I pre-thought sides to go with the chicken: Salad (the kind that's a kit and just so happened set to expire on the exact date we were going to eat it, but it was still crisp and didn't smell like rot, so I went ahead and made it). Rolls (the kind that go from the freezer to the oven in one step and you really can't screw up, but I've burnt in the past, so I promised myself I'd stay close to the oven that night so the meal would turn out semi-okay-ish).

I removed the chicken dish from the refrigerator and sent it to the 375-degree-preheated oven in one smooth motion.

I was rather proud of myself. One meal every season—and this was to be it. One meal that I don't royally screw up.

And I walked away for the 35 minutes that the chicken needed to bake through.

It smelled good. I was so looking forward to it.

Hubs comes home, right on time. While he's getting cleaned up for dinner, the timer dings—and I was standing right there to hear it (another win). I pulled out the chicken, and put in the rolls. Perfect.

Then I turned my attention to the bubbling, steamy main dish.

And wondered why the cheese topping looked weird.

And why there was a strange, crystalline crust around the edges of the 9X12.

I stuck a fork in one of the chicken pieces closest to the crust to test for doneness and to see what the crust would do when it was poked.

(You have no idea how many times I have to poke things in the kitchen—just to be sure...)

The chicken was most certainly done. But the crust came off in one long strand.

A strand Saran Wrap would be proud of.

My heart sank. The Hubs would be done soon and hungry for supper.

Think, think, think.

And what happened next, I blame Little Miss Muse. She was on fire during the earlier writing session, and she wasn't quite done yet, and a little aggravated that I'd stopped writing to actually do day job stuff. And prep food.

"Just scrape it and redo the topping." She sat on the countertop swinging her chonky legs, her purple stilettos banging against the cabinet.

"Yeah, but what if it hurts him?"

"So, you eat it too, and see what happens."

"It's just plastic, right? I mean, in our decades of marriage, he's eaten worse."

"I'd assume so, given it's you that's been cooking." (She can be a real snot, even though she speaks the truth.)

"And we use plastic wrap in the microwave, and the stuff sometimes gets melty, right?"

"I've seen you do that. Both of you." Little Miss blows a grape-flavored bubble right over the chicken. When it popped, I could see tiny moisture particles land all over the dish. I shooed her away.

Then I succumbed to the Muse's suggestion and scraped all the topping off the chicken. No way Saran Wrap bled that far down into the dish. And to be honest, the crusty crystals were only around the very edges and clinging (as good brand-name Saran Wrap should) to the top and outside edges of the 9X12.

I reapplied the cheesy topping and slammed the dish back into the oven with the rolls to melt the topping.

And when the dinger went off the second time, we filled our plates and both partook of my mistake.

It was good, I must say. Though I did chew very carefully, waiting for that bite that wasn't chewable, but it didn't come. Just chicken and cheese. I waited too, for Hubs to say something to the effect of "what's this?" while pulling a 12-inch stringy mess from his plate. But he didn't.

It was good.

So good, in fact, that my dear husband went back for seconds before he'd even finished his rolls or the by-the-skin-of-our-teeth-use-by-date salad.

I cringed. Seconds was pushing it.

Then, he says, "I wonder why the cats aren't begging. They're usually all about demanding chicken."

And I almost died. Because the cats *knew*. The cats overheard Little Miss Muse's plan, *and they watched me carry it out*. Cats don't like Saran Wrap. They let us mere humans have it to ourselves.

I dismissed myself to clean up the kitchen before my face gave away my trespass.

What prompted dear Hubs to sprint down the hallway to the bathroom shortly after dinner could only be one of a few things:

- It was going to happen anyway—due to the nature of his issues.
- It was the too-close-for-comfort salad.
- It was the grape bubble gum residue from Little Miss Muse.
- It was self-inflicted by the second helping.
- His wife can't cook and fed him plastic.

Like I said at the start of this confession:
"It Didn't Kill Either of Us, Did It?"
"It's Just How Things Are"
"I'll Be More Careful If There's a Next Time"
"I'm So, So Sorry"
Dinner out is on me tonight, Honey. Your pick. Love you. Don't hate me.

Looking Back: I'm sad to say that this was the beginning of a long round of bad culinary mishaps. I'll leave you to read them as they come.
One that didn't warrant a blog post all by itself just happened last week. It involved disintegrating stuffing mix and a very unhappy husband.
I'm so, so sorry.
Whatever future date the Hubs reads this, I won't be cooking that night either.
Little Miss Muse prefers Mexican cuisine in the actual restaurant as she likes swinging from their ever-hanging Christmas lights and eavesdropping at other tables.
"Free dialogue ideas."
I can't argue with her.

189

TAKE ME AWAY

I'm suffering from commercial fatigue. Advertisement angst, so to speak. From our streaming service's "watch free with ads" options to the banners that pop up on Facebook, the marketers have been hard at work trying to get me to part with my money.

Facebook certainly has my patterns figured out. Any and all things writing-related: cool t-shirts, craft courses, publishing podcasts... you name it. All I have to do is hover my finger or pause my scrolling for one microsecond and the next time on the platform, I'm bombarded with a fresh influx of "opportunities."

It wants my money, and no doubt a team of techy marketing gurus is hard at work finding out your pain points, as well.

Streaming services don't have the luxury of personalization, so they must aim for the masses.

Prescription drugs to address your ailments so you can go on that 19-hour plane ride to an exotic location.

Vehicles to take you to exotic locales—or those that will park themselves along the sidewalks snaking in front of glistening skyscrapers.

Insurance to protect your belongings while you're away in an exotic locale. (I don't mind the insurance commercials so much.

Allstate's Mayhem and Geico's Gecko are better actors than some folks on the shows we've been watching lately.)

Fast food, lunch meat, and Oreos. To keep body and soul together as you travel to and from your exotic locales.

Now, I understand the drug commercials—I either have or care for someone with an ailment that those products might address. I understand vehicle commercials as I've driven and ridden in vehicles more than a few times. Insurance—no problem. Food? Well, even if I've never eaten at a particular restaurant or tried a certain brand of lunch meat, I can guess what flavors might be opened up to me should I decide to try what they're offering.

Oreos? Yeah. I'm hungry now...

But, I'm clearly not in the target audience for perfume ads. Those ads fall way short and irk me, even. I've never been to the moonlit beach or the hot springs oasis to know what those places smell like, but I doubt they've bottled up damp nature and stuck it in a glass jar.

According to those commercials, one little squirt and you'll be adorned in bejeweled black-tie attire, dancing on a moonlit beach or doing the salsa through a hot spring oasis—with a model, no less.

I know, I know, it's all about brand awareness. Marketers hope if I hear "Chanel" or "Hugo" enough, I may want to pull on my sweatpants and hoodie and head to a certain fragrance-destination department store. They hope I'll test out the testers with a high-pressured salesperson (some prissy young thing, no doubt) who pretends to be my best friend while silently judging that I dared approach her smudgeless glass case while wearing an outfit straight off of "What Not To Wear."

Marketers hope I'll purchase a bottle for myself and one for a loved one. So we can smell good together. (Ooph. If you're close enough for me to smell you, you're probably too close.)

While I'm at it, I'll have to shop for that black-tie apparel because, well, sweatpants and hoodies aren't exactly exotic locale attire. Neither are jeans or t-shirts, and that's all we wear around here.

If toiletry marketers want my money, they'll have to do better.

They'll have to relate to my real-life issues.

They'll have to take me away. Away from real-people problems.

Picture this:

The camera pans across a living room that needs to be swept because three cats live in the house, and one feline likes to rip up cardboard and scatter it like confetti. There's a cobweb above the fireplace with a resident spider who has forwarded his mail to the mantel below.

The camera angle widens, and you see a middle-aged-ish woman adorned in a t-shirt she scored at a garage sale and a pair of ripped jeans frantically waving a dishtowel in front of the stove because something's burning in the oven. She's also having a hot flash. Sweat drips down her temples, making her bifocals parkour down her nose.

An even wider angle shows three days' worth of dirty dishes about to topple to the floor. On the adjacent counter, the woman's novel-in-progress sits unfinished in loose-leaf format... and will need to be edited soon.

There's a knock at the door because the doorbell is busted and has been for years. The mailman hands the lady a package, all sympathetic smiles because he's delivered to this house so often that he's used to seeing the middle-aged-ish woman in such a state and likewise accustomed to the aroma of over-done dinner.

The woman closes the door and slides to the floor in the entry-way, cardboard box in hand. Two cats join her because, usually, life is all about them, and the box could hold a new toy or catnip. The other cat is still tearing up a cardboard box from a previous delivery and eating a tax receipt.

But alas, she opens the box and pulls out INSERT BRAND NAME HERE perfume. One of those fancy bottles with the little bulb that you squeeze. She doesn't know where it came from. Doesn't remember ordering it, and really doesn't care.

She squeezes the bulb, and out comes a fine mist, landing on her still-sweaty forehead. It's a subtle fragrance, barely noticeable above the burning dinner, but her spirits lift ever so slightly.

She rises from the floor and sprays it again. Two cats flee down the hall, returning with broom and dustpan and begin sweeping up their own mess.

Another squirt. The third cat appears, giving a sweet leg hug to the lady, and politely waits her turn for the broom and dustpan before collecting all the cardboard confetti and depositing it in the trash can.

The lady, amazed, wonders if INSERT BRAND NAME HERE will do wonders in the kitchen, so she sprays it once again. The oven sucks the smoldering cloud of singe from the air and pops open its door, offering a perfectly-browned turkey, baked potatoes, and a raspberry pie.

Another spray, and the dishes wash, dry, and stack themselves. The novel's loose pages lift and swirl and coalesce into a pristine paperback with not a typo to be found.

As the soft aroma reaches the corners of the living room, the spider gathers his mail, packs up his cobweb, and heads outside.

One more squirt of INSERT BRAND NAME HERE, and the lady's hot flash is gone. She's calm, cool, and collected, and, though she's still adorning her garage sale shirt and ripped jeans, she's happy about her lot in life—no exotic locale needed. With plenty of time to spare before the Hubs comes home, she grabs her kitties, a fuzzy unicorn blanket, her new paperback, and settles down on the couch to enjoy some soul-filling quiet time.

Now *that's* a product I'd brave a prissy department store clerk for.

But alas. That's not a perfume.

That's a magic wand.

Looking Back: Since no such product is on the market, you know, one that you can use to squirt away what irks you, I've decided I'll have to take myself away.

Physically away from the CIRCUS and the cats, as much as I'll miss the felines.

Granted, two trips are to fulfill the bucket list items for the Hubs and a friend, but hey! Away is away and I don't cook on vacation, so that's a win in and of itself.

I've got a "me" trip planned to a weekend writer's conference in Nashville which should be a blast.

Back Guy, after discovering several more discs which are harboring "great amounts of stress" suggested alone time in a cabin by a lake.

"As long as Uber can deliver the meals," Little Miss suggests.

"Alone time. As in, no Muse."

"Well, what fun would that be?"

Probably no fun at all, actually. I guess we'll have to find her purple suitcase. The big one. With wheels.

190

EAT MY ERASER DUST

How many of you are completely over 2022?

I know I am. Have been for a while.

To the point where I started ripping out pages from this year's calendar back in July, tossing them in the garbage, setting them on fire, or handing them to Little Miss Muse so she can tie them to a bottle rocket and send them into the great beyond to live out a happier existence than they had on planet earth with me scratching out, underlining, erasing, and whiting out.

I do believe I went through five bottles of Whiteout before fall arrived. Why, you ask?

The CIRCUS!

Doctor appointments, surgeries, drama fests, follow-ups for surgeries, and doctors and drama fests. And all the recovering.

And the CIRCUS still hasn't packed up and left town yet.

Looks like it's here to stay, and I'm still wrestling with acceptance.

And likely, when/if the rings do die down, there will be permanent scarring of the earth beneath from all the elephant stomping, poodle peddling, and general foot traffic any circus generates.

In the meantime, I'm rebelling.

Big time.

I'm ripping out calendar pages by the week.

Good riddance.

I'm also trying to look forward, as much as possible, to the new year ahead.

One of the upcoming projects is the sequel to *Life Along the Way*. That included the first 100 blogs I wrote as B.A. Paul. This is blog #190. It's time to start reviewing and compiling that second batch of 100 blogs. Because, if the CIRCUS has its way, it may be the only project I *know* will get done next year.

So I'm starting early. Little Miss Muse is adding her own commentary to each review this go-round too. Jury's still out on whether her input is helpful or a hindrance. Perhaps a little of both.

At any rate, we've reviewed blogs 101-140. And we've noticed a pattern.

"You like to make goals." She's sitting on the edge of my desk, swinging her purple heels back and forth so they bang against the wall. The wall needs to be painted, so I guess I don't mind. But the banging is giving me a headache...

"Yes. Goals help me focus on something other than the chaos."

"But you usually fail." She says this with no judgment at all. Just matter of fact. She pops a nasty grape bubble in my face. "Or you have to rework the goal. Or only get halfway on something." She says all this in a whiny voice. "Why can't we just be freeee?" She flits away, glitter dripping from her wings. She's shining a bit brighter today because we did get some fiction words in earlier. And, in typical Little Miss fashion, she's taking the credit.

"Hey, that halfway thing is mostly on you, you little ADHD imp. And I prefer to think I'm failing forward." I do tend to set lofty goals. Or goals that don't consider the amount of mental energy the CIRCUS will require of me. Or who in the CIRCUS I'll have to stand in for this week. Will I be the ringmaster? Will something force me into the dunk tank with the clowns or up the tightrope with the acrobat? Perhaps I'll be scooping elephant poop.

One never knows.

So sometimes, the goals get tweaked or forgotten about entirely.

Since October, I have made a concerted effort to spend Thursdays writing away from the house. That's helped a great deal. Checking in with a friend weekly and setting smaller goals is also a motivator.

Learning to forgive me for my "failures" is an ongoing process. If I didn't get the 5,000 words I wished for this week, but I did manage 2,000 despite a brand-new Clown on the payroll, well, hey. I failed forward.

Little Miss floats back into the office and dumps a pack of grape-scented erasers on my desk. "Maybe try these instead."

Yesterday, she saw me attempting to do some goal-setting for 2023. "You know ink isn't going to work." She nods her curly head toward my stack of gorgeous fountain pens. "Save those for your stupid plot scribbles." She hates it when I plot. She likes free reign, in case you hadn't noticed.

I picked up the erasers. I'd given them to her in her Christmas stocking several years ago. They're unopened.

"I don't need them. I don't make mistakes." She boasts and lands her tutu-clad behind on top of the office door. Her heels now clang against the wood while she balances herself by placing both of her sticky chubby hands flat against the ceiling.

"Goals aren't mistakes—" I start to argue, but she flips herself backward off the door, her wings flitting in time to catch her from clonking onto the floor.

"Yeah, but flexible, erasable goals would be better. For me at least."

Well, all right then. As long as the Muse is happy.

I pull out my new 2023 calendar. I clean off the dry-erase board on the wall. And I begin to scribble some writing plans for the new year. Word counts. Project titles. Publishing targets.

And then I carefully, carefully transcribe my wall plans to my calendar—in pencil, grape erasers close at hand. I may have to make a little pocket inside the calendar to store an extra grape eraser just in case the CIRCUS.

So, an early goodbye to 2022. A preemptive strike on next year's chaos.

A promise to myself to say "No" more often and guard my writing time a little more closely. Something more than only Thursdays...

And anyone who doesn't like it can eat my grape-flavored eraser dust.

Looking Back: Closing in on the home stretch of reviewing the second one hundred blogs. I've got a rough draft of the cover for Life All Over Again, *and most of the edits are done for blogs 101 through 180. Yay!*
"So, we've done 89 of these now. How's my input been?" She's found grape-flavored Pop Rocks. Her mouth sizzles when she speaks. This is new.
"It's been... Real."
She's happy with this answer and proceeds to dump five more short story ideas into the To-Be-Done folder.
Yeah. Erasers. Those are a genius idea.

191

NOT FIT FOR COMPANY

I tried a new recipe.

For any normal human on the planet, this would not be news. But I'm not normal.

And if you're a regular to the blog here, you just fell off your seat. Or, at the very least, your eyebrows raced up to your hairline pretty quickly.

I hate cooking, but with the ever-expanding CIRCUS and the barreling down of the holidays, I needed a quick, go-to breakfast that was less pre-packaged and more nutritious, even if it does have cream cheese in it. (Side note: Did you know that if you soften cream cheese for a little bit too long in the microwave, you then have to clean the microwave?)

Enter Red Lobster Cheddar Bay Sausage Balls.

I figured cooking a batch of something protein-heavy once to reheat each morning would be simpler in the long run. Far better than me risking life and limb over the stove *every morning* before the sun comes up to fuel the brain for the day job.

Fewer dishes, too.

Well, I thought fewer dishes until the Hubs walked through and asked what happened to all of our big stirring/flipping utensils hanging above the countertop. Then I realized I was only on Step One and full of regret. The recipe suggested using a countertop mixer, but I figured I could strong-arm the dough since what in the world would I do with a countertop mixer?

I figured it'd be even easier to stir because, instead of softened cream cheese, I had straight-up liquid.

I figured wrong. Not one stiff-ended spatula or large spoon or even the potato masher would get through this stuff.

I ended up putting baggies on my hands and trying to knead the dough (I think part of my cooking aversion is an aversion to touching raw meat—too many salmonella medical dramas on television). My fingers poked through the baggies, and I touched the raw meat anyway.

After wrestling and wrestling with it, I finally got the stupid balls onto the baking sheets and put the first batch in.

Waited the 20 minutes.

They came out... crispy.

I tried one. That blasted ball sucked all the moisture out of my mouth on the second chew.

Second batch went in for two minutes less, me hoping the whole time that was long enough to kill the salmonella, E. coli, or whatever else lurks in uncooked pork. I also drank a bottle of water.

The second batch came out... crispy. Perhaps they're supposed to be crispy?

I tried one.

Grabbed another bottle of water.

At this point, I only put the third batch in out of spite and because I could hear Grandma from her mansion above shouting through the clouds, "Don't you waste that! It'll hold body and soul together if nothing else."

Body and soul together... that was her go-to when she wasn't thrilled with what she offered for a meal or snack.

My body and my soul got together, alright, and told me this would be the last time I tried a batch of anything I'd never cooked before.

The last thing I tried to cook that I'd never cooked before ended up with a nice Saran Wrap glaze... You'd think I'd learn my lesson.

The dinger on the oven went off (and yes, I stayed close to the stove this whole process—I had a whole plethora of dishes to do and raw meat to wash off my hands, remember?).

Guess what? Crispy again.

I did NOT try a third one. I figured the body and/or the soul would go on strike, and I will need them both to get through the next week.

I bagged them up and tossed them into the fridge (again, with a vision of Grandma standing with her arms crossed, daring me to throw them away).

This morning, after a fitful night's sleep because of all the WATER, I pulled a few out of the bag. Heated them in the microwave. And... still crispy. Still required 16.9 fluid ounces of help. But they don't taste as disappointing as they did last night.

Chili and stew do that, too. Get better as they set (until a certain point, then you'll be sitting in the ER).

But I'm not hungry now. And they weren't entirely awful.

I suppose that's the point of any sustenance.

They're not fit for company, though, unless company is of the canine variety—and even then... (I'm remembering a real-life Schnauzer that wouldn't eat my enchiladas). Envisioning a guest with one of these balls in their hands makes me sweat. It's much like my writing-during-the-CIRCUS-life process lately.

I want to. So I do it. Then I stand in regret realizing how much I've dirtied up. Half-baked plots. Twisted characters. Too-crispy dialogue.

Keep going anyway.

Keep trying new things anyway. Three batches worth, as a matter of fact. Determination, that is.

Pray someone doesn't pick it up in its current state and start going all judgy-judgy on it.

Let the work set. Walk away. Do something else.

Sleep on it. Dream about it.

Try it again the next day and realize...

Yeah, the story's still not fit for company, but it'll hold the dream and the determination together in the meantime.

Grandma would be proud.

Looking Back: I'm letting several things "sit" as I clear out mental clutter from the CIRCUS. When I go back and read what I've done, I'm shocked—shocked, I tell you—at some of the things that have fallen from my fingers onto the keyboard.

Some things are surprisingly... good (Is this shameless self-promotion? A pat on the back? Those aren't in my nature, but if someone else had written that story I'd say it's good. So. Some things I write I like).

Others? Yeah. Those won't see the light of day.

And I have a whole file folder of stuff I snipped and pared away from the current novel's manuscript. Stuff that makes absolutely no sense, but Little Miss Muse says we might need them and refuses to let me hit the delete key.

"You never know. Keep the snippets."

I never knew my muse was a hoarder.

192

THE DAY OF THE SIBERIAN GOOSE KAZOO

This post goes live the day after Christmas. Once it hits your eyeballs, it could be the 26th of December or the 8th of July for all I know, depending on when you clicked the link. (Or when you picked up *Life All Over Again*.)

As I write this, it's 12-23-2022.

It's nine a.m. now, but The Day of the Siberian Goose Kazoo started much, much earlier than that.

1:00 a.m.: The cold front arrives, and with it, the winds, reminding me our front door has needed to be replaced for over ten years. The first windy day in this house, we thought someone was literally standing on the front porch whistling. When the winds kick up, the Unseen Whistler's high-pitched tune can be heard throughout the house.

This morning it woke me up.

Since the temps have dropped to sub-zero, I get out of bed, do a faucet/pipe check, turn a few taps on to drip, toss the cats their three a.m. Salmon-Flavored Temptation treats two hours early, and go back to bed.

2:00 a.m. I'm still awake.

3:00 a.m. The Unseen Whistler hasn't left the front porch, blowing his high-pitched melodies through the cracks in the front door. The cats have forgotten their 1:00 a.m. treats and believe Temptations are still due them.

I'm now another episode into the legal drama I've been binging. Since I have to work today, I decide a minuscule dose of melatonin can't hurt. Just one milligram. For reference, some children's versions have a full three milligrams.

6:30 a.m.: I sit straight up in bed, eyelids not obeying me because of that less-than-child-sized dose of an over-the-counter sleep aid, my heart pounding in my chest. I must've heard the sound before my sleep-deprived brain could determine what it was.

Someone handed our Unseen Whistler a full-blown kazoo. Or it could've been a disoriented Siberian goose sporting a kazoo that chased our Unseen Whistler from the porch. No doubt one of the orange-haired CIRCUS clowns from my out-of-control freak show had something to do with it. The direction of the wind (or multiple directions of the wind—it's really bad out there) produced more of an out-of-rhythm buzzing honk than anything resembling a whistle.

I lie back down and try to calm down, but just as I thought I might be able to sleep off the rest of that milligram, the cats happened.

Stella Marie finds the kitchen cabinet door ajar (dutiful homeowner here, trying to prevent frozen pipes) and begins spelunking through the cleaning supplies, knocking them onto the floor. When I get to her, she's found a secret passage over to the Hub's lunch cabinet and is stomping around in his box of cheese and peanut butter crackers. I shoo her out because those belong to the Hubs, so he can goo up the pages of my paperbacks with cheese smudges on his lunch break.

I pick up the cleaning supply chaos and call Hubs to make sure he made it to work okay in the pre-dawn whiteout. I try once again to rest, but sleep doesn't come at this point. May as well officially start the day.

7:30 a.m.: Eggs sound good. (Regular readers of the blog will know this is where the day really goes south, despite the 6:30 a.m. goosey kazoo. Because eggs must be *cooked*).

7:35 a.m.: Eggs in the skillet, cheese and bacon bits, too. A little caffeine to counter the effects of that residual melatonin milligram. Things are looking pretty good when I notice that my solar-powered dancing unicorn in the kitchen windowsill is covered in snow. I think this will make an interesting blog post, or Facebook update... something.

7:40 a.m.: I plate my eggs, lest they burn, retrieve my phone and snap photos of my chilly figurine. Take breakfast to the office and clear emails, post on Facebook, start the day job...

7:45 a.m.: Stella Marie happens again. Her bellowing drowns out the ongoing Siberian Goose Kazoo. Her raspy voice and snarky swish of her tail tell me she is definitely unhappy and no amount of pets and kind words from me will assure her everything is fine. She leaves the office. Comes back again. Over and over. Louder.

And louder.

Until...

7:47 a.m.: I smell it.

7:47 ½ a.m.: I find it.

In my melatonin-induced brain fog, and because I am who I am, I'd left the burner on. The skillet with the cheesy egg residue, along with my scrambling spatula, succumbed to my carelessness. The spatula had contorted into a twisted mess, much like the acrobat in my CIRCUS show. I turn off the burner, flip on the stove vent, and debate opening the kitchen window. I could rescue my snow-covered solar-powered dancing unicorn and allow the melted plastic fumes to escape.

But the -35 degree windchill notice on my phone suggests I just use the vent.

7:50 a.m.: Stella is still bellowing. Malachi can't even with her noise and tries to get her to shut up by gently head-bumping her into the walls.

8:00 a.m.: Amara, the boss cat, now attempts to calm Stella down. This ends in a hallway-long scuffle which sends clumps of hair into all rooms coming off the hallway.

8:30 a.m.: The faucets are still dripping, and Amara, figuring Stella will eventually stroke out on her own, turns to the fine art of the water-drop-bat-then-flick-it-everywhere game.

9:22 a.m.: We've now caught up with the beginning of this post that I started 22 minutes ago. Stella has finally ceased her cries and has taken up post on my desk, the dutiful office cat she is. Amara pounds around in protest, parkouring off the walls, since I turned the faucets off and dried her paws.

Poor Malachi has disappeared. He fears the Day of the Siberian Goose Kazoo is just getting started and he's gonna need a minute.

I fear the same because I've still not worked off that last remaining milligram of melatonin.

And, at 9:25 a.m., the Siberian Goose Kazoo has awoken Little Miss Muse...

Looking Back: I'd forgotten all about burning that skillet and spatula up. Didn't even bother trying to salvage it. It's been through enough. May it rest in peace.

The cats have saved the house from the fire department at least three times since Christmas. Just the other day I was boiling eggs. Left the kitchen. Forgot I was boiling eggs. Then poor Malachi couldn't even with the boiling-over water jumping from the pan onto the burner. Stood in the middle of the kitchen squalling until I fixed the noise.

Melatonin is now only used pre-eleven p.m. and only if I don't have to drive anywhere the next morning. Evidently my precious snowflake system can't handle it.

Little Miss Muse is rummaging through the freezer—again
"For crying out loud. What are you looking for in there?" All I see of her is her purple tutu barely covering what it needs to.
She pops her head out and with a huge smile declares, "I think you and I should write a cookbook."

"Uh... no."

"It'd be shelved in the comedy section. And not really be a cookbook."

Well, with enough melatonin/caffeine combo deal, I could probably make that happen.

It isn't lost on me that she dodged the question about the freezer.

193

BAM! POW! BOOM!

I t's a brand New Year!

A brand new chance to make changes and resolutions! To lose weight! To read more! To do more of what you love! Like reading!

And, for some nonfiction writers I've been editing for lately, to use fewer exclamation points!

Please!

Oh. My. Word!

Despite all the typos you can find in my blog (which I don't pay to have proofread before I send live) I do have a full-time day job editing nonfiction for marketers who build business web pages — from plumbers to proctologists (another type of plumber?).

My job is to make sure Google can find these pages based on the language used in the piece and make sure human beings can read the article without needing to Google definitions and without turning into bobbleheads who click away to a competitor's website.

It seems after the first of the year, the new batch of writers hired for one marketer's project is very excited about the assignments — and they also have a knack for stating the obvious. Like, every single idea is super exciting! And so *obvious*!

Toilets are an essential part of your home! You need a plumber if your toilet is malfunctioning! Quick! Before you get a clog!

Without electricity, your home won't be as comfortable! Hire an electrician to inspect your wiring today!

Regular bowel movements are necessary for good health! Contact Dr. Procto Plumber Today! We look forward to serving you! Today! Quick! Before you get a clog!

I can't help but picture some of these sentences tucked inside comic book panels with BAM!, POW!, and BOOM! floating above the characters' heads in psychedelic colors as they hold their shiny wrenches, amperage testers, and enemas!

You're probably already worn out by now with all the exclamation points. Punctuation, spacing, and paragraphs affect readers, whether they're aware of it or not.

The general rule for professional content is to use zero exclamations or just one well-placed exclamation point. That's it. No matter how excited you are about plumbing or proctologists.

Not one thing in any topic is that exciting *all the time*. Sorry. Especially anything regarding pipes.

For fiction, it depends on the situation. Sparingly is still best, or you exhaust your audience. Let the action and emotion of the content wear them out, not the punctuation.

For example, if I wanted to promote my new short story collection, *Dark Minds*, I'd tell you that New Year's is a great time to pick up the pace with your reading. Or explore new genres, like twisted mysteries that make you wonder if B. A. Paul needs a special session to sort out some issues. (She probably does, but that's a topic for another post. And if she ever goes to a session like that, she'll blame Little Miss Muse anyway...)

The stories in *Dark Minds* include:

Awake
Bonfire
Backroad Driver's Ed
Nondisclosure
Often and Endlessly

and *Coral Cove,* which was first seen in Black Cat Mystery Magazine.

You can find it on Amazon for now; I'm slow to get it onto bapaul.com or other distributors. I've been too busy taking out exclamation points from the day job pieces.

See? All promotional without one exclamation point.

It can be done.

Now, go get your copy of *Dark Minds*, and

BAM!

POW!

BOOM!

READ!!!

Looking Back: By the time you read this, Little Miss Muse and I will have had a session or two, likely many time slots, with Couch Lady.

As I write this, I won't have any idea the outcome of those sessions yet, but I feel they'll be promising.

Keep the CIRCUS from overtaking all the brain cells.

Keep the brain cells on task.

Keep the tasks manageable.

Little Miss Muse is now hung up on the cookbook idea, a possibly manageable but completely ridiculous task which may go the way of several other of her ridiculous ideas.

I still want to know what she's been doing in the freezer.

She still won't tell me.

194

NEVER AGAIN, BETTY

On Christmas Eve, I tossed a hot, bubbling berry pie from Marie Callender all over my kitchen floor. The Hubs and I literally stood over it in a moment of silence before we sprang into action to clean up the boiling goo before one of the three cats singed off their bean toes.

And you'd think that after all the cooking for Christmas that I'd give it a rest. But, somehow, one must continue to eat, even if one is sick of cooking.

Or no good at it.

You'd also think a pre-made angel food cake wouldn't cost six bucks. I mean, I already threw an eight-dollar pie on the floor. I'm not spending six on one, even if it means fading visions of the fresh strawberries I was going to put on it.

But then I found an angel food cake mix. On sale for a buck.

Betty Crocker, even.

And the front of the box said, *and I quote*, "Just Add Water!" (With the exclamation point and everything.)

Alright, Betty. We'll give this a try a long as water is all it will take to satisfy my sweet tooth. And I saved five bucks, I did, I did.

So, I pull out my round pan that I only use at Christmas when I make pull-apart monkey bread (I did that job okay, but it's been years of practice to get it right) and spray it with nonstick cooking spray. Like you're supposed to.

I grab my handy-dandy measuring cup and my mixing bowl.

Here we go.

Step 1: Rearrange the entire configuration of your oven so the cake will set as close to the bottom heating element as possible.

Well, that's a step I'd not seen before. But, okay, Betty. Oven racks all over the place... The cats think we're moving.

Step 2: Preheat to 325. Do not grease the pan.

Oops. Apologies, Miss Betty. I should've read through this first. Wash the Bundt pan.

Step 3: Beat the mix and water in an extra-large glass or metal bowl.

I look at my bowl. It's not glass. It's not metal. And it's not extra-large. It'll surely be okay, even though there's a little nudge from my mind's dark, dusty recesses where I stored some of my chemistry classes... I bet the make of the bowl is important, but I don't have what I don't have.

Now let me tell you, if the Betty Crocker company went to the trouble to tell you to use an extra-large bowl, use it. That mix frothed up like it had rabies. Then it continued to rise. But alas, my plastic medium-ish large bowl seemed to work fine. Don't know what the glass/metal thing had to do with it. They should give explanations on this stuff. Teach a fool a thing or two. Tell me WHY.

They should also explain that raw angel food cake batter DOES NOT taste the same as regular cake batter. Fun Tip: Skip licking the beaters...

Step 4: Pour into the ungreased pan you just washed because you greased it when you weren't supposed to.

Step 5: Measure your pan. It can't be smaller than 10x4.

That would've been nice to know right up front. Like on FRONT of the box, Betty.

Step 6: Bake until the top cracks and browns, is not sticky and do NOT UNDERBAKE. (Literally all caps on the box, people.) I feel good about this step. I tend to crisp and burn everything. Underbaking is not my problem.

Step 7: (Here, it's my own steps until #14, when we get back to what Betty said to do). Set the timer and grab lunch. Forget your drink, return to the kitchen five minutes later for it and turn on the oven light.

Gasp.

Step 8: Freak out and ask two friends on opposite ends of the globe if my angel food cake is going to blow up. You know that scene in Ghostbusters when the Stay Puft marshmallow guy did his thing? Yeah... that was happening in my oven. The batter grew before my eyes, and I watched for it to sprout limbs and ears and noses and such.

I paced a little bit until France Friend says, "It looks good." So I relaxed. She knows what she's doing.

Indiana Friend knows, too, but nothing from her yet.

Step 9: Cue Stella to begin wailing the first verse of "We're All Gonna Die!" in deep, sorrowful meows. Actual fire. In the oven. The cat knew it before I did. (Poor thing has the opportunity to sing this tune at least once a month... She's looking into having her adoption revoked.)

Step 10: Send photographic proof to France Friend that it really did blow up.

Indiana Friend finally chimes in with sad emoji and the too-late advice: "pan's too small."

Nooo... You don't say?

Right here, I want to say I did not measure my pan back in Step 5 because I'd ALREADY PUT THE BATTER IN. Besides, the BACK of the box said tube pan or two loaf pans. I only have one loaf pan, and that frothing batter didn't look like it wanted to wait to be baked. It was becoming sentient at that point and demanded heat.

But, I suppose, if the Betty Crocker Company took the time to write the pan size right there in step whatever, that you should probably measure your equipment. My bad.

I still think something like this should be up there on the FRONT with the "Just Add Water!" remark, but hey.

Step 11: Turn on the vent and crack some windows. Cue Stella to start her second verse, where she sings that Mom should crack windows and open vents *long* before she turns on the stove. This verse is longer and louder than the first, so add extra time for this step and take some Tylenol.

Step 12: Finish your lunch because you'll need the energy to clean the ENTIRE oven later. The Marie Callender method is much easier. Step One: Pie into the oven; Step Two: Pie on the floor.

Step 13: Remove the pan from the oven and get your oven mitts all messed up from the overflow.

Step 14 (Back to Betty's suggestions): Immediately turn pan upside down onto a glass bottle to cool.

See, Betty. I don't have a glass bottle. All of mine are plastic. I don't have a metal bottle, either. This is yet another piece of equipment that should've been listed on the FRONT. Along with a difficulty level of 5/5 for fools like me who don't kitchen well. Just add water my foot. That's like telling a writer struggling with their manuscript to "Just Add Words!"

Step 15: Spend way too much time trying to create a contraption to allow my mutilated angel food cake to cool upside down. Mumble under breath that it's easier to write novels than bake a cake. Upside down on a glass bottle... what a precious snowflake.

Step 16: Turn off the vent, close the windows, and toss Stella a turkey-flavored Temptation for her agony as she finishes the third verse of "We're All Gonna Die" where, alas, the family lives, but an ominous note at the end says this will all happen again next week. Dig into the Christmas candy for a white chocolate Reese's for my own agony, because I won't likely be eating cake.

The cake—if you can call it that—is now cooling, hanging upside down from a spatula anchored into my Yeti thermos. There's nothing at all angelic about it. It's the food version of "What Not To Wear."

Step 17: Glance at the box. The very last direction says to cut with a serrated knife using a sawing motion or use an electric knife.

Hey, Betty? Don't tell me how to cut my cake, k?

You don't see Marie getting all pushy about her pies, do you?

It's my cake. I'll cut it how I want.

Come to think of it, Betty, I may not even cut it at all.

I may just sit with it in the middle of the kitchen floor right there where I dumped the berry pie a few weeks ago and eat it with my fingers. Even if I did have a white chocolate Reese's already. Don't judge...

I spent a whole dollar on it, after all. It's mine.

And I don't have time to search for a serrated knife, anyway. I have novels to write—which from start to finish take fewer steps than Crocker's cake mixes.

And my books don't make my cat cry, Betty.

I don't care if I did save five bucks...

Never again, Betty. Never again.

Looking Back: So far, "Never Again, Betty" is my number-one most read post ever. Probably even wider read than the short story fiction pieces that appeared in Ellery Queen or Pulphouse Fiction Magazine.
I still have folks in the community telling me they laughed until they hurt.
Or the post made their toes curl.
Or, please call me before you attempt anything else in the kitchen. Anything at all.
Or, here, you poor dear. Here's some angel food cake that you don't have to buy or make.
"And this is why we should co-write a cookbook. Stuff like this. A cookbook that isn't." Little Miss pulls her glitter stash from the waistband of her tutu and heads to the freezer.
I grab her by the arm. "So basically, you want me to attempt new recipes with the very real risk of burning down our house in order to make profit off of our words?"
"Now you're getting it." She tries to wiggle free.
"What are you doing in the freezer?"

"Getting ready."

"Ready for what?"

She slips out of my grasp and dives head-first into the cold, knocking out a bag of frozen peas and a box of Eggos on her way in. She slams the door behind her, and when I open it again, all that's left of her is a trail of purple haze.

195

TIE IT ON THE DOG FIRST

I grew up with Boston Terriers. It was a generational thing on my dad's side of the fam, with at least grands and great-grands owning one—or several—throughout their lives. There was one in the house to greet my newborn self (Daisy), and there's still a sweet little one kicking around with the Aunt to this day (Dawn). That's a lot of Bostons.

Anyone who knows the breed knows they're as full of personality as they are of gas. Really bad gas. But the loyalty is worth the occasional rancid air. I've not had a Boston during my adulthood, since I'd be more likely to rescue some mutt from the pound than to purchase a purebred (overbred) anything from a breeder.

Oh... Wait a minute. There's another reason, too, right?

I've turned into the crazy cat lady. So there's that.

But back to Little Beth and the Bostons. There was Daisy, Boomer, Blossoms, and Bandit.

Blossoms was my absolute favorite, a tiny little female who followed me around as though we were sisters from separate litters. And, as an only child, Little Beth was more than happy to have such a friend.

One of our favorite things to do was to play dress up. My Aunt had given me a tall doll, complete with gorgeous ball gowns of lace and sparkly fabric. They poofed out like the square-dancing dress she'd given me. I'd wear my dress and Blossoms would wear the doll's clothes. Off we'd go on one of my many imaginary adventures, probably accompanied by Clark Kent, Mr. Rogers, and an Ewok. (Cut me some slack—I was, after all, a neighborless, only child back in the era before the internet. I often mashed up the genres).

Little Miss Muse wants everyone to know it had actually been *her* idea to let Ewoks and Mr. Rogers co-exist. Little Beth wasn't aware of the Muse yet. And, here, I tell Little Miss to be careful lest we fall into copyright infringement issues with Lucasfilm. Or Disney. Or D.C.

Good grief. Muses are so much work.

These dress-up adventures lasted until Blossoms outgrew the doll's clothes.

Then Bandit came. A wall-eyed, goofball boy pup my dad added to our family.

So, I put the dresses on him. Happy with my accomplishment, I coaxed the dog out of my bedroom, him tripping over the lace hems and wobbling the whole way to the living room.

There was just one problem with this... Blossoms was in the living room.

When that girl saw the newcomer in her outfit, she went berserk. She bit him on the head, running rageful zoomies all over the house. On her final return trip to the living room, she full-on plowed into Bandit. He never saw it coming, given his wall-eyed status.

I peeled the dress off Bandit and promised my Blossoms girl no boy would ever wear her dresses again—even if she was too fat to wear them herself.

To make her feel better, I started tying on some of my hair ribbons around her neck (those fat, thick yarn ones that itched when they brushed your face). She pranced around the house, Queen of Fashion once again. Bandit didn't get to wear anything but his God-given tuxedo (and was too dumb to know he was missing out on anything, so it all worked out).

Sometimes, I'd even tie the ribbon on Blossoms' neck before tying it in my hair. It was easier to get the bow right. I've heard of guys allowing their doggos to help them get the knots just right in their suit ties, too.

I imagine a feline's neck would suffice, but the tie would end up in shreds before becoming an accessory to anyone's outfit. Depends on the look you're after, I suppose.

I've been hard at work on my novel-in-progress, a good-guy versus the system type of tale—with dogs, even (none of them wear clothes, though).

It's been fun. Until it's not.

I dress up a character, from actual wardrobe to the intricacies of quirks and strengths and send them out into the scene.

But there's a problem. There's always another character in the scene pitching a fit that *they* want a character trait like that. Or a cool quirk.

Where's *their* genre-appropriate wardrobe of flaws and strengths? To tell them they're too fat for the wardrobe or that they're a secondary character (or heaven forbid an extra) is to be met with war.

The secondary runs around in the script in a raging case of the zoomies, completely uncooperative and edging on violence.

I look to Little Miss Muse for advice.

"Not my department." She picks at her peeling purple toenail polish.

"What do you mean, it's not your department? You're the one taking credit for the ideas."

"Yes, the big, fun ideas are mine. You're the one responsible for dressing it up." She flips her tutu and pops a grape-flavored bubble in my face for effect. You'd think with as many stilettos as she has, she'd love dressing up the characters.

So, I've taken a quick step back from the manuscript. I've written some character sketches—behind-the-scenes stuff to flesh out attitudes, quirks, and, yes, what kind of shoes someone needs. Because despite what Little Miss Muse believes, emergency room doctors and dog groomers are unlikely to grab their highest of high heels and head off to work.

Basically, I'm tying stuff on the dog first. Straighten out the knots. Right the bows. Then, I'll carefully pull out what works and stick it in the novel, all nice and straight and everyone dressed for the scene.

No purple tutus or rage zoomies required.

Looking Back: The novel-in-progress mentioned here is Triage. *It's coming along, though with square wheels. Little Miss Muse and I have decided my current CIRCUS brain is causing some issues with the main character's personalities. We're letting them sit down for a minute, gather themselves, then we'll be back at it full force when* Life All Over Again *is in final proofing.*

The issue with the secondary and tertiary characters happens to me frequently, even when the cast is only short-story long. Those "background" dressings want full-blown parts and personalities. A promise of a sequel all to themselves and the Netflix special to boot.

"If the tertiaries get a special, I definitely get a cookbook." Little Miss is up in arms. With bottle rockets in each chubby little fist.

I can't even with this imp.

196

THE OTHER SHOE

Several of you have asked about the state of my CIRCUS. Thank you for that, I appreciate the concern.

I painted a picture of my chaotic behind-the-scenes life in the post "Acceptance" back in August. If you've not read it, the following may seem odd, perhaps as though I should seek professional help.

You'd not be wrong. It's all odd. And I likely do need a pro to play around in my head for an hour at a time at least twice a month.

Sometime after writing "Acceptance," more and more rings were added, and I decided from that point forward to capitalize the entire word given its always-in-my-face status. I was waiting for it to pack up and leave town, but this seems more of a permanent gig.

So, the CIRCUS.

Here's the update:

The long, metal bleachers are empty except for me. Remember, no one wants to buy tickets to this show — I couldn't even pay anyone to watch. I put my top hat next to me. The brim has a hole and a couple of singe marks from where I lit the concession stand on fire, and the tails of my tux are tattered. My feet ache. My head hurts. My soul is weary.

I try to catch my breath, but it's not coming yet.

Some would say I'm waiting for the other shoe to drop. All tensed up and ducking.

That's accurate, but this is more precise: I'm waiting for the next showing under the Big Top.

Yes, yes. Step right up, ladies and gentlemen. Witness drama, drama, drama, like you've never seen before. We can't make this stuff up, folks! Hurry, hurry, hurry!

But, before the announcer tries to sell seats for the next round to a nonexistent crowd, I wait. And try to catch my breath behind ribs crushed with sadness and exhaustion.

And as I long for the next breath, The Ring participants are catching theirs.

A dozen monkeys in bright red vests are lined up front-to-back in Ring One, each one picking nits and examining the coat of the monkey before him. The monkey in the front of the line picks at his own toenails with an intensity any pedicurist would envy.

Over in Ring Two, the poodles crashed their unicycles into the clown cannon, the wheel of one cycle still spins, giving off a squeak. The dogs pile in a heap. A couple of them snore and chase rabbits in their sleep. I look a little closer and can see a purple-haired clown hanging from the end of that cannon. At first I thought it was Little Miss Muse, but she's otherwise occupied behind the tent with some other author's muse—the Sultan, I do believe.

We'll have to talk about that later.

Ring Three smolders from the mishap with the cannon in the last act.

We won't talk about that later.

The elephants crashed hard in Ring Four, all their ball tricks and trunk swinging wearing them to the bone. They sleep lying on their sides. I watch them breathe. A yellow-haired clown sleeps on one elephant, enjoying the rhythmic rise and fall of the pachyderm's rib cage.

My tightrope walker finally extricated herself from the wire where she's been hanging upside down for months. She sits on the support scaffolding, propped against a pole, dangling her legs in the air. A snore erupts from her tiny frame, and her chin hits her chest. Her head bobs back against the pole. Her legs never stop moving.

Opposite her, on the other high-wire support platform, a problem brews.

It's a clown.

An Awake.

Aware.

Alert.

Obese.

Clown.

By the look of his posture, he needs no nap or grooming or downtime. He's all oxygenated.

He's good to go.

He perches on the platform's edge and swings his feet through the air. His pants are striped in primary colors. His shirt is polka dotted in reds, yellows, and blues. He wears a striped tie as wide as his beefy neck. A black curly wig is topped with a blue hat adorned with daffodils on one side.

I hate daffodils. I'm allergic.

He knows this.

He catches me staring at him. A wicked, red grin creeps over his white face and he cocks his head at me. A daffodil falls from his hat and flutters to the CIRCUS floor.

He's taking off a shoe. A shoe wider than his thick thigh. His footwear is grungy with the dust from Ring Four where the elephants do their thing.

On second thought, perhaps that's not dust...

He holds this one giant shoe out past the platform in midair.

And he waits.

I don't know how long he can hold that stance, maybe minutes. Maybe weeks, given the amount of backup padding he's packed onto his skeleton.

And I wait with him.

Waiting for that shoe to drop.

Because when it does, that monster clodhopper's gonna land

right on the poodle pile. The dogs will rise and mount their cycles. The slumbering slob atop the elephant's ribcage will saunter over and light a fuse, sending the purple-haired clown in the cannon across the Rings. The sonic boom will startle the tightrope walker back to the wire, where she'll hang for who-knows-how-long. Her wail of surprise will wake the gray giants, who will gather up the line of monkeys in their trunks to escort them to their starting positions.

The announcer will come over the shorting-out speakers, voice garbled... "—ep right up. Step right up."

And the second showing of the CIRCUS will begin, whether or not I've had sufficient time to mend my tails and patch my top hat.

Or breathe.

In the meantime, just as before, I'll laugh when I can, rest when I can, write as much as I can (if I can get Little Miss's attention away from the Sultan), and be grateful for all the blessings in my life.

I'll use that joy and rest and creativity and gratitude to mend wounds and put one foot in front of the other.

I may even call in a pro to play around in my head for an hour at a time twice a month. Sit on a big, comfy couch for a while instead of these hard bleachers.

Because my CIRCUS ain't over.

...That fat clown still has another shoe.

Looking Back: I've a sneaking suspicion that whatever's happening in my freezer has something to do with the Sultan. Ages ago, Little Miss Muse pitched a fit and went on a walk about, leaving me all alone. The Sultan had been involved in that adventure.
He's not a bad guy, from what I can tell. He likely has his own author that he must put up with, and Little Miss and he have a lot in common.
But I would like to know if he's taken up residence in my freezer.
Because that would add to the CIRCUS.
And cause that fat clown to drop a shoe.

197

BLOOD-PUMPING GOOD NEWS!

I t was unfortunate timing, really.

Last Tuesday, the Kickstarter for Thrill Ride Magazine went live.

I also had a doctor's appointment that same morning.

Doc Guy asked about my life. Visions flurried of my crazy CIRCUS and that one clown hanging around up by the tightrope just waiting to drop his shoe...

And I thought: *No. No. That will earn you a new pill to swallow. Stick with the good news.*

But when the good news is thrilling, what do you do?

Doc asked for my left arm. (Why do they do that? Why not ask for the arm first, THEN have you explain clowns and story submissions?)

Doc and his nurse took turns pumping up the cuff on that arm, then the right. Until they were both satisfied that I was quite a few numbers off normal.

I earned bruised biceps and more than one new pill to swallow.

I blame my CIRCUS.

And Kickstarter.

And Thrill Ride.

And Little Miss Muse, who nearly wet her tutu when one of the graphics for the promotions had a tank on it. A TANK.

Can you imagine my Little Miss Muse driving a tank?

"It could shoot purple glitter along with the cannons. And lavender dust would follow our wake. We could spraypaint purple lettering on the side: THE MUSE RIDES AGAIN!"

"*Again?* When have you ever driven a tank?"

"There's a lot you don't know about me." She got one of her wings stuck between the wall and the sharps container. After a couple of seconds, she pulled it loose, spraying glitter all over the wall.

She bopped from chair to chair to the exam table and then to the top of the supply cabinet, where the tongue depressors went flying. I hate waiting in rooms with her. It's a lot to explain to the medical staff that I wasn't in here alone playing with cotton swabs and bandage rolls...

I pondered just how lucky I was to drive on to the pharmacy instead of being hauled off in a straight jacket...

At any rate... I'm thrilled to be a part of the Thrill Ride Magazine Kickstarter. My Story, "The Waiting Room" (no, it's not about a doctor's office—different kind of waiting area), will appear in Issue #4, *Betrayals*, this winter. I share a table of contents with some super-talented writers from across the globe—more blood-pumping news.

What is a Kickstarter, you ask?

It's a platform where creatives can fund projects from gadgets to games to publishing endeavors through the help of fans like you.

Over the last couple of years, I've backed quite a few campaigns, found some new favorite party games (Exploding Kittens, Ransom Notes), and scored great reads from talented writers.

Basically, Kickstarter helps project creators kickstart their dreams.

What is Thrill Ride Magazine, you ask?

It's a debut magazine edited by M. L. Buchman and packed with thriller stories.

I don't consider myself a thriller writer, more mystery than anything else. But the setting for this story lent itself to Issue #4's theme of Betrayal, and from that, I figured I could do some twisted psychological tale and maybe the editor would like it.

He did! (Thanks, Matt!)

Little Miss was rather proud of it too, but now believes it should have a tank in it.

Little Miss will have to come up with another story that has a tank in it.

You can throw some love at the Kickstarter here and get in on this publication's first year of thrilling reading. The authors get a share of the profits after the project funds, and you can score some great reading for your own TBR pile.

I'm sure the stories will get your blood pumping. Hopefully, your doctor won't tell you to swallow extra pills from reading these issues, unless you, too, have a CIRCUS like mine.

And hopefully your tutu-wearing Muse doesn't have "drive a tank" on her bucket list...

Looking Back: That Kickstarter funded, and by the winter of 2023,
Betrayals will be available.
Other good news is that the increased ticker medication seems to be calming things down a notch.
Little Miss still wants to drive a tank. Probably not good news. Chuck it in there with the cookbook idea. A friend of ours posted on Facebook the other day that he wishes he owned a tank. I'd be happy if he did. It would be fun to run over things. Or blow things up.
I can understand Little Miss's fascination with bottle rockets. It may be time to purchase some fireworks and head out to a remote field and light some stuff on fire. Therapy, we'll call it. In addition to the Couch Lady sessions, this activity may prove helpful.
Come to think of it...
"Hey, your Sultan friend, does he drive a tank by chance?"
She grins.
And heads for the freezer.

198

IN THE EVENT...

After the fiasco with the angel food cake, the Hubs had returned home that evening asking what smelled like burnt cotton candy and tried to offer encouragement. But alas, nothing he said could wipe out the disturbing thought that hit me as I stood at the kitchen sink scrubbing the wire oven racks.

In the event of the demise of humanity as we know it, you know, with the toppling of the grid and the internet and Amazon delivery and such... I possess no real survival skills.

This thought plagued me again when we had a death in the family. A great-aunt passed away, the last of my paternal grandmother's sibling group. I remembered how self-sufficient they all were. With the cooking, and the sewing, and the growing things. All of my grandparents and their siblings were a hardy bunch. Growing. Sewing. Cooking. Building.

I can't cook. That's been well established. Once the canned goods run out, we'll be hungry, because if I tried to run a canner, the apocalypse will be the least of our worries.

I also can't grow things.(See "Water Your Unicorns"—one sprig left of that once-thriving, multi-spriggy succulent, and that's only because I've literally not touched it since my dear friend told me not to touch it). Spring is 43 days away as I write this. I'll get an urge to go play in the dirt, but then…. Yeah. Everything will die unless the Hubs steps in.

I can't sew. Buttons and simple seams, yes. But past that, we're naked.

I'm not good with mechanical things or building stuff. I mean, I can change lightbulbs and the filter on the fridge, but if the real end of the world comes, I don't think bulbs and fridge filters will be a thing… And as for the construction, just ask my kids what happened to their Lego creations any time I tried to "help."

I'm certainly not made of the same stuff as my ancestors—that's a cold, hard fact. I blame the internet. And Amazon.

I can't run fast (also the Internet's fault). So if the end of things happens to be a zombies-after-brains/stampeding-herds-of-rabid-cattle/Roombas-gone-wrong sort of deal, I'll be the first to throw myself into the oncoming melee, giving those around me a fighting chance at escape.

Because I can sacrifice. One less mouth for the cooks to deal with.

If I do manage to survive the initial chaos, I'll be the one sent down to the river with loads of nasty laundry from those who *do* know how to cook and clean and grow things. Or, I'll be the one scrubbing some makeshift kitchen or cleaning up the campsite.

Because I can scrub things. A skill that comes in handy when one regularly blows stuff up in ovens.

Or—and this idea was given to me by another friend who told me I could win "Nailed It" with my disastrous cooking—I could be the record keeper.

Because, I can write stuff. String words together for fun and profit.

Why not string a few together for posterity's sake?

In the event of the end of the world, I'll be the old woman in the hut on the edge of the village. Folks will come from all around to tell me their stories because they know I have the largest hoard of office supplies that require no electricity. Pens and pencils and legal pads and notebooks. I'll serve as the scribe, recording our new reality, how things used to be, and make stuff up just for the heck of it. You know, to really throw off the alien archaeologists who'll discover our settlement centuries from now.

I'll store the pages carefully for the generations to come in archival sleeves (yes, I have these sleeves, just in case, you know).

You and I can work out some sort of bartering system: Two pages of a memoir for one knitted sock. Five pages for the pair.

Potatoes from your garden? That's ten pages of family history or a brand-new fantasy tale to tell your children. I'll throw in a sci-fi short if those potatoes are already cooked.

If my hut door is falling off its hinges after the last gaggle of Roombas burst through? That's five chapters of a thriller novel if you fix the door. I'll finish the thing if you rethatch the roof.

So, I suppose, in the event of the end of the world (unless running is necessary for survival), I'll scrub your pots, beat your underwear on river rocks, and write your words.

A quick glance around my office tells me the beginning of the Roomba Rampage is nigh if I don't get up and do some scrubbing of my own.

But if this *is* it, and the State Board of Health unleashes the sucking robots on us all, I'll just sit right here, write about it, and wait for you to bring me your laundry.

Looking Back: I tend toward the cataclysmic—whether writing stories or thinking about real life in my head. I need to work on that—at least in the real-life vein.
So, in the event that things start looking up, I might take up a hobby that would teach me a survival skill, so I'm not completely dead weight on the new world order.
In the event that CIRCUS out back loses a ring or a clown or two, perhaps I'll be too busy writing away to develop any new skills, the words happily pouring from my fingers.
Maybe even work on "Little Miss Muse Cooks a Book."
Oooh. That's the title. Right there.
"See? My ideas are just what you need in the event that things go right."
Well, when you've been living in a state of things going sideways, south,

and zig-zagged for three years, having such a thought that things could go right is... bizarre at best.

"I want a byline."

"Of course. If you tell me what's in the freezer."

She stops cold—no pun intended—and stares at me. That look. That look that's cost me thousands of dollars in all things purple. Shoes. Gum. Soda. Erasers. Purses. Tutus...

That look that's also awarded me some pretty amazing ideas for those efforts.

She's got that look.

I sit back in my office chair, cross my hands behind my head and wait her out while the gears swirl in her head.

Let the bargaining begin.

199

ROUND 'EM UP!

"Do you think the couch will be purple?"

That's what Little Miss has been asking since we were placed on the waiting list for a legit Couch Person back in December. I finally got the okay to be seen in person.

It's a girl, by the way, so I'll call her Couch Lady. We'll just add her to the Gang.

The Gang that helps me keep the CIRCUS from burying me alive under the Big Top.

A friend of mine was shocked to hear that I would discuss therapy here on the blog. "People will... *know*." She whispered the *know*.

You know what? Everyone who knows me knows I need all the help I can get. I'm twitchy on a good day and ugly-crying on the bad ones. Last year, I wasn't a crier and could function in the cat food aisle at Walmart.

This year? I avoid the cat food aisle at Walmart, and, evidently, I'm now a crier.

Don't ask.

And I already tell you people about my overworked ticker and my nonfunctioning endocrine system and my angry spine (where Back

Guy told me just last week is, how'd he put it? hoarding stress?). So yes. Therapy is indicated.

And if someone else sees a hint of themselves in my chaos (isn't that the great thing about reading—finding yourself revealed in someone else?), and if my openness about my struggles helps them reach out to their own Gang for the help they need, it's worth every jot and tittle in this blog.

Help is a good thing, even if it comes in the form of a purple, white, or polka-dotted couch.

Well, as long as Couch Lady doesn't let the clowns in the room at the same time. I'm not up for group therapy with the CIRCUS Performers at this time.

I won't be disclosing on the blog the deep and dark conversations I will most certainly have with this lady. That's no one's business. I do suppose Little Miss will overhear the sessions if she can't cool her ADHD jets in the waiting room. Maybe I'll send her packing with some other writer's muse for the day. I can't imagine if Little Miss must come into the session with me and starts acting up. I'd have to explain why on earth I'm arguing with a being Couch Lady can't see.

Trying it for six months. After that time frame, we'll reevaluate whether I notice a difference. But, given the CIRCUS, I'm sure there'll be so much to chuck in the therapy bucket that six months will become a longer-lasting gig.

Unless I wear out Couch Lady and must break in someone new. I mean, Back Guy already cut his hours down to two days a week, which puts a cramp in my schedule and leaves a certain number of cramps in my back unattended. Nurse Practitioner Lady went down to one day. And Web Guy? Don't even ask. Little Miss and I have a track record of retiring and/or downsizing professionals in all industry fields.

Since I was given an appointment time after a long waiting period, I have had a whole new round of anxiety.

Are my problems legit enough to warrant the fuss? I peek in the backyard. The CIRCUS is still there. So, yes. I believe I have legitimate issues to discuss.

What if she breaks my brain? What if I can't write anything ever again? What if the tangled mess of emotions is exactly what's driving the creative process?

What if she prescribes group therapy with the Cannon Clown, Elephant Tamer, and the Poodle Master?

What if she wants to get really serious and talk to my whole Gang?

"Round 'em up!" Little Miss goes galloping across the office, one hand slinging a bottle rocket above her head as if there's a lasso attached to the end of it, the other slapping her tutu'd fanny. I struggle to keep my head from hitting the keyboard in a frustrated moan.

Can you imagine?

Group therapy with Back Guy, relatively New Doc Guy, Nurse Practitioner Lady, Eye Guy... May as well throw in Proofreader Gal, Web Guy, the Peacock Friend, and all of France. Every one of them knows more than enough to add months to my treatment plan. Give Couch Lady a real warm how do you do welcome to my life.

I'm getting ahead of myself here.

Most of what I worry about is completely ridiculous and will never materialize.

I need to turn down the volume on the "crazy" and focus on putting words together in an order that makes sense (unlike real-life events that make NO sense) that others might want to read.

Perhaps shake a few titles out of my fingers before Couch Lady rounds *those* up.

Wait. What if she reads my stories? How far into them would she "read"? I mean, I write some twisted stuff.

Another forehead moment on the keyboard. My eyes pop open wide and I jerk upright. What if she reads the blog?

What if she tells me the whole blog is just my brain's twisted way of wrapping hard-to-deal-with events in sarcasm and dry humor in an attempt to cope? (Well, she wouldn't be wrong...)

Little Miss is back from her gallop around the house. (I'd just vacuumed, and now there's a fresh dusting of cat hair all over the place from Little Miss's attempts at herding cats.) She reads the last couple of lines over my shoulder.

"I'll just have to go in with you." She plops down on the desk and lets her bare feet swing. She's recently painted her nails (how does she find the time?), and a tuft of Stella's fur sticks to some of the wet varnish.

"What? Oh, no way. You're in the waiting room. Or in the car."

"Well, it'll just save you time and money if I go in and explain that all those twisted ideas are mine and that—"

"No. You're in the car."

"I won't disclose any confidences." She leans in close and pops a purple bubble in my face. "There's an unwritten law, a sort of Muse-Writer confidentiality agreement." She's got a sparkle in her eye that I don't quite trust.

I shoo her off my desk and rummage for the number of a writer buddy of mine. Surely she has a muse Little Miss can occupy herself with while I'm in appointments.

She catches on to my plan.

"You do remember what happened when you left me at the Shark Pool in the Golden Nugget Hotel, right?"

Why, yes. Yes I do.

"And the casino?"

I sigh. "What'll it take?"

She grins. I'm her hostage.

"I'm out of grape bubble gum, lavender polish, purple hair bows with the gold sparkle sequins—"

She's just getting started.

"—bottle rockets, lighter fluid, a one-size bigger tutu in eggplant—"

I better go round 'em up. My diagnosis depends on it.

Looking Back: The couch was black. The front door of the therapist's office, though, I kid you not, is as purple as it could possibly be.
The tissue box was purple. The tissue box was empty when I left after that first session. But Little Miss agreed to stay home (after much bargaining)—

no doubt hanging out in the freezer, so the meet-and-greet first session with the Couch Lady was fruitful, I think.

I struggled quite a bit with this post. Whether to write it. Whether to promote it. But, in the end, if it helps someone else take steps to get help of any sort for whatever flavor of circus they have, it was worth the extra anxiety.

I'm going back to sit on that black couch. At least until I can better cope with the CIRCUS and don't feel as if I'm falling off the roller coaster into a pile of un-lined-up ducks Every. Second. Of. The. Day.

Speaking of bargains, Little Miss has agreed to disclose the events going on behind the freezer-burnt ground beef and Tyson chicken strips if I do a mock-up cover of "Little Miss Cooks a Book."

I agreed, but requested that whatever being likes my freezer so well must come out and meet me.

In person.

And, I hate to have to say this, but you can't leave anything to chance when a Muse (possibly more than one Muse) is involved: The Freezer Being must be fully clothed.

Negotiations are ongoing.

200

PLAGUED

Mr. Bob Ross and I have been hanging out quite a bit lately. Something about his baritone voice and the tisking of paint brushes and scratching of the knife against the canvas is quite calming. Come to find out, my reaction to this particular show is based in science: ASMR (autonomous sensory median response). I'll spare you the details—if you're curious, you can look it up.

I was in a coffee shop not too long ago where I'd drug in my laptop for a quick writing session. The store was streaming *The Joy of Painting*, and about twenty minutes in, I wondered why I could barely hold my head up. Because I've trained my brain to use Bob Ross to relax... I nearly fell asleep on my keyboard.

The effect he has on me is soothing. A twenty-five-minute "hush, world," if you will.

Lots of happy trees living in the brushes.

Lots of free and happy little clouds.

Lots of happy little accidents.

Lots of Bob cleaning the brush against the leg of his easel, declaring "Beat the devil out of it."

"I bet there's a lot of stuff you'd like to beat the devil out of." Little Miss Muse annoys me as I'm trying to write this post. She's eager to get on with another of our projects, and this blog was not at the top of her to-do list. So she hangs behind me, wings flapping in mid-air and reads over my shoulder.

"Yes. Some days, you're the one I want to beat the devil out of." She slows her flapping and lights on the desk. All polite like. And innocent. As if.

Anyway.

One of Bob's phrases has become my go-to inspiration lately: Plagued with dissatisfaction.

He explained letters from aspiring painters wondering how to determine if a painting is "good enough." In other words, when to stop fiddling with it and call it ready for a signature.

He grinned at the camera and said it again. "I hope you're plagued with dissatisfaction."

That feeling that it's never good enough keeps you going. If you've painted your ultimate masterpiece, what's the point of painting ever again? No artist at heart is ever totally satisfied with a creation, so they must call the current work done, then begin fresh on a new canvas.

Dissatisfied but happy.

The next time, our mountain will be crisper. The next time, our evergreen won't smudge. The next time, we'll add more layers of depth to the background. The next time, we'll take the happy little accidents and turn them into... magic.

There's grand inspiration in this plague.

In writing the next story to practice a new technique or explore a new "what-if."

In writing the next blog, because the last one was just so-so.

And another. In case my life can brush against yours, and we can learn from each other.

Another story collection.

Another attempt at cover design.

I hope I remain plagued with dissatisfaction. Enough so to write, release, and repeat.

To be plagued with the next idea. And the next. Because I'm not the best writer I can be yet.

I hope I never am.

I hope I'm so plagued that I never quit learning or striving for the next milestone.

Here are B.A. Paul's (and Little Miss Muse's) stats as of March 2023:

Novels: 1

Short Stories: 97

Short Story Collections: 13

Shorts to outside publications or published anthologies: 11 published, 2 pending.

Honorable Mentions from Writers of the Future: 3

Creative Nonfiction: 1

Blogs: Counting this one? That's a whopping 200!

Two-hundred! I've been doing these since the summer of 2018. The first hundred were pulled off the site and compiled in *Life Along the Way*.

So, it's time for the second creative nonfiction "blog book": *Life All Over Again*.

By the time this post goes live, the manuscript will be in the final proofing stages and, if all times out well, it'll be ready by April.

One thing I've discovered along the way: The Writing Bug behaves much like any disease-causing pathogen.

It takes hold and spreads to one area of the brain, then the next, and the next. It's all-consuming.

But it is, by far, the most fun you'll ever have with a plague.

Looking Back: Those stats are what plague me today. That Novel number is quite low, given the fact I've got three, THREE! In progress as I write this.

Plagued with dissatisfaction, certainly. I apparently also suffer from perfectionism, procrastination, and the inability to write in chaos. Some of that I can control—some of it is up to time and the Couch Lady to help me sort out.

*I've had a few folks ask me since I've hit the 200 mark on the blog will I
keep going?*

Short answer: Why not?

It brings me joy. It gives me a space to vent and dream and be silly.

It brings the readers a mini escape and maybe a smile or two.

It gives Little Miss Muse a place to air her grievances. Which are many.

Speaking of...

*After much bargaining, Little Miss Muse agreed to a meet-and-greet with
the Freezer Being.*

And wouldn't ya know it? It's the Sultan.

*Surprise, surprise. Knee-high to a horse, only slightly taller than Little Miss
Muse, he's wrapped in traditional Turkish garments, robes of purples and
tangerines flowing in all directions. As he steps out of my freezer, three cats
spin wildly in all directions, longing for traction on the hardwood floors. I
won't see any of them the rest of the day.*

I'm glad he's fully clothed, at any rate.

*I had him pegged all wrong. I thought he was some other writer's muse this
whole time. Years, actually. That he and Little Miss had "a thing," given all
the secrecy.*

Nope.

*Turns out, my Little Miss decided way back—in month two of our current
working relationship—that she was never going to make it as my full-time
muse if she didn't engage in some kind of therapy of her own.*

*The Sultan, who's set up portals in authors' freezers all over North
America (and parts of Mexico), is Therapist Supreme to under-
appreciated, over-worked, and slightly twitchy muses of all makes and
models.*

Imps (winged and wingless). Birds. Cats. Sirens. Narwhals. Iguanas.

All of them.

*Because to be a writer, you must be a bit twisted, but to be a writer's muse
takes more gumption than any one being possesses. Especially when your
author is plagued by so many issues.*

*"Now, wait a minute. Didn't you just try to get me the name of his therapist
a while back?"*

"Yeeeesss." She drips with attitude. "Because you can't use MY therapist.

Sharing would be..." she wraps her chonky arms around her front "...
weird."

I lean toward her and whisper, "I thought he was some other author's
muse."

The Sultan overhears this and shrugs. "I lead a full and fruitful life. I have
many responsibilities." He hands me a card he retrieves from under his
massive headdress. "Just in case your Couch Lady goes on vacation or
becomes a full-time writer." The card sparkles in my hand. It's embossed
with bright yellow feathers and reads "Canary Counseling."

"Let me guess, the therapist is a—"

"A flock of highly qualified, fine-feathered professionals." The Sultan stands
up as tall as he can—which isn't very. He's quite the proud little man. With
all his responsibilities and such.

"How much is he costing me?" I grit through my teeth at Little Miss.

She grits back, "Just keep the bottle rockets coming — and be glad he didn't
bring his mule this time."

"This time? There's been a mule in my house?"

She clams up. I can't even with these beings.

Not to be rude, I tuck the card in my back pocket and thank the mini
Freezer Being. He bids me farewell and disappears behind a box of corn dogs
that's been in there longer than, well, probably longer than the Sultan's
been holding therapy sessions for Little Miss.

"So about that book." Little Miss Doesn't waste any time.

"What book?"

"The one you promised me we'd do. 'Little Miss Cooks a Book.'"

I stick my head in the freezer. No sign of Sultans or canaries. "Don't you
even. Don't you even procrastinate one more project by cleaning out that
freezer." She flits around my head with her hands on her purple tutu'd hips.

"There was a mule. A mule. In my freezer. It needs to be cleaned."

"We had a deal. And you have THREE novels in progress!!!"

I supposed we did have a deal. Lots of negotiations to meet the Sultan.
Lots of negotiations to keep my brilliant, glittery Little Miss on the payroll,
so to speak. Lots of words to write.

I close the freezer door and find my hoodie. The temp in the kitchen dropped
ten degrees during our meet-and-greet.

She buzzes my head, pulling a bottle rocket from behind her back, and the noisy lute from the band of her tutu, fearing even something as simple as finding a sweatshirt could derail me.

I get the point.

We'll get to work.

In the middle of life all over again, CIRCUS and all, we'll move onward to the next project...

always plagued with dissatisfaction.

LINKS AND WEB ADDRESSES

Bapaul.com: Current blogs, news, Little Miss Muse-isms, and B.A. Paul's full list of available titles.

Blog 101:

wmgpublishinginc.com

WMG Publishing offers online and in-person writing classes from Dean Wesley Smith and Kristine Kathryn Rusch. They also have links for the Holiday Spectacular publications mentioned in later chapters.

Blog 105:

kickstarter.com

Kickstarter is a wonderful site that helps creatives get a start on their projects via crowdfunding. Thanks to some brave writers, Kickstarter is also becoming a "shop for your new favorite writer" spot. Check out their publication tabs. Lots of projects rotating through there, from magazine startups to anthologies to full novels.

Blog 118:

The Lawyer Cat Video: www.youtube.com/watch?v=lGOofzZOyl8

The Indian Priest Video: www.youtube.com/watch?v=iGdlZ1C1hVg

Blog 134:

Black Cat Mystery Magazine: bcmystery.com/magazines-for-sale

Blog 135:

Nora Roberts info: https://www.theguardian.com/books/2019/apr/25/nora-roberts-files-multi-plagiarism-lawsuit-alleging-writer-copied-more-than-40-authors

Blog 164:

rwwallace.com

R. W. Wallace's author page for *The Ghost Detective* stories. (Just clean your cheese-puffy hands first!)

Blog 180:

naughtycatcafe.com

duckriverbooks.com

The Adult-ish Man Child's Castiel Monroe:

Little Miss Muse crafted by Number One Fan, Miss L:

ABOUT THE AUTHOR

Beth enjoys chucking words into sentences then standing back to see what magic—or mayhem—falls out, crafting tales in mystery, sci-fi, fantasy, and general "slice of life" fiction. She couldn't accomplish this without the help of her tutu-clad Little Miss Muse and Trudi the Concrete Office Goose, who's partial to superhero capes.

Her stories have appeared in multiple publications, including Pulphouse Fiction Magazine and Ellery Queen Mystery Magazine, and in multiple fiction anthologies. She's received several Honorable Mentions from Writers of the Future. Her lighthearted blog peeks into the writing life as she pokes fun at herself and her circus of a life.

Follow the antics of Little Miss Muse and Trudi, read Beth's blog (she might have burned down her kitchen last week), and discover the stories at bapaul.com.

ALSO BY

Short Story Collections

Spunk and Spice, Volumes 1 and 2: A Collection of six short stories celebrating timeless wit and wisdom.

Out There, Volumes 1 and 2: A Collection of six short sci-fi and speculative tales.

Mystery Minutes, Volumes 1 and 2: Six short mystery stories

All the Feels, Volumes 1, 2, and 3: Collections of inspiring short stories

Just a Tick of Whimsy, Volumes 1 and 2: Collections of fantasy shorts.

Hijacked Holidays: Definitely not your warm-and-fuzzy winter tales.

Dark Minds: Toe-curling twisted mysteries.

Blog Compilations: Slices of the writing life with lots of laughs and bumps in the road.

Life Along the Way

Life All Over Again

Novels

Triage

Young Adult (or Young at Heart) Books

Switch: Book 1 in the Oliver Andrews Trilogy

Check out B.A. Paul's first novel, a heart-felt adventure for both Middle Grade and Young Adult – or simply the young at heart.

SWITCH

Book I in the Oliver Andrews Trilogy

Never having the stomach for conflict or confrontation, Oliver Andrews isn't upset about the extended school year in the small town of Fallston. Classroom dilemmas are easier on the nerves than an entire summer with feuding relatives.

His parents threaten divorce—and a move back to Chicago which would uproot Oliver from the grandfather and farm he cherishes and rip him away from his only friend in the world.

Maybe for good.

But when the family's crisis hits a boiling point, Oliver discovers there's more to the issue than everyday family drama—and a whole lot more at stake.

Set in motion generations before he was born, Oliver falls into a tight grip of magic and mystery that threatens all he holds dear.

Now he must team with unlikely—and eccentric—characters on a quest to repair his family.

And save the life of his best friend.

KEEP IN TOUCH!

BAPAUL.COM

Take a glimpse into B.A. Paul's writing journey, including the ups and downs of managing family, "real jobs," ducks in wobbling rows, and chasing down her Little Miss Muse. New blog posts go up Mondays, with the first Monday of the Month reserved for a free fiction short story available on the blog for a limited time.

Newsletter Signup!

Get the latest release information, author updates, and exclusive content by signing up with your email. Check out bapaul.com.

www.ingramcontent.com/pod-product-compliance
Lightning Source LLC
Chambersburg PA
CBHW070900120626
46546CB00001B/83